Myopic Me!

Love, Love, Love,

[signature]

Myopic Me!

The Dividing Wall of Hostility

John D Lane Jr.

XULON PRESS

Xulon Press
2301 Lucien Way #415
Maitland, FL 32751
407.339.4217
www.xulonpress.com

© 2021 by John D Lane Jr.

All rights reserved solely by the author. The author guarantees all contents are original and do not infringe upon the legal rights of any other person or work. No part of this book may be reproduced in any form without the permission of the author.

Due to the changing nature of the Internet, if there are any web addresses, links, or URLs included in this manuscript, these may have been altered and may no longer be accessible. The views and opinions shared in this book belong solely to the author and do not necessarily reflect those of the publisher. The publisher therefore disclaims responsibility for the views or opinions expressed within the work.

Unless otherwise indicated, Scripture quotations taken from the Holy Bible, New International Version (NIV). Copyright © 1973, 1978, 1984, 2011 by Biblica, Inc.™. Used by permission. All rights reserved.

Scripture quotations taken from the Holy Bible, New Living Translation (NLT). Copyright ©1996, 2004, 2007 by Tyndale House Foundation. Used by permission of Tyndale House Publishers, Inc.

Paperback ISBN-13: 978-1-6628-1523-2
eBook ISBN-13: 978-1-6628-1524-9

Before you embark on a journey of revenge, dig two graves. Confucius, 504 B.C.[1]

"Revenge is a dish best served cold." Marlon Brando, The Godfather[2]

"My name is Inigo Montoya. You killed my father. Prepare to die." The Princess Bride[3]

An eye for an eye will only make the whole world blind. Mahatma Gandhi[4]

The Beatles' Come Together, the lead song on the Abbey Road album, prompted a court dispute by Morris Levy (Chuck Berry's agent) against John Lennon of the Beatles. Levy later sued Lennon in a contract dispute, receiving less than $7000. Still seeking payback, Levy adapted some of Lennon's musical material in his own album, and Lennon sued. Levy lost $85,000 in that court battle. Net result: $78,000 the poorer. "Levy's Revenge"[5]

In January 2017, Madonna spoke at the Women's March in Washington, DC, a mass demonstration for women's rights and progressive causes centered on opposition to the newly sworn-in president. She called Trump's election a "horrific moment of darkness" and said she had "thought an awful lot about blowing up the White House" (a phrase she later clarified was intended as a metaphor). In response to her actions against a duly elected President, President Trump referred to Madonna as "disgusting."[6]

"You have heard the law that says the punishment must match the injury: 'An eye for an eye, and a tooth for a tooth.' But I say, do not resist an evil person! If someone slaps you on the right cheek, offer the other cheek also." Jesus Christ[7]

"Repent of your sins and believe the Good News!" Jesus Christ[8]

Table of Contents

1: The Impetus for Writing *Myopic Me!* 1
2: The Dividing Wall of Hostility.. 9
3: Father Wound: The Shriveled Potato. 25
4: Root of Bitterness:Three Incidents. 35
5: The Syrian Desert Flower. 51
6: Shadow of the Baptist Church. 59
7: Beautiful Woman with Potato Chips. 65
8: The Body Speaks. 71
9: The War in the Womb. 85
10: Medium Security Prison. 103
11: Chinese Orphanage. 111
12: Born to Be Free! 123
13: The Hernandez Murder. 133
14: History & the Mall in Washington. 143
15: Factional Hostility. 161
16: Persecution of Christians. 177
17: The Black Angel. 183
18: Confess your sins to one another. 195

Permissions for Stories included in this book: 201
Bibliography/References: 203
Endnotes 211

1

The Impetus for Writing *Myopic Me!*

> Is there any encouragement from belonging to Christ? Any comfort from his love? Any fellowship together in the Spirit? Are your hearts tender and compassionate? Then make me truly happy by agreeing wholeheartedly with each other, loving one another, and working together with one mind and purpose. Don't be selfish; don't try to impress others. Be humble, thinking of others as better than yourselves. Don't look out only for your own interests, but take an interest in others, too.[9]

"This is my book," I announced to the prayer team. It was Sunday morning in 2014, and we were sitting in the cold hall in front of the door to the *Answer's Fitness* portion of the former corporate center for *CVS Drugs*. I handed the seven-hundred-plus pages to Brenda, my faithful prayer partner at Waters Church during the year we had been in this new Roger Staubach-managed building.

In 2004 the initial twelve people had called themselves Living Waters Church, meeting in a Christian bookstore before moving into the basement of Fisher College. The beer-scented carpets in the Cinema Pub provided another temporary Sunday meeting place for the presentation of the Gospel message.

They then gathered in the small clapboard and steepled building on Kelly Boulevard [where Ann, Christopher, and I got involved, coming

Myopic Me!

from an Attleboro church], until it became evident that it would be too small very soon.

I loved thumping the congas during worship, regularly bringing prophetic words, as the Holy Spirit permitted, and enjoying the Word of God that flowed into our lives like Living Water at Jacob's Well. We could have stayed there forever, except that the crowds were filling every pew.

From that fun period with around a hundred people, we found a larger open facility which needed refitting for church functioning. During the months-long construction period before moving in, we shifted to another temporary spot in the Middle School in North Attleboro where noisy spring-loaded auditorium seats punctuated our rising and our sitting down during worship and departures.

During this time our amazing volunteers were installing the metal studs and sheetrock, the electrical runs, and the plumbing upgrades for bathrooms, the amazing Cafe and kitchen in the new 20,000 square foot facility a few miles away. Meanwhile, we continued worshiping God in childlike ways in that Middle School! We received Jesus' blessing during that brief season.

> One day some parents brought their children to Jesus so he could lay his hands on them and pray for them. But the disciples scolded the parents for bothering him. But Jesus said, "Let the children come to me. Don't stop them! For the Kingdom of Heaven belongs to those who are like these children."[10]

God continued to free us from religion during this waiting period, as we embraced the Good News like those children whom Jesus blessed. We enjoyed coming into the presence of our good Father week after week. Becoming more child-like in our faith, it was hard to imagine that four-hundred soft seats in our new facility would ever be required since we were around seventy-five in number.

Our Roger Staubach rental area seemed so large to us while the construction continued. "Have we bitten off more than we can chew, spiritually speaking?" Our question had been answered by the God who saves, the God who calls, and the God who speaks. Now, we were

The Impetus for Writing Myopic Me!

in that cold hallway in that gigantic building, and I was standing there with my bundle of printed pages. There was no room for the prayers to be spoken, but in this hall.

> "I have combined my daily blogs to create this book. I finished them, making them flow from chapter to chapter, and I printed them all last night!"

As I handed the bundle to them for perusal, we were preparing to pray for our third of five weekend services! All the seats were not only filled with worshipers in one service, but we needed five services to handle the overflow. God is bigger than our imaginations, and He is the mover of mountains!

The average weekend crowd had grown to around two-thousand from the original twelve who gathered in that book store. In a region where many church buildings were closed for a lack of parishioners, we now had more than four-hundred volunteers involved in kid's ministries each weekend. The offices were full of staff, and a fabulous Cafe was staffed by volunteer workers as well, cooking eggs, bacon, and hash browns.

With five services and no prayer room the handwriting was already on the walls for another expansion in a few short years! We rolled out our borrowed chairs into the hallway where we prayed, believing that everything good in God starts with prayer.

Jesus actually said, "Pray with me for one hour that you not be tempted."[11] His call to prayer reminded us of our frailty. He reminded us that our Father's name is hallowed, and His kingdom and glory is where our life is found in forgiveness and forgiving, while we trust Him to shield us from temptations and the schemes of the evil one. He also reminds us that we are His hands and feet.

> "I tell you the truth, anyone who believes in me will do the same works I have done, and even greater works, because I am going to be with the Father. You can ask for anything in my name, and I will do it, so that the Son can bring glory to the Father. Yes, ask me for anything in my name, and I will do it!"[12]

Myopic Me!

The fulfillment of **God's** mission in North Attleboro inspired us to seek God's will and purpose every day, leading believers into worship, praise, and thanksgiving for family, community, and for our city positioned between Providence and Boston.

To see God, it is essential to forgive others whether they ask or not. With our eyes opened wide by prayer, we could see that the time promised by God had surely arrived. He had opened our eyes as we prayed for His glory, as we prayed for Jesus to speak to us, reminding us of the urgency of repentance after John the Baptist was arrested. Nothing about that urgency had changed in two-thousand years.

> "The time promised by God has come at last!" he announced. "The Kingdom of God is near! **Repent of your sins and believe the Good News!**"[13]

We agreed with Jesus that the Kingdom of God is at hand through the forgiveness of sin; through the Cross; and so, we focused all the more on the repentance from sin and and dead works, while forgiving others. Revenge has no place in God's Church. As James exhorted, "Tell your sins to each other. And pray for each other so you may be healed."[14]

We prayed for everyone to receive the Good News of the Kingdom. We knew that hundreds of people each weekend had really never heard God's plan for redemption, even though some were church-goers for years. They did not know they could give their resentment to God, their anxieties to God, and their failures to God.

They did not know that Peace was possible. Many had no idea that God loved them so much that He sent His only Son to die on the cross so that anyone who believes in Him will not die but will have eternal life. So many had been in those rote services without understanding that God did not send Jesus to condemn them—but to save them through Him.[15]

We had many visitors who told us, "I learned more in one service than I learned going to church for my entire life." We prayed that our regulars and the newcomers would "see Jesus" during the worship, during the teaching of the Word, and during their encounters with authentically loving people who cared about them and their families.

We prayed for God's provision and protection for leaders, families, and young people.

We prayed that no one would be deceived by the persuasive arguments of this world. Many realized they had built their lives upon the convincing sermons from the world, from the media, and from the culture. They had been indoctrinated in the vain-glories of self-aggrandizement and the benefits of greed and materialism.

Their daily rituals had become deeply rooted into their stuff, into dead religious rites, and into repetitive rituals of **REVENGE**. With that common background of failure, self-loathing, anxiety, and personal brokenness, the Good News was stunning to them. Their sins could be forgiven, forgotten, separated from them as far as the east is from the west. All they had to do was ask Him to save them. All they had to do was believe in Him!

Now, Brenda was reading my first typed page from the thick bundle I had placed in her hands, and I would quickly learn that those three-hundred thousand words from seven-years of blogging could never become the book God wanted me to write.

Oh well, the journey is more important than the prize anyway; but when I heard them pray for my writing project, I knew that God would take over. They asked God to encourage, guide, and give favor for this project which could only be for the glory of His Son.

Those blogs represented my disciplined daily focus upon the Good News, shining a strong Light into every dark crevice of the bad news coming out of the world during that seven-year period from 2007. This initial effort would become five books, with the main title of *Myopic Me!* Almost nothing from that original seven hundred pages survived the hundred editing processes that followed that morning in the hall. Jesus would continue to lead me into all Truth.

> "If you love me, obey my commandments. And I will ask the Father, and he will give you another Advocate, who will never leave you. He is the Holy Spirit, who leads into all truth."[16]

Jesus also told His disciples, "I am the way, the truth, and the life. No one comes to the Father except through Me!" All truth is found in

Myopic Me!

Him. He is the center, and He is the Advocate, the Counselor, and the Comforter in every one of my projects. Some of that God-given help came from the serendipity of meeting a consultant at the bookstore. She helped me find my voice, bringing some tangible description into my parables and stories.

She helped me to see "the beautiful book" which God wanted me to write. Her background at Chicago's Wheaton College came as my authentic deus ex machina—God dropping down from the heavens to show me the way to proceed through my project. Soon, I found a helpful publisher, and I got much needed feedback from my wife, Ann, and from John Buchanan, to get me moving in a good direction.

Having someone to read what you have written is no small first step in the process. There is an audience that you need to reach! Their reaction is crucial. Meanwhile, Tim Keller and Tim Hatch, my two favorite theologians and brothers in Christ, helped me press into the Gospel for every personal story told; Eric Metaxas showed me the Gospel's pivotal role in America's miraculous arrival in the wild woods of colonial North America.

When my wife recommended we have coffee at Jeff Kinney's brand new Bookstore and Café in Plainville, I found my writing nook. I said, "Yes! Let's do," but I thought, "I don't really want to go stand around in a bookstore with nothing to do!»

Myopic Me! demonstrated its essential selfishness even before the name for the book series had even been coined! "What will I do while she shops?" I wondered. Like those toddlers I would see there every day, I wanted to stay or go, to have or to have not. I could not help that I released my adult versions of their selfish screaming into my collar. Theirs was louder by far, but mine had to be tamed by the Holy Spirit who would teach me to appreciate every interruption during the four years that followed.

Of course, I found an inspiring atmosphere for the writing of the five books, establishing a five-hour-per-day writing ritual. I found my daily working, worshiping, praising, and thanksgiving hangout until Covid-19 struck down the gathering, talking, and sprawling there with French-roast coffee and grilled sandwiches, delicious soup, and green wraps full of turkey and bacon.

Jeff Kinney's *Diary of a Wimpy Kid* series of books[17] was already selling across the world in multiple languages, and his personal example inspired me to create the *Myopic Me! Series* of five books. The title was coined after the "Selfie-Stick" had been included among the best inventions of 2014.[18]

The Senior Pastor had preached on the obsession with self, constantly stoked and encouraged by social media platforms that make *Me* the star of the show. I could imagine a happy Narcissist holding his iPhone in the air on the end of one of those selfie-sticks, grinning, and exclaiming, "Look at *Myopic Me!*"

That might have become the slogan for a series of slick ultra-4k ads flashing on our retinas forever with the flutter of multiple self-portraits, self-videos, and skits by a pretty young girl whose irresistible grin repeated the phrase, "*Myopic Me!*"

The sudden fame of the selfie-stick seemed to arrive when every exhibitionist across every social media platform was featuring their daily activities. All of this unfolded while *Myopic Me!* was being written down in personal parables from the journey Home.

The view from my myopic mirror revived that ancient Humpty-Dumpty character from children's literature where the thin-skin-of-sin always collides with the marble-floor-of-Truth! I learned that *Myopic Me!* craves self-exposure, self-justification, and self-actualization, while failures and posturing pile up all the more.

Myopic Me! wants to be enough, but is drawn into the ancient futility of identity surfing: Like Pilate, before the Lamb of God in Jerusalem asking God's Son, "What is truth?" But nothing is ever enough, like Solomon, Beloved of God, stopping along the road to Moab and Syria every month for thirty-five years to bring home another beautiful girl with her idol tucked under her arm.

I learned that our sins are not what we imagined on those long afternoons when we wiped the mirror dry after our hot shower or bath. Our sins are much worse than we could ever describe using any known written language.

Sin is the impenetrable *Dividing Wall*, like that complex web of the writing spider spun up in the afternoon sun after the rains subside. That web of Sin cuts us off from God's Love, rolling us up in its

Myopic Me!

necrotic lust. But God solved the infinite hostile wall of sin, making fruitful our formerly empty lives.

> For Christ himself has brought peace to us. He united Jews and Gentiles into one people when, in his own body on the cross, he broke down the wall of hostility that separated us.[19]

2

The Dividing Wall of Hostility.

The woman was convinced. She saw that the tree was beautiful and its fruit looked delicious, and she wanted the wisdom it would give her. So she took some of the fruit and ate it. Then she gave some to her husband, who was with her, and he ate it, too. At that moment their eyes were opened, and they suddenly felt shame at their nakedness. So they sewed fig leaves together to cover themselves.[20]

When they came near the camp, Moses saw the calf and the dancing, and he burned with anger. He threw the stone tablets to the ground, smashing them at the foot of the mountain. He took the calf they had made and burned it. Then he ground it into powder, threw it into the water, and forced the people to drink it.[21]

For the sin of this one man, Adam, caused death to rule over many. But even greater is God's wonderful grace and his gift of righteousness, for all who receive it will live in triumph over sin and death through this one man, Jesus Christ.[22]

It finally happened one day at the bookstore. I was sitting in my regular chair when I experienced the corollary to the frightening tale of

Myopic Me!

the rebellious Israelites at the base of Mt. Sinai. The evil got twisted around the good I had been enjoying for years. Remember that fortieth day when the golden calf came from the melting of their jewelry, and they danced in a sexual orgy, twisting together in a frenzy of lust?

Hundreds of days had passed, with five hours a day in that same leather chair that Jeff Kinney had toted over his head on that second day. During the five-thousand hours since then, there were no apples taken, and no golden calves worshiped. There were no sexual orgies weaving through the new book racks, and there were no stone tablets smashed on the hardwood floors that came down from those regional factories that had closed their doors decades before.

But in this odd twilight of morning, sitting all alone in silence, an attractive young woman landed on the bar stool one foot above me. With her knees nearly touching the plate glass window on South Street, I was sitting with my chair back against the brick wall on East Bacon Street.

She was so close to me in that empty cafe, that rotating her tall stool ninety degrees counterclockwise would have put her knees in my face. Her perfume swept over me, and the heat off of her bare legs radiated so that I could actually feel it on my face. Suddenly, every forgotten idea seemed more urgent.

The "two of us" were there "together," and she relaxed, like nothing had happened, poking her phone and sipping her fancy coffee. Meanwhile, my fingers froze a few inches above my keyboard, and I watched her knees flex each time the passers-by looked through the glass at her. She posed herself on her tall stool like one of those Greek Sirens shrilling in the rocky shoreline of Corinth.

> The very name Corinth was synonymous with debauchery, and there was one source of evil in the city which was known all over the civilized world. Above the isthmus towered the hill of the Acropolis, and on it stood the great temple of Aphrodite, the goddess of love. To that temple there were attached one thousand priestesses who were sacred prostitutes, and in the evenings they descended from the Acropolis and plied their trade upon the streets of Corinth, until it became

The Dividing Wall of Hostility.

a Greek proverb, 'It is not every man who can afford a journey to Corinth.'[23]

Though she made zero effort to smile or speak in my direction, she hung there in her shot-glass skirt like a bright red apple in an unlikely orchard. Having written a chapter describing Solomon's eighty versions of the fool, I realized the fool was ***Myopic Me!*** Frozen in the haze of sensory overload, this frontal assault was mercifully brief, and then it was gone.

She soon tired of checking her Instagram account, and she made a phone call. Within a few minutes, another young woman arrived to fetch her from her stool, and they left together, babbling and hugging each other like long-lost lovers. I let out the air trapped in my inactive lungs, and I never saw her since.

The deceiver left his faint footprints in the sanctity of my holy work place, and in the edges of my marital covenant. He had done his best to twist his shame of adultery, of covetousness, and idolatry around my mind and body and life. I was "ready to follow her home," leaving behind my faith and family, when God intervened with the rest of the story.

Why did it happen? Or did it happen? If no one hears the tree fall, did it remain vertical in the forest? Since I had not "actively" sinned, would a tree fall to clutter the aisles in the bookstore when I went home four hours later that afternoon?

The enemy comes to twist his lust around the axel of covetousness. And Marriage, that "thing with feathers flies away, and never asked a crumb of me."[24] And I do apologize here for the profane juxtaposition of Christ's blood with that evanescent heat which belittles His power and love.

> This time Paul was coming to excommunicate those who refused to repent of their sins. He would only do so on the basis of two or three witnesses. The person who then refused to repent would become an outcast, sent back into the world, without the support or covering of the church. Basically, these would be returned to Satan, from whom they had come. Paul would make clear to

the church that there are two masters, and two only. We can worship God or Satan. When Jesus answered Satan, "It is written," for the final temptation in the wilderness, the real issue was worship. Satan was offering Jesus the whole world if He would worship him. Jesus answered that God was a jealous God. He commanded us to worship Him alone.[25]

It is an affront to the greatness of His redemption. But on this one morning, on that sanctified hardwood of the Cafe, I could already hear the strident cries of Adam and Eve. The air around me had filled up with the noise of blaming; and Satan's argumentative agenda had been faintly disguised in that seductive woman whose arrival had heated me up and frozen me in one undocumented moment. Some would say it never happened, that I drifted off, and endocrine and testosterone had erupted in a fleeting dream, or nightmare, but Paul and I disagree.

> [John], a final word: Be strong in the Lord and in his mighty power. Put on all of God's armor so that you will be able to stand firm against all strategies of the devil. For we are not fighting against flesh-and-blood enemies, but against evil rulers and authorities of the unseen world, against mighty powers in this dark world, and against evil spirits in the heavenly places.[26]

The one-flesh of marriage is joined by God for the raising of the children, for the family's unity, for the moments of joy, excitement, and affection, and for the knowing which is intimate and wonderful. The Serpent understands full well that this ***knowing*** can be readily manipulated, to add the ***Hiding*** and the ***Shame***.

Satan got right to the point in the Garden of Eden, telling Eve, "God knows that your eyes will be opened as soon as you eat it, and you will be like God, <u>***knowing***</u> [עֵדִי] both good and evil." [27] Satan ***knew*** the implicit sexual meanings.

The good and the evil potentialities of the Hebrew word, עֵדִי, "to know," were twisted by Satan when Adam and Eve consummated their relationship, joined together in "sexual relations" [עֵדִי].[28] Cain was conceived as the evil son, and Abel was conceived as the righteous son: And so, the evil got twisted around the good, and Abel's blood cried out to God from the ground.[29]

First lesson from the Garden: God brings blessings and life, while the Serpent twists the evil around the good, producing shame and death! God breathes life into our lungs, and the Serpent asphyxiates with the lie. Both are intimate acts, and both bring powerful connectedness: One connects us to the Good Father, while the other connects us to the Father of Lies, the Destroyer of souls.

Today, the very mention of Adam and Eve triggers spontaneous embarrassment or enmity, driving us to hide behind our fig leaves. Rather than thrive and multiply, we withdraw, covering our nakedness with all manner of emblematic clothing. Today, it is not the lamb or goat that dies, for it is our children, working in the sweat shops around the globe.

> In 2019, global retail sales of apparel and footwear reached 1.9 trillion U.S. dollars, and were expected to rise to above three trillion U.S. dollars by 2030.[30]

Our identity springs from our posing rather than our character. The beautiful actress puts on see-through clothing, inviting the whirring cameras to feed voracious appetites across the various media markets. Satan attacks the synergy built into man's sexual impulse and God's Command: "Be fruitful and multiply."[31]

Second Lesson from the Garden of Eden: Satan always seeks to undermine God's Commands: "Don't eat the fruit of the Tree of the Knowledge of Good and Evil." Satan twists this Command, providing the undermining arguments.

> "You won't die! [Give me a break!] God knows that your eyes will be opened as soon as you eat it, [God doesn't want you to know what He knows!] and you will be like God, knowing both good and evil [This is your secret power—knowing both the good and the evil]."

Myopic Me!

Myopic Me! is always nearsighted, and this malady of the *EYE* arrives when Eve sees that the forbidden fruit is not only beautiful but is also good to eat. She is oblivious to every eternal consequence of her disobedience.

Just look at the Ten Commandments, and you will see this problem each time the Law is presented. Three thousand died after the Law had been scribed on stone tablets by the finger of Yahweh on top of Mt. Sinai. Then Moses returned to the base of the mountain to discover Satan twisting the truth around the golden calf in the encampment of the 600,000 Israelites.

Three-thousand chose the lie of idolatry, and they perished. The Israelites learned that listening to God brings a fruitful life, while listening to Satan brings rebellion, shame, and death.

> Moses saw that Aaron had let the people get completely out of control, much to the amusement of their enemies. So he stood at the entrance to the camp and shouted, "All of you who are on the LORD's side, come here and join me." And all the Levites gathered around him.
>
> Moses told them, "This is what the LORD, the God of Israel, says: Each of you, take your swords and go back and forth from one end of the camp to the other. Kill everyone—**even your brothers, friends, and neighbors**." The Levites obeyed Moses' command, and about 3,000 people died that day.[32]

How deadly is this twisting which Satan performs? Just look at the story above. The list can even include your family members who will turn against you and will try to kill you. God will come to smite them for their complicity in the enemy's schemes.

The Hostility launched in the Garden of Eden was amplified when Cain rudely answered God's question about Abel's whereabouts. "Am I my brother's guardian [keeper]?"[33] [**He had just murdered his brother!**] Cain did very few things right, but he did ask the right question. Cain's voice still rings across human history with his cynical interrogative.

The Dividing Wall of Hostility.

When the Serpent twisted the evil brother around the good brother East of Eden, Cain was surely asking the right question. But his bitter heart mirrored the Curse that was already woven around his life. In that sullen exchange with the incarnate God, Jesus had become the only efficacious Curse-breaker. He was, and is, and ever will be, the only remedy for the quid pro quo built into every one of our ***Myopic!*** relationships.

When my friend took me to the airport through a fit of ugly traffic in Philadelphia, he alluded to this quid pro quo. At the airport gate, I thanked him profusely, and he responded: "Not necessary. I will be compensated well for driving you today." He was talking about a very explicit payoff for his good deed.

He had not yet read the Sermon on the Mount which reveals that God's divine generosity far exceeds the three wishes of the personal Genie. "God blesses those who are poor and realize their need for him, for the Kingdom of Heaven is theirs."[34]

> You are jealous of what others have, but you can't get it, so you fight and wage war to take it away from them. Yet you don't have what you want because you don't ask God for it. And even when you ask, you don't get it because your motives are all wrong—you want only what will give you pleasure.[35]

What an indictment by Jesus' half-brother, James! William Tyndale wrestled with this same cruel grin of ***Myopic Me!*** Tyndale spoke of this powerful dissonance that comes with our constant obsession with satisfying these malignant appetites.[36] ***Myopic Me!*** turns sensations, flavors, and feelings into gods.

The shortsightedness of ***Myopic Me!*** leads to Death, jumping the fence of God's Commandment and landing feet-first in the quicksand of Gravity. Our prayers are ruined by our false gods' appetites. So, remind me again why we should listen to the ancient William Tyndale? The first translator of the New Testament into English, Tyndale put the Gospels of Jesus before the eyes of a billion English-speaking readers.

The Church officials of the day [sixteenth century] twisted his neck around his New Testament. They burned him at the stake for his righteous contributions to the English church. They did not want us to see

Myopic Me!

this Good News that would certainly threaten their wealth and power![37] Self-interest by these religious leaders got William Tyndale killed.

Before they could silence him, Tyndale observed that the Law discourages this very self-interest, shifting the focus from the god of *Myopic Me!* to the *Other!* [38] For the first time, we may broach the possibility of caring for our *Neighbor!* Tyndale explained that these Relationships are intrinsic to the Commandments.

> "Thou shalt not kill [your neighbor, William Tyndale], steal [from your neighbor], covet [what your neighbor has], bear false witness [against your neighbor], commit adultery [with your neighbor], or murder [your neighbor]. Thou shalt honor your parents [blood-neighbors], worship your God [Creator and Father, Brother, and King], and scrupulously abstain from the making or worshiping of idols [manmade things, instead of the Word, through Whom all things are made, in Whose image we were made]. You will keep the Sabbath day holy [Entering into the rest of the Father, established and demonstrated on the seventh day of the Creation]."[39]

Tyndale had highlighted this divine paradox that brings a man to exchange self-concern for the concern for the neighbor—the concern for this high priority of God, which is "one another." The Bible contains one-hundred and nineteen references to "one another." Tyndale understood that attentiveness for "one another" depends upon a supernatural shifting of the eye of *Myopic Me!* "Such disinterestedness [in *self-interest*] is precisely what the moral law demands [but only God's grace can inspire in us]."[40]

My father, Emeritus Professor of Literature and Journalism at Clemson University, called me into his tiny pine-paneled study. I felt honored to be with him in this personal encounter. Though he hugged me with those overgrown whiskers every evening after climbing the steps from the basement garage, I felt distant from him. It was in me, not in him.

He informed me [1953] that Ernest Hemingway had just published a short novel named, *The Old Man and the Sea*.[41] He wanted me to write

The Dividing Wall of Hostility.

down the story after reading the old fisherman's struggles. "I will pay you three dollars when you finish the project, writing *The Old Man and the Sea* in your own words."

He said that he was concerned about all the comic books I was reading, and he wanted me to read this amazing battle between the deep sea fisherman and the great swordfish. "Pay special attention to the boy who waits for the old man to return to the shore. Imagine that you are that boy watching every day near sunset, with no fishing boat appearing."

I was nine years old when I accepted his offer. A movie ticket in 1953 was 25 cents, and today the price is $9.00. So, the payoff in 2021 dollars is $108.00. I went to work reading and writing my own version of *The Old Man and the Sea*, and that started a quest which I guess has culminated in the writing of this five-book series. I had no idea in 1953 how hard it would be to write one book! What marriage can survive the writing of five books.

Undaunted by these challenges, my books chronicle the Grace, as well as the Warfare, that has occurred in five different states, and six local churches, during this fifty-three year journey to the ultimate Shore [as the Romans might have said], to this ultimate Port-of-call [as the seafaring Corinthians would have recognized], and to the ultimate Home [which Dorothy sought with all her heart in the Emerald City].

She was actually looking for a City whose builder was God—not being impressed at all with the Wizard or his Emerald City, or his gold streets. She found Hollywood instead. So, too often, do we settle for Hollywood instead of God's City where the streets are paved with His blood-bought transparent gold.

> Abraham was confidently looking forward to a city with eternal foundations, a city designed and built by God . . . But they [offspring of Abraham through faith] were looking for a better place, a heavenly homeland. That is why God is not ashamed to be called their God, for he has prepared a city for them . . . No, you [believers in Jesus through faith] have come to Mount Zion, to the city of the living God, the heavenly Jerusalem, and to countless thousands of angels in a joyful gathering.[42]

Myopic Me!

    The smorgasbord of demons is incredibly attractive at first, until the doors lock behind us, and the voices start, and destruction is unleashed in every direction. When the little child is also infested with the demons' voices in her head, it becomes crystal clear. The tears can't wash it away when this happens. Only God's Spirit can come to thrash the unbelievably persistent grip of hell spreading throughout your family.

    I have learned that God's favor alone can make the new creature from all the rough stuff of every man who believes in the Son. I can't take credit for any good thing that has come, for God made sure no one could boast.[43] Boasting is never in God's vocabulary,[44] and He has offered nothing for me to boast about other than Jesus. After all, He is the Benchmark, performing His miracles throughout Judea:

> "I tell you the truth, the Son can do nothing by himself. He does only what he sees the Father doing. Whatever the Father does, the Son also does. For the Father loves the Son and shows him everything he is doing. In fact, the Father will show him how to do even greater works than healing this man. Then you will truly be astonished."[45]

    After raising Lazarus from the dead, Jesus continued to prove His humility and faithfulness: "Father, not My will, but Yours be done." He modeled faithfulness in the littlest things for me, so that I could catch a glimpse of my own flawed nature—even when I was eight-years-of-age. My first published book of poems contained all the ingredients for my grown-up efforts today. I remember that little dog-eared book containing my famous poem about my first goldfish:

> Once I had a goldfish
> That swam around so free.
> It swam inside the fishbowl
> Staring back at me.
> I touched the glass.
> It moved away.
> I hadn't fed it for a day.
> It died,

The Dividing Wall of Hostility.

And stayed that way.
Forever.

We laugh, not understanding death. The woman in the Stark-Bayer Cafeteria laughed as we watched live as the Trade Towers fell down on that day of 9-1-1. Three-thousand were dying, while she laughed. The children in my wife's classroom also laughed when those Towers fell.

Many children will experience death for the first time in the same way that I did with the goldfish. They don't know whether to laugh, but their hearts feel sick inside. It is surreal and memorable. It is eye-opening and frightening. That dysphoria I experienced at eight years had to be written down in order to mark the formative event.

More than sixty years later, I realize that the same themes from the childhood poem should be revisited in the ***Myopic Me!*** *Series.* That poem speaks of freedom—within imperceptible boundaries. It celebrates the fragile gift of life and the importance of faithfulness in little things. When God asked me, "What happened to your goldfish?" I could feel the twinge of Cain: "Am I my fish's guardian?" Mumbling today, I confess to God, "I flushed the goldfish into the Seneca River."

The welfare of the "Other" comes back as a painful memory from the too-familiar story. I can see that Cause & Effect is constrained from playing favorites, operating as a law across the depth and breadth of the universe, impinging upon the fishbowl, the boy, and the helpless goldfish.

Though the matter-of-fact style of the poem implies an absence of empathy by the narrator, the poem can also be read as the author's confession. There is little the narrator can do to rescript his story, for it is too late to amend the outcomes. Do you get my meaning? This is timely for me, and I am sure for you. The reader is presented with every terminal intention of entropy and death. Failure is a road littered with our broken relationships.

The role of the evil one is not mentioned in this story written by a child, for the child does not yet understand the Serpent's twisting of the evil around the good. In every known and unknown failure-mode of man, the Father of Lies is standing in the shadows nearby.

Without the clear and right perspective of Grace, any reflection across the unalterable past would bring a veil of darkness over the mind;

Myopic Me!

but viewing these events through the lens of the Cross and the empty tomb brings hope and refreshment through the Holy Spirit.

The Cross reminds us that we are not alone, and we need a Savior to ameliorate the shattered eggshell of our lives. "Amend, ameliorate, correct, upgrade," are words that fail to account for the blood of God's Son. "Reconcile" is the word that comes closest to describing what the Cross has done to transform our Past, Present, and Future. "Enrich" will always fall short of the mark, and even the word "Revolutionize" will fail to appropriate the miracle of His forgiveness.

My stories, after all, are not really about *Myopic Me!* They are really about Jesus. I'm not the center of the story, so if you don't like what Jesus has done, then this will be a hard or baffling journey for you. These stories are about His glory, and not mine. The entire focus shifts from my impotence to His finished work of redemption. It is a paradox of Substitution which brings daily miracles.

Today, I can look back to study that little poem for its wonderful brevity, but the most important insight from the past is the Grace arriving through a clear lens. The New Creation is Grace personified, not works from striving. I have learned the hard way, that it is impossible to give Grace away if you haven't received Grace. Grace is a gift—it is undeserved favor from God.[46]

In utter darkness, the Light of the World burst forth at 3:00 p.m. when Jesus gave up His Spirit on the Cross. What had been destroyed in the first Garden was restored in the second Garden at Gethsemane. The Light that went out East of Eden was turned back on again when Jesus rose from the dead. He stepped from the borrowed tomb to speak His final instructions to every disciple who would listen to Him.

I am therefore a bit wiser today than on that day when I flushed the goldfish down the toilet into the Seneca River. The significance of that silent gold fish stirred my soul, for I accounted the little creature as having a life. My part in its death was painful for me to face as an eight-year old. I only vaguely understood my complicity in the little creature's death.

Today, I bring annual plants in from the deck in the winter, keeping them alive until spring. This over-compensation likely comes from my experience with that goldfish, having a better understanding today of God's great desire to breathe life into all men everywhere.

The Dividing Wall of Hostility.

The Seneca River awaits us all, but God's love is more important than the Seneca River. When the Seneca, Tugaloo, and the Savannah Rivers were repurposed with dikes and the Hartwell Reservoir's dam, twenty-one miles of bottom lands were flooded in the late 1950s. But a much greater flood covered the whole earth twenty feet above the tallest mountain, and God carried Noah's family in the Ark to a safe landing on Mt. Ararat a year later.[47]

Adam had long ago flushed our eternal life down the Tigris & Euphrates Rivers, but God is restoring everything that was lost. His Son Jesus chose to raise the most eloquent white flag in the Garden of Gethsemane, surrendering life and breath unto the Father's plan for our redemption.

Jesus cried out, sweating blood, "My Father! If it is possible, let this cup of suffering be taken away from me. Yet I want your will to be done, not mine."[48] He prayed fervently in the winepress of Gethsemane that the sins of all men would be transferred to His body, and that God's righteousness would be transferred to us sinners through His blood on the Cross.

The purpose of that winepress was to bring great pressure upon every vintage grape, exploding the juice through the flesh and the skin. On that Thursday night, the pressure became so extreme that new wine exuded through the Lord's skin.

Arriving at that point of no return two thousand years ago, Jesus set aside His divine privileges, saying, "Yes, Father, Your will, not mine be done." Jesus made a way for me, at age twenty-three, to raise my tattered flag in Smyrna, asking God to save me. At Church of Our Savior, on Highland Avenue, I prayed:

> "Forgive this idolatry that is taking my breath away, for I have made another human being into an idol. Take this sin that is smothering me, for I have ignored Your commandments and Your warnings in the shower in Clemson. Let your will be done in my life, not mine. Pour out your new wine, the Blood of the Lamb who was slain for me. Remove this Curse that has sealed my destruction. Show me now how I should live my life. In Jesus' name, Amen."

Myopic Me!

Of course my prayer was far less than eloquent then, for I was living in "Cain's World." Cain's World is all about victimhood, unfairness, sullenness, and mandated tolerance for the one who murdered his own brother. In Cain's World I was a marked man—marked by God Himself. Though God protected Cain, Cain carried the curse of the second death, and the self-destructiveness of ***Myopic Me!***[49]

Cain is a wanderer without a country, so he commits his life to destroying everybody else's country. He has no city, so he seeks the destruction of everybody else's city. He is the man of revenge, so vengeance is new every morning. He pulls a mask down over his face at night, and his childhood "wounds" erupt with violence and the hurling of stones. Revenge is his consistent motivation, and fear stalks him forever.

Saul [Paul] never intended to become the hit man for the Pharisees, though he did volunteer and recommend himself to the Chief Priest. This proud religious man, this coveter, was persecuting the risen Christ. Worst still, he persecuted the body of Christ. Throwing rocks had come naturally to him, and he held their coats while they bruised Stephen to death with stones.

Like Cain, he still had the rock in his hand when he met Jesus Christ on the Road to Damascus. Saul imagined that revenge could fulfill the Law and the Prophets as he approached the houses of those who followed the Way in Damascus. On that blinding road, Saul met the fulfillment the the Laws and the Prophets when Jesus knocked him from his donkey, exceeding every expectation that he had for the Lord of Life.

The Light of the World blinded this self-righteous Jew, that he would learn to see. Saul's eyes were covered with scales like a fish. The Chief Priest's hit man soon found himself on Straight Street praying, and his prayer would change the known world. That prayer would overflow across the oceans and over mountains, impacting the distant islands and dry deserts and frozen continents.

God put His Good News in a blind man's eyes to guard like a junkyard dog. "Cursed is anyone who preaches any other Gospel beside this Gospel we are giving you." The Hit Man had become the Guard Dog, pronouncing a Curse upon anyone who altered the Gospel of the risen Lord of Life, the One True Living God, Jesus of Bethlehem **and** Nazareth.

The Dividing Wall of Hostility.

I include Paul's words below for every man or woman who is searching for peace, while the world is leveraging revenge like a drug. Paul, the would-be Guard Dog, asks Jesus Christ: "Who are you Lord!"[50] That question never left his searching and his knowing, and he found the Way through forgiveness and unmerited favor from God.[51]

If ever there was a reason for revenge, Jesus had that reason. But He said to leave that ugly vengeance to God's pristine justice. God adds the mercy, but He applies the Law which Jesus never undermined. Jesus upped the ante, saying, "Return a blessing to those who mistreat you."[52] It is impossible to do what he recommends unless you first receive that forgiveness, that Grace, authenticated by the blood of God's Son.

> Do all that you can to live in peace with everyone. Dear friends, never take revenge. Leave that to the righteous anger of God. For the Scriptures say,
>
> "I will take revenge; I will pay them back," says the Lord.
>
> Instead,
>
> "If your enemies are hungry, feed them. If they are thirsty, give them something to drink.
>
> In doing this, you will heap burning coals of shame on their heads."[53]

3

Father Wound: The Shriveled Potato.

> If you honor your father and mother, "things will go well for you, and you will have a long life on the earth."[54]
>
> Fathers, do not provoke your children to anger by the way you treat them. Rather, bring them up with the discipline and instruction that comes from the Lord.[55]
>
> When you follow the desires of your sinful nature, the results are very clear: sexual immorality, impurity, lustful pleasures, idolatry, sorcery, hostility, quarreling, jealousy, outbursts of anger, selfish ambition, dissension, division, envy, drunkenness, wild parties, and other sins like these. Let me tell you again, as I have before, that anyone living that sort of life will not inherit the Kingdom of God. But the Holy Spirit produces this kind of fruit in our lives: love, joy, peace, patience, kindness, goodness, faithfulness."[56]

That little boy from my friend's ancient past had been deeply injured by his father's constant criticism and harsh treatment while he was growing up in Africa. His father had been rigidly religious and moralistic, exhibiting none of the grace of God.

His father must have thought John, the Apostle, had misspoken, for he seemed to be convinced that God intended to bring condemnation

Myopic Me!

upon every household across the world. He seemed to be holding his own son accountable for every sin of man. He punished him constantly, for the things he did, and for the things he imagined that he did.

He apparently never heard that "God sent his Son into the world not to judge the world, but to save the world through him."[57] He was surely thinking during his early years in the horrors of World War II that the Tank he lived in was God's metaphor for living: Climb into the thick steel hull every day, and look for something to destroy with the copper clad shells they stacked inside the beast.

In his tank brigade in Northern Africa, he had witnessed unspeakable things which he could not utter, and he dared not remember. Now, he took his nightmares directly to his own son's back and legs with a whip and a ragged switch daily. "The world is condemned already," he was sure, "and my job is to beat every evil intention out of my son's heart, no matter how loud he screams!"

The boy was convinced that his father couldn't be right, but he muttered, "I deserve this whipping. I'll never be any good, no matter what I so!" Dad and son were both correct, for Grace alone would be able to mend their father-son relationship.

When I started writing down this story, I thought it was really a story about him, and about my relationship with him. But it was actually a story about every father as well. It raised the question, "Why does a father fail his son? Why is a father cruel to his own little boy? And finally, does the boy's father reach across time and distance to whip that boy's childhood and adult friends? Does the father's whip appear, leaving welts, in all of his relationships for the rest of his life?

I love the grown man as a brother, but these deep revelations have come as we looked together at the dimensions of the father-wound that is far too common in the men I consider as friends. When he told me his "Parable of the Wrinkled Potato," I looked through a dark window to see the damage done in his childhood days.

He dealt with demons that came and went, twisting first the father, then the son. He would always fall short of the mark his father set or failed to mention. Even if he had been Jesus Christ every day, his father would have crucified him with sticks and rulers and vile words.

This tale of the badly wrinkled potato became the only picture for revealing the damage done by constant negative feedback enduring until

Father Wound: The Shriveled Potato.

his father's death decades later. Even as a boy in school, the wound had become vividly known in his classroom. My eyes widened in wonder as I heard his intricate plan for revenge.

The hideous outworking of this powerful generational curse had consumed him in the first decade of his life. As we remembered the pain, sipping our coffee, I could see God's grace being unwrapped for our adult eyes to behold. We could easily acknowledge God's great mercy preserving the two of us from many things handed down by our fathers and grandfathers.

His parable brought together these interconnections of the wounding and the unforgiveness—the bitterness, anger, and perfectionism—infesting a boy's childhood heart. It affected his academic life, and his psychological and spiritual life. He strove to become the perfectionist his father demanded, and a terrible balancing act had been choreographed by the devil himself.

Religion is the chalice the enemy tells us to drink from when we can't seem to satisfy our father's commands. Perfectionism is the spiritual reflux we suffer when nothing ever makes the father happy. We drink down to the dregs, embracing the humiliation and the pain. We swallow the enemy's toxic brew of foul flavors mixed in the very gates of hell.

His father left him with no alternative, and the son embraced vengeance as his most precious and trustworthy religious rite. The pressure demanded Cain's revenge for every Abel whose work is approved. A terrible ripple, seemingly beyond his control, had been released into his childhood rituals, and into this formative classroom.

When he judged that his teacher was responsible for making him the butt of many jokes, he felt justified in getting revenge. She could have protected him from their laughter, but she had promoted it. Since it was the tradition in her class to bring a final gift at the end of the year, the boy chose to communicate his own fierce wrath. He wanted her to suffer, to be laughed at, and his gift would surely achieve this goal.

He selected a badly wrinkled potato as her gift. An older woman, her deeply wrinkled face left a powerful impression in the minds of every student in her classroom. His choice would be more than symbolic. It would present a kind of replica of her face and neck which every student would immediately understand.

Myopic Me!

There would be no doubt of the meaning of his gift when she opened it. Though her students rarely risked speaking of her wrinkled face, her appearance had become burned into their collective memories. As he described her to me in the bookstore, I remembered my Latin teacher in high school. She too had those deep wrinkles that identified her from every other teacher in the school.

By himself at home, the nine-year old boy got busy wrapping the perfect gift for this teacher who deserved what she would get. She would understand what it feels like to have everyone laughing at her. He sat alone in his bedroom with the badly wrinkled potato, wrapping it with growing excitement. The deep wrinkles perfectly matched her appearance.

He wrapped it with five, six, seven layers of different wrapping papers until he was satisfied with this initial phase of his urgent process. Then he placed the wrapped potato into a box; and once again, he started wrapping the box with six, seven, eight different wrappings, using different colorful papers.

He grimaced as he finished phase two of his intricate process. He was setting a bold trap to humiliate his teacher. He hated her, and he did not want this process to ever end, enjoying the delicious revenge it promised. He would finally see her humiliated in the same way that he experienced it.

She would finally become the butt of the joke, and the shoe would be on her foot. He could barely wait until the next day to deliver the perfect gift to her desk. Revenge would be so very sweet. After a fitful night of sleep, he awoke to dress and grab the present, taking it with him to the school.

Finally in her classroom, it was his last class of the day. Waiting had been so hard, and he wanted to tell someone why he was so excited all day. He delivered his decorative box to her desk with all the other wrapped gifts from the students.

As it would happen, his box was opened last, and it took her quite a time to unwrap it, while he watched with growing tension, for he knew the final paper would unveil his masterstroke for the others to see. As she uncovered the potato, layer by layer from the box, then all seven layers from the potato itself, there remained a mound of wrapping paper there

Father Wound: The Shriveled Potato.

on her desk. The students had already started laughing at their crazy classmate's excess, not yet seeing his cruel trap.

When the wrinkled potato was finally revealed, the teacher was stunned. Her hand visibly shook, and recoiled, as the potato fell from her hand to the desk with a soft thud. When they saw the wrinkles, the entire classroom gasped, and then there was complete silence.

The nine-year-old version of my friend flushed with shame as he witnessed the vengeance he had poured into this cruel sacrament. He had humiliated her in front of her classroom. He was shocked when he saw the savagery that had caused her face to recoil in horror. He saw that he was the author of this revenge conceived in his heart and his mind. At age nine he could easily understand that he had done something evil.

It was shocking to revisit this event in his history that morning at the bookstore where we often talked. Remembering those events, we both understood the paper wrappings to be the layers of his buried anger toward his father and toward himself. He had learned to project this deep anger in the direction of ANYONE who demeaned him or laughed at him.

Under the many layers of unforgiveness and bitterness, he had wrapped the deep father-wound in so many layers, it was difficult to discern in the light of day as an adult man, and man of God. Sometimes the colorful wrapping papers had made it possible for him to pretend that the father-wound did not even exist. But those layers were visible to everyone who knew him—though no one understood fully the root cause of his emotions that might flare for no reason at all.

For many years those layers had disguised intact the wound until he found a spiritual context where he could begin to unwrap that terrible box, baring his wrinkly potato inside. The potato represented his own shriveled up soul—his own deep injury, and the wrinkled face of that scapegoat—his teacher.

He would retaliate many times over the years without understanding the wrappings over those wrinkles deep inside his soul. At age ten, seventeen, and thirty, he buried that potato deeper and deeper. He buried it while it grew new potatoes from those eyes underground in his soul. The wounds were so deep, and so painful, and so arousing of his intermittent wrath. His father never relented.

Myopic Me!

It was inevitable that he would revisit those layers in a completely different and revelatory context. Many years later, when he entered the medium security prison as a minister, he had to pass through multiple layers of security that held those men's crimes in check. They were quarantined deep inside the multiple layers and walls and locking doors.

They became the wrinkled potatoes he might deal with one by one in the dark rooms in Norfolk Prison, each one wrapped in dull layers of steel and concrete. Through many walls of hostility and through many locking doors, he entered that prison to find his own father-wound wrapped in multiple layers.

Disguising their crimes from the other prisoners, these men had wrapped their packages securely, never intending for anyone to come along to open them up in any classroom ever again. Their stories had actually terminated for many of them in these private rituals behind steel bars, in isolation, and in their quiet pain vibrating inside, with no way out.

When my friend understood their need for Christ's freedom, it opened his own eyes wide to see the tightly wrapped anger, bitterness, and fear. Helping them with their insecurities, deep inside that prison, he gradually arrived at a more secure place concerning his own deeply buried hostilities. He helped them unwrap each layer of their wrinkled souls. He could vividly see the cruel potential of bitterness.

Instead of condemnation coming for these wrinkles God uncovered, he found forgiveness and reconciliation behind every folding of that buried world of pain and anger inside those prison walls. Instead of demanding inhuman feats of self-discipline from these men, Jesus had already made a way for each one of them to boldly come to the throne of grace.

As an adult, God handed my friend a hall pass for the prison he had willingly entered as a boy of nine. Though he could still be the most intolerant person on the face of the earth, God was filling him up with Grace. God revealed that there is nothing more narrow-minded, more bigoted, than His own perfect solution for our vengeance.

But God will not leap through our cultural hoops as He accomplishes His miracles. He sent His Son as the only Way for us to unwrap His gift of forgiveness. God entered the macabre wrapping papers of

Father Wound: The Shriveled Potato.

our fallen nature to save us. He never approves our cruelty born out of our personal father-wound.

He staunches our vengeance with His forgiveness, taking the torment of evil men: "Father, forgive them for they know not what they do!" The scandal of Jesus' forgiveness had long ago crushed my friend's entitlement. Jesus blood had flowed down over his constant grotto of revenge!

How could God's forgiveness accomplish the impossible task of unwrapping all the layers covering up his wrinkled soul? God never intended that we would complicate it with Freud's sexual antecedents, taking my friend to the foot of the Cross, cutting through the red tape of sin.

When he surrendered to God's solution for his solitary and unconscious confinement, he experienced peace for the first time. Though his freedom is certain and complete, the Holy Spirit is the teacher now. He does not humiliate His students, but leads them into the full pardon and healing that comes in Christ's name. Now, he can pray with confidence:

> "I will never be able to satisfy my father's righteous or unrighteous demands! I don't have to. Jesus has set me free from my sins, and from the damage done by my father's sins against me. Jesus even frees me from the screams of death and murder I have heard so many times in my inner ear. I don't have to be afraid of my father's wrath any longer because Jesus has shielded me from the wrath of God. My father's wrath was often unrighteous, but I don't have to hide from him anymore. No longer cowering, I don't have to avoid him like the Covid plague. I don't have to rush him, like some madman. I am free to live in peace with all men!"

The hard part, of course, lies ahead for him. He has seen God's forgiveness in the faces of the men he meets with in the prison. Their bitterness, shriveled up like old potatoes, can be pitched into the InSinkErator. He sees these men through Jesus' eyes, and Jesus' eyes are looking back at him. He can't earn his salvation by giving his time, but Jesus has already given him eternity through His own blood.

Myopic Me!

He is able, slowly, to see his father as Jesus saw him. He died without being reconciled to his son, but God has shown him a compassion for the man that he did not have before. He no longer sees his father's cruelty in every face and every voice speaking into his life.

He had to forgive his father—not pitying or holding on to the bitter root of contempt for him; he also had to let him go in death, allowing God's judgment to prevail with perfect justice. Meanwhile, he is learning to return a blessing for the cursing he received. In our conversations, he revealed that having a normal conversation was still difficult for him.

He never experienced a father and son discussion where he was permitted to speak. That and a number of other issues can arise because of this father-wound which affects so many of us human beings.

1. Low self-confidence
2. Anxiety
3. Depression
4. Rigid boundaries
5. Loose boundaries
6. People pleasing
7. Emotionally empty relationships
8. Emotionally empty parenting[58]

My friend learned to store up anger and shame until his father tired of berating him. Transferring this pattern to his few friends, he had to discover that they were not coming to tear him down. Rather, they consistently sought to build him up. They continued to befriend him, in spite of his red-hot face and argumentative spirit rising up to correct their every word.

His reactions to them came out of that spiral staircase down into the quarry of his deepest sin, down into the bitter rooting in the soul of a little child. "Let the little children come unto me!"[59] The journey out of that pit is not my friend's to accomplish: Only the Holy Spirit can lead him or me into all truth.

Myopic Me! is not silenced immediately, but is driven out by the Grace and Mercy of God shown to us daily. "If God is for us, then who can be against us."[60] Psychology has no power to save us, but God's forgiveness is the only Door. "Father forgive them, for they know not what they do!"[61]

> Bless those who persecute you. Don't curse them; pray that God will bless them. Be happy with those who are happy, and weep with those who weep. Live in harmony with each other. Don't be too proud to enjoy the company of ordinary people. And don't think you know it all! Never pay back evil with more evil. Do things in such a way that everyone can see you are honorable. Do all that you can to live in peace with everyone.[62]

4

Root of Bitterness: Three Incidents.

> Look after each other so that none of you fails to receive the grace of God. Watch out that no poisonous root of bitterness grows up to trouble you, corrupting many.[63]

Fourteen years ago, I partially awakened to find dark specters from my past in my nightmares. Vividly replaying past events in my mind, I was there—three decades before—and my body erupted with adrenalin as I intended to kill the perpetrators of my humiliation. Three personal insults had coalesced into this single nightmare that shocked me to a stupefied wakefulness in the dark.

Each ancient spirit had come back from decades before, and a python had wrapped around my throat, filling me with hatred and murder toward the three people from my past who had humiliated me. Each event had occurred while I was with friends, in safe public settings, more than thirty years before; and each incident had occurred at night.

- Tenth High School Reunion
- N. C. School of the Arts performance
- Arrival at Pastor's house in Midland

With my heart pounding, I was still asleep, but half-awake. I recalled three buried murders from decades before, and my blood pressure was one million over five million. My heart rate was a billion. I could feel a stroke standing on tiptoes on the high diving platform where strokes

Myopic Me!

always dive from, and I was so enraged I imagined these murders with intricate details in my wakeful-dreaming state.

The first event had occurred forty-four years earlier in Clemson, South Carolina at the Tenth High School Reunion. Those reunion events are always fraught with strong emotions anyway, and this one was no exception. "They" gave out awards to three or four alumni, and my name popped up among the winners. They voted me the "Ugliest."

Why was there an "Ugliest?" Why not something like, "Most Successful?" or "Funniest!" This was like a spear into the ugliest part of my character. It exposed me to the abject vulnerability of my still-forming, too often ugly, face in the mirror. I was so angry that I wanted a fist full of revenge to quench my instantaneous feelings of shame.

I wanted to demonstrate by some proof that I was not the Ugliest. I wanted everyone to see that I was anything but the ugliest. But this spear was left dangling from my pride like one of those knives cast into the bull's hide by the toreador. I wanted to prove them wrong by some exploit. Like that enraged bull, I would finally die from the tiny wound in my hide, and the easy sword into my heart from the skillful Toreador, Satan in tights.

The next day, on cue, the beautiful former girlfriend showed up at the New Year's Eve party on Lake Hartwell. She walked right up to me with laser-like eye contact. Knowing I was married, and that Ann was somewhere close beside me in the roar of that band, she provoked me with a classic question, "Are you happy?" It was the corollary of that question the serpent posed to Eve. Genesis describes the scene this way:

> "The serpent was the shrewdest of all the wild animals
> the Lord God had made. One day he asked the woman,
> 'Did God really say you must not eat the fruit from any
> of the trees in the garden?'"[64]

I looked at my former girlfriend's pretty face, and I saw that she could provide my monumental need for approbation. In that moment, I was swept into an overt assault upon my marriage covenant—she looked me in the eyes with such affection as she seemed to be asking me a most provocative question. "You can just leave your wife, and you can go home with me!"

Root of Bitterness:Three Incidents.

I had thought I might marry her a couple of years before, when she slipped away like smoke to her medical school in Ohio. There, she studied to be an obstetrician: "Catching babies," as she reported to me right there in the middle of the roar of the band that night. I had dated her during the years before I met my wife, to whom I have been married for over fifty-one years.

In that noise at the Barn that night on Lake Hartwell, Ann seemed oblivious to my distracted situation, unaware that the earth had been tilted to a 45-degree axis. She survived many such moments watching the shadows of adultery and lust flash across my face. In the roar of that New Year's Eve band, she likely did not hear her bold question inserted into her two-year-old marriage: "Are you happy?"

That question jarred me like the 600-volts from my first physics experiment at Clemson University, when I built an electromagnetic grid around a laser in order to determine Planck's Constant. That shock went through me late one night when I carelessly handled the bare male banana plugs that were inserted into the female banana jacks on that electromagnetic grid I had created.

At the Barn dance, I had responded to her shocking question and her barely disguised high-voltage probe into my marriage. I thought out loud in the roar of the band, "I am **not ugly** after all. This beautiful girl made a beeline to me to invite me home with her." She had just confronted the lie that I was ugly, while reminding me about those bare parts in the lab where nothing could have insulated me from the jolt of the "Ugliest Award."

With her arrival, my ugliness had suddenly become beautiful, and my beautiful marriage had become ugly. This pretty young woman from my past had grabbed my antennae as if she had been hired by an undercover TV crew with cameras whirring. It vaguely crossed my mind that I was being punked in that rough barn where the band howled and the waves softly lap the shoreline of our beach on Lake Hartwell.

That beautiful apparition from my past nearly ruined my immature marriage. In one night of insanity, someone came for me, for I was being punked by the flaw in my character—the deep wound in my flesh. Partly because of this evening, I would wait forty more years before diving into the pitfalls of a Fiftieth Reunion.

Myopic Me!

A full decade later, and a few months before we departed North Carolina for Texas to be part of a church-planting, several of us traveled together to the nearby performance at North Carolina School of the Arts. A friend and brother in Christ had attended that school, studying in their acclaimed performing arts department.

His gifted performances with the clarinet had gained him opportunities to play in more than one symphony orchestra for several seasons after his graduation from the University of Michigan performing arts department.

We had arrived at our seats in the balcony section overlooking the pit and stage on our left below us. This setting would be a welcome break from working on the house I was building [they were helping when they had time]. Not wearing the full armor of God, I was caught completely by surprise when a second insult occurred.

Getting settled into our seats for the curtain opening for the dramatic dance performance in a few moments time, a young man behind me blurted out his loud and rude command: "Sit down, you big-nosed xxxxxx!" [I won't include this forbidden word, used nonstop within our culture].

I had spent hours that day working to refinish some old furniture for our house, and I had drifted too far from God's presence during that same day; now, on that balcony, this personal taunt struck me somewhere very deep inside, in a place that I had forgotten.

It inflamed me with murderous anger. I felt the most powerful urge to turn, grabbing the offender, throwing him off the balcony railing right in front of me. In my mind, I had hurled him to the seats thirty-feet below.

My younger brother in Christ, Jerome, who is the present-day missionary to nearly fifty countries, told me afterward that he had a powerful mental picture in his mind. He watched me hurl the rude man to his death. Had I actually killed him? I can't describe him because I didn't really get a good look at him. Will the police be looking for me in some Cold Case file?

These close friends likely started praying instantly for me at that moment, as the demons jabbed their fingers into some deep wound in my soul—I found myself in this place full of potentially destructive outcomes. Through the grace of God, and through their prayers, I did

Root of Bitterness:Three Incidents.

not become a pawn for the devil's scheme. The Pharisees in Jerusalem had become pawns, and Jesus told them so.

> For you are the children of your father the devil, and you love to do the evil things he does. He was a murderer from the beginning. He has always hated the truth, because there is no truth in him. When he lies, it is consistent with his character; for he is a liar and the father of lies.[65]

Not very many months later, Ann and eleven-month-old Christopher and I traveled the two-thousand miles to arrive in West Texas, walking into that fine house which my Shepherd [pastor] had built on a vacant lot on the western edge of Midland. There, in that place for celebratory hugs and joyful reunions, the third insult struck me. All of our friends were facing us as we entered the large room expecting their hugs.

I had been working to finish the house in North Carolina, forced to put the unfinished house on the market, and leaving a Realtor to try to convince prospective buyers that it would be beautiful when it was finished. Ann, baby Christopher, and I had moved all of our possessions to Texas in a big moving-van. When we entered the large room, the pastor struck me in the face with some unexpected words.

"I'd forgotten how <u>ugly</u> you are!"

My shepherd, my pastor, and my friend, greeted me after many months with my second "Ugliest Award!" Once again, I was the "big nosed xxxxxx!" Three times the cock had crowed over my ***ugliness***. The pastor's personal disparagement of my appearance greeted me like a third hard slap across my "ugly" face.

I wish I could say that I remembered what Jesus endured after His mock trial; but on that night, I did not think once about the insults He endured so that the murder in my heart might be forgiven.

> Some of the governor's soldiers took Jesus into their headquarters and called out the entire regiment. They stripped him and put a scarlet robe on him. They wove

Myopic Me!

> thorn branches into a crown and put it on his head, and they placed a reed stick in his right hand as a scepter.
>
> Then they knelt before him in mockery and taunted, "Hail! King of the Jews!" And they spit on him and grabbed the stick and struck him on the head with it. When they were finally tired of mocking him, they took off the robe and put his own clothes on him again. Then they led him away to be crucified.[66]

Nothing in my life could pass muster with Jesus' suffering in the profane and violent treatment by the Jews and the Gentiles alike—the very ones He was dying to save. One of His precursors, King David, had also faced a bit of mistreatment, handling it very well.

I did not think of King David once during my own personal humiliations. Unlike David's response when the kibitzer hurled the rock at him,[67] I had grimaced with my private anger, stinging once again from the personal insult. David had practiced dodging King Saul's spears, but I would unwittingly plant a seed of revenge for my deeply buried nightmare a few decades later!

What was happening to me? Isn't that what you and I always want to know? "Why is this happening to me!" we ask our mirror or our close friend or our confessor. Why was my physical appearance being directly attacked across thousands of miles and over more than a decade in South Carolina, North Carolina, and in Texas?

What human or demonic purposes were being choreographed by these disparate people who brought their insults to bear on my ugly facial inheritance? How could—why did—I wake up years after these events to struggle with the murder in my heart still?

My post-nightmare autopsy concludes that in each timeframe, I had been struggling with an ancient idolatry. I hope you realize that I had to search my heart—allowing the Holy Spirit to search me—to see if there was any wicked way within me.[68]

I deduce that each time I was in a season when I was twisted by an ancient personal idolatry—a thorn in my side to humble me. The return of those specters were related to those struggles with pride and idolatry. In each instance, major life-choices were underway, and that

Root of Bitterness: Three Incidents.

idolatry erupted to war against the good that God was about to bring into our lives.

Having left everything behind, we had arrived in Texas with nothing, and this rude greeting in front of my friends felt like the most bitter of blows after all I had endured. The arrival of the good always comes with pain, but this was not what I expected.

I'm not sorry you have to read this personal account, for I believe it can become an edifying window into human nature, and into the nature of Satanic powers attacking God's plans in your own life. It is a window into the Pride that always comes before the Fall.

Satan comes to steal, kill, and to destroy. He doesn't care about our well-being, but wants to destroy our souls. We are vulnerable and fragile people, and it hardly helps to mention it, but Jesus is Lord of All. In this "fifth Gospel" account of Jesus, which is full of the details of Jesus' life and ministry, we find Isaiah the prophet "**insulting**" Him.

> **There was nothing beautiful or majestic about his appearance, nothing to attract us to him.**
>
> **He was despised and rejected**—["I forgot how ugly you are, Jesus!" the prophet seems to be saying] a man of sorrows, acquainted with deepest grief. We turned our backs on him and looked the other way. He was despised, and we did not care. Yet it was our weaknesses he carried; it was our sorrows that weighed him down. And we thought his troubles were a punishment from God, a punishment for his own sins! But **he was pierced for our rebellion, crushed for our sins.**[69]

I often wonder if my troubles in life come because of my sins. Outside of Christ, troubles are the direct result—the cause and the effect of sin. But in Christ, they come as the discipline from God who pursues us through it all. It is an expression, of the first order, of His love for us. It is a Father's love for us. But Jesus, truly, took our pain upon Himself when He was loaded down with our sins, falsely accused and charged, whipped with the cat-o-nine tails, mocked, and crucified naked in front of His mother.

Myopic Me!

The prophet states clearly that Jesus was pierced for "my rebellion." My rebellion springs from my pride. When my pride is wounded, murder or suicide ensues. When I returned to North Carolina after the insult in the shepherd's new house, I had lain down alone in that sixteen-inch ceramic bathtub full of hot water in an unheated house in winter. I had returned to complete that house for sale.

I had screamed into that darkness that surrounded me that night, not caring if anyone heard me, while asking God to show mercy. Finishing our four-bathroom house, I was overwhelmed with lonely tasks, and my bloodcurdling cry might have been heard by my distant neighbor through the woods. He was a wonderful friend who immigrated from Hungary, who had his house built by a contractor about a hundred yards away.

I cried out to God asking for deliverance from the unbearable project, and from the bitter and crushing burden pressing on my chest. I begged Him to release me, so that I could become a part of the new church-planting in Texas. This was one of those really important relational moments when God said, "Okay."

My shepherd had delivered his intentional insult in front of my friends, and I couldn't laugh, though it begged for my embarrassed chuckle; but there was something else twisting in his strident greeting. Some ulterior motive he never revealed had prompted this cruelty?

What bitterness hid under his tongue when I arrived in the room? "Take that!" he seemed to be saying. "See how that feels?" Was this his revenge for my late arrival in Texas behind the others? I will never know, for I never asked him. Did he bring this rebuke to silence the idolatry that had beset me?

Yet, how could those words spill out of him in front of everybody? Had I humiliated him, made him look bad with his new shepherd; therefore, did he determine to get his revenge by humiliating me? Was it that simple a thing? It didn't matter because it happened. The die was cast in my soul, and my own "revenge" would be hatched thirty-four years later in my bed during a nightmare in North Attleboro. How cunning is the evil one? How perfect is God's timing, setting the captive free?

"Don't let the sun go down while you are still angry, for anger gives a foothold to the devil."[70] A foothold for the demons, huh? What does a foothold look like? Does a foothold hide for decades before erupting with fantasies of murder and a near-stroke in my bed?

Does a foothold make an older brother kill his younger brother? Was Cain's failure with his offering to God with tangled motives very much like my failure to fully forgive and repent, to recognize and acknowledge my wounded pride and unforgiveness? Cain's idolatry was his curse that followed him for all his days—blaming, blaming—from pillar to post as the victim.

Fact is, I never thought of these three events again after they had happened. I had no idea they were buried in a fitful bed of unforgiveness. I had always spoken well of the shepherd, always defending him, always praying for him—even after I told him that our shared ministry was over. I never thought of that night at the theater again, or that Reunion. Revenge? What revenge? Do you see the subtlety of sin? It hides in the covers of our beds until the nightmares awakens us.

What God was doing in me had little or nothing to do with revenge, for I had not sought revenge in either case. He wanted to deal with the pride and vanity which had left me fragile and afraid—self-conscious and impotent in certain settings. My physical appearance could not become a door left open for the enemy to twist me, incapacitating me, or even killing me.

Self-control is important, and I demonstrated that to some extent. Shame over physical appearance is pure vanity, a chasing after the wind, meaningless. Vanity does not decide my future, wounding me in public settings. Public speaking is a call of God in my life, and vanity has no place in that venue where physical presentation is important but should never be crippling.

When self-consciousness is obsessive, then pride is preparing the fall. God wants to heal this fragile vanity in every one of His little ones. He wanted to heal this devil-disease, first sighted in Lucifer before his fall from heaven into hell.

> "In the place of the dead there is excitement over your arrival. The spirits of world leaders and mighty kings long dead stand up to see you.

Myopic Me!

> With one voice they all cry out, 'Now you are as weak as we are! Your might and power were buried with you. The sound of the harp in your palace has ceased. Now maggots are your sheet, and worms your blanket.'
>
> "How you are fallen from heaven, O shining star, son of the morning! You have been thrown down to the earth, you who destroyed the nations of the world. For you said to yourself, 'I will ascend to heaven and set my throne above God's stars. I will preside on the mountain of the gods far away in the north. I will climb to the highest heavens and be like the Most High.'"[71]

That same Satan, fallen angel, had sent his demons too find an easy entrance into my dreams. Their powerful nightmare woke me up from a near stroke or heart attack; and immediately, I had recalled the three occasions, one on top of the other. Three disparate events combined for my supernova dream of revenge. These events, and the offenders of my pride, were served up in pristine memory on my ugly platter of revenge.

I shiver today, recalling how my pride had swirled into my orbit on those earlier occasions—each time at night. Inside these nightmares, merged as one, I revisited the shuddering thunder of revenge that waits for the perfect moment to follow the crackling-electric-flare and lightning of my personal humiliation.

"Ugly" had become a hot button, my lightning; and vengeance had become my thunder following every flash. "You Ugliest, Big-Nosed, Uglier than I even remembered" xxxxxx was my triple-lightning, with triple-thunder of revenge exploding in my bed!

Satan's Stradivarius had deftly played Berlioz's, "Witch's Sabbath," and only afterward did I realize that Satan always plays that scherzo for my destruction. Still dreaming in the shepherd's new house in Midland, I saw his feet dangling in mid-air against the wall. The spirit of murder stroked my ego, and I could almost see Satan's evil grin.

> Let God's curse fall on anyone, including us or even an angel from heaven, who preaches a different kind of Good News than the one we preached to you. I say

again what we have said before: If anyone preaches any other Good News than the one you welcomed, let that person be cursed.[72]

Though he led us all from the profligacy of the early 1970s, the **pastor's** engine got hooked to money, and his heart got hooked to self-aggrandizement. His father's anger had filled him up with phantoms, and his father's rage had brought him low. His soul had been severely damaged, but God can forgive even that. Now, the same Destroyer arrived in my bed reminding me of my self-destructive contracts signed in the heavenly realm.

My reaction to those cruel words of my pastor could have resulted in more than one death, with vast harm to many lives, like ripples in a polluted pond. My younger brother in Christ who was in the room that night might never have visited the forty-plus countries carrying the Gospel of Christ, teaching leaders across the globe. He might never have raised an amazing family, with two sons and a beautiful daughter.

The other younger brother in the Lord might never have raised his beautiful family, a daughter and a son, leading his law firm in the seeking of justice and mercy every time he set foot inside the courtroom. His son might never have become the brilliant musician playing in orchestras and trios and quartets around the world.

Two young women present that night might not have raised families, with one finding her husband in Carlsbad, New Mexico. I would not have officiated at their wedding in my final service in Texas before moving on to New England. They might not have followed the admonition of Christ in Ephesians 4 to love one another through it all; praying together and leading many freedom journeys at their local church, leading many out of bondage.

Their beautiful daughter might not have gotten her Master's degree from Brandeis University in Waltham or her doctorate from Liberty University. She might not have become a powerful influence for sexual purity from her teaching position impacting an entire city with the message of God-ordained sexual relationships through Grace. Ministering to many hundreds of young people, she has always pointed them to the God who made them beautiful in His own image.

Myopic Me!

Ann's close friend, and our long-time family friends [all of these] might never have raised two beautiful girls, with one becoming a brain surgeon, and the other a pharmacist. One would pray publicly to receive Christ in Midland the same day that eventual-President George Bush prayed privately with Arthur Blessitt. Each of these young women have raised wonderful children, serving their communities and their many friends with love.

My wife might never have become the healing force for all of her young students who could not process language on the written page, who were outcasts, failures, rejects, laughed at and scorned—until she mentored and taught them to find the hidden codes in the word, and the sentence, and the syntax, and the vocabulary full of telltale sounds which they could use to decode their broken lives. She taught them to read, and now the Words of Christ no longer arrive at their eyes as curses crawling off the page, but they come with a blessing.

My son would not have grown up bringing love into every context he enters, and everywhere he goes, serving, humbling himself, and coming into a deeper relationship with his Lord and his God. The devastation of my actions might have destroyed the planting of God in his little life in Midland. That church we planted in Midland might never have happened; and the two-hundred thriving churches today might not have been planted on that same caliche and tumbleweed plateau in the Permian Basis.

Ann might never have heard her father, the famous Cardiologist from Duke Hospital fame, say that vanity is meaningless. He had spent his life very much aware of reputation, appearances, and standing in the field of medicine. He had imposed some of this chasing after the wind on his daughter in moments of weakness or anger. As they walked on the golf course road together, after she had helped him pack his life into cardboard boxes, he told her his new truth: "None of that striving really matters at all. Our relationships are the only things that matter."

The weirdest thing about that night in my bed in North Attleboro, was the way those three disparate events arrived for one final visitation—years after her dad had died of a heart attack at eighty-seven years of age, on the same day he would have traveled to Costa Rico for a vacation.

I prayed, forgiving my shepherd who had also died, taken from this life by cancer. I forgave that unknown assailant on the balcony, as well

Root of Bitterness:Three Incidents.

as that unknown classmate who had designated me to be "the ugliest" returning graduate from D. W. Daniel High School. Within forty-five minutes in that bed, sitting in the covers still, the war in the heavenly realm had passed over my head, and peace was restored to my heart.

That Revenge was gone. That ugly vanity had been disarmed. That night I did not have all these revelations about causes and deeper meanings. Writing helps with that part of the process. This is why journaling is so very important for the Christian.

On that night, I placed my three stones from Cain's field on the floor beside the bed. I put the stones down at the foot of the Cross. I could not fix anything, for Grace is the sole terrain of forgiveness and redemption. The soul's topography is best left to Christ's choreography. After all, He faced the mockers so that I would not be ashamed, wounded by words hurled into the darkness.

I was certain when I lay back down in the bed that night, that I would revisit the place of peace reserved for God's beloved. I was sure that the Holy Spirit would once again guard my dreams. Does it really matter that I forgave those folks, those people made in the image of God? What does Jesus say about this kind of forgiveness? Do you know? I know, and I have no excuse nor claim of ignorance. "Forgive, or the Father in heaven will not forgive you! Forgive, or your prayers will be hindered."[73]

God was showing me that night that He wants no roots of bitterness making their nest in my soul. He wants no vulnerability to vainglory to remain there in my soul either. He only wants healing—bringing appropriate discipline as an emblem of His love for me and mine. And He wants me to give this revelation away so that you will let him search you for any wicked way that might still be hiding in your dreams.

He wants me to remind you that He permitted Joseph's story to unfold in Egypt. The evil intentions of Joseph's older brothers were part of the story, but healing and provision was God's intention all along. When Joseph wept and kissed his cruel brothers, he revealed to us the love of Christ come to save us. It is the choreography of God in our lives which we fail to appreciate. What Satan meant for evil, God meant for our good.

His older brothers wanted him dead because of their jealousy. Their father loved him best, and they wanted him dead. They sold him as a slave to a caravan which took him into Egypt. When Joseph interpreted

Myopic Me!

Pharaoh's nightmares from his jail cell, he had been falsely charged with rape of Potiphar's wife. God showed Joseph that the famine would come, and he would store grain in silos for the lean years.

The real famine God was dealing with, was the spiritual famine in Jacob's own house. His sons were spiritually corrupted by their selfishness and carelessness toward the call of God on their lives. Now, God placed them in the control of the one they had betrayed, but they didn't recognize Joseph in his Egyptian garb. Joseph had their fate in his hands, sending them to prison or to freedom, to life, or to a sudden execution by his own hand.

Joseph's story is an open window into the deliverance of Christ, the Son of God, who will come hundreds of years later into Jerusalem. God is forever purifying His people, preparing them for the fulness of His plans. When Joseph forgave his envious and cruel brothers, it was a foreshadowing of Jesus on the Cross.

During Christ's day in Jerusalem, the Pharisees have become like Joseph's brothers, sending Jesus to the Cross on trumped-up charges. But once again, what Satan meant for evil, God meant for great good. Entering Jerusalem, Jesus wept over His lost brothers, Israel. He embraced them, giving His life for them, though they had laughed at Him and mocked Him.

Joseph's tears, weeping over his brothers, is a picture of Jesus Christ setting aside the vengeance we deserve, for He could have slaughtered us all with a word from His mouth. With a word, Joseph could have executed his brothers; but God sent the Lamb to die on the Cross in their place. Judah is a foreshadowing of Jesus, the Lamb of God.

> Judah answered, ". . . My lord, we have all returned to be your slaves—all of us, not just our brother who had your cup in his sack . . . So please, my lord, let me stay here as a slave instead of the boy, and let the boy return with his brothers."[74]

With God, there is ALWAYS a larger plan which only a few will really perceive as it happens. Joseph understood God's plan when he spoke grace to his brothers.

> "But don't be upset, and don't be angry with yourselves for selling me to this place [Egypt]. It was God who sent me here ahead of you to preserve your lives."[75]

God showed me a better way that night, a more healthy, edifying way. His Way is always more edifying, and God is pleased when we prove our faith in Jesus. Faith will always see that God's Way is good. The risk and reward of faith causes us to say, "Father, I'm all in with Jesus. He is the Way, the Truth, and the Life. He is the only Way for us to know you and to please You."

> It is impossible to please God **without faith**. Anyone who wants to come to him must believe that God exists and that he rewards those who sincerely seek him.[76]

5

The Syrian Desert Flower.

> Since God in his wisdom saw to it that the world would never know him through human wisdom, he has used our foolish preaching to save those who believe. It is foolish to the Jews, who ask for signs from heaven. And it is foolish to the Greeks, who seek human wisdom. So when we preach that Christ was crucified, the Jews are offended and the Gentiles say it's all nonsense.[77]

> "Look, I am sending you out as sheep among wolves. So be as shrewd as snakes and harmless as doves."[78]

A seventy-mile-long spiritual desert was described in 2014 national polls—in general, it defines the geographic landscape from Providence to Boston. This region is chilly to the Gospel of Christ. It has nothing to do with the snow that is outside my window, falling for a day and a half. This is a region in which there is animosity toward God's Son, His Words, and His Church. At that time, there wasn't another region so reticent to hearing and receiving the Good News of Jesus Christ.[79]

This is a region, then and now, flooded with Catholic crimes committed by priests who exploited altar boys for their sexual pleasure. It is a region familiar with the Cardinal's church-ordained authority being used to sexually exploit seminarians who were preparing for the ministry as priests.

Officials of the church have famously been vocal in condemning the abuses without doing very much about it. Mostly unresponsive to public pressure or legal claims, these figures of authority in the global religious organization have maintained radio silence concerning their fallen priests. One Cardinal was moved, and promoted to a new post in the Vatican when his home city was crumbling all around him.[80]

The inconsistent handling of these stories of hundreds of boys who were abused while serving as altar boys has not enhanced the image of the so-called "church" in this region. Catholic church buildings are nearly empty, and many have already been closed. This murky history has propelled the region into a deeper darkness, contributing to the rise of opiate deaths.

Young people rarely look to the church to help them resolve their internal struggles. They choose the powerful euphoria of the addictive pills and the heroin syringe to accomplish that job. Many young people today consider themselves to be "none's," rejecting religion in all its familiar branding, with Catholicism at the top of their list.[81]

Our neighbors laughed derisively when we invited them to our services, and their response was the same sarcastic and cynical attitude we have heard many times. The more religious they are, with rituals of family, entertainment, sports, and career, the more cynically they will speak to the issue of God or Jesus in their lives. "All the churches are empty."

Our Mission in New England from the beginning has been to reach the None's. When we say we are here for those not yet here, it is in direct response to this pattern of withdrawal by young people who no longer seek God. Our vision has always been referenced to this spiritual blindness of the region, speaking into the latent spiritual hunger that longs for Good News! A spate of new believers weekly increased our faith.

> For I am not ashamed of this **Good News** about Christ.
> It is the power of God at work, saving everyone who
> believes—the Jew first and also the Gentile. [82]

You see, it has little to do with Catholic or Protestant, Methodist, or Nondenominational emphasis. The Good News bespeaks the ultimate theology of freedom through Christ's name, offered to all men, unhindered by religious trappings of **any** sort. And there are many sorts. The Gospel shows no favoritism to any group, any geography, or any social status.

The Syrian Desert Flower.

Twenty-seven years ago, God orchestrated our next move, this time under the disguise of Texas Instruments. We arrived in our second consecutive desert vineyard, having lived in the near-desert region of Midland-Odessa Texas for eleven years—we would soon become cultivators of a frail crop of "tiny yellow flowers" we found breaking through the cracks in the dry spiritual landscape of New England.[83]

Truly, we found a great spiritual thirst for the Gospel of Hope! Everyone is looking for hope. Cynics are looking for hope. The yellow flourish of new life has become a powerful metaphor for me since hearing the story from a missionary who came from South Africa to speak with our group in Norwood, Massachusetts.

Today, the polls have improved slightly for the Boston and Providence areas; and Holyoke to our west, has become Number 1 in its cold-shouldering of the Gospel.[84] Into this kind of negative spiritual atmosphere, the Gospel fearlessly moves. The context and meaning of the yellow flowers came to us from the personal testimony of a South African church-planter speaking to us about his own daughter's journey into Syria.

When his daughter married an African man, the couple moved to the war-torn landscape of Syria where God had shown them to plant a Christian church.[85] Her father had spent his life teaching others to be sensitive to God's still small voice—especially in the command to share the Gospel, planting churches around the world himself for decades.

He explained to us that he had faced myriad dangers along the way, but nothing could compare to the danger his daughter was now confronting![86] When his ivory-skinned daughter and her ebony-skinned African husband informed dad about their plans to build a church in the Syrian desert, he blanched with fear for her.

He found himself privately overwhelmed. It was his son-in-law's fervor for the Lord that frightened him. That fervor would carry his little girl into a desert alive with ISIS fighters! Famous for cutting off the heads of Christians, or for crucifying them, or for raping the women, this image of them going into such a vulnerable place terrified him.

Nothing good had happened in Syria for decades, and deadly hostilities were lurking everywhere as they arrived there for their visit. Christians had been systematically driven out, or exterminated, by the

Myopic Me!

local people or by ISIS.[87] So, on his visit to the desert with them, he was flooded with anxiety that almost sloshed when he walked.

He tried to hide it from these two bold young people while he searched for God's confirming message from an entirely desolate landscape. They traveled together to the actual site for their church-planting, and his desire for encouragement sank even lower when they announced, "Here's the spot!"

Their wide smiles belied their own fears about the future, for the danger was very real to them as well. Looking in every direction the land lay as flat as a concrete slab. Nothing green interrupted this horrifying moonscape. The missionary's heart shriveled in the baking sunlight that had killed every plant and animal which had sought to live there. No realtor would bring a client to this place saying, "This is your building site!"

In this blinding sunlight, he tried to squat down to keep from falling down. He had preached about difficult situations in people's lives which gained miraculous outcomes, but this stopping point on the surface of the earth seemed devoid of any hope. As he struggled to get his bearings on this rough and sandy soil his hands pressed against, he saw it for the first time. God's message was right in front of him.

A tiny yellow flower had pushed through that same hard-packed earth. The flower stood confidently in the dead soil. How could such an exquisite thing survive in this terrible place of death and despair? How could this tiny messenger send forth such abundant hope, indifferent to the hostile environment? He checked his cell phone involuntarily. There were no bars.

Yet, this yellow flower instantly rang in his worried spirit as he bent low, as if in prayer. He stared at the detailed texture and shape, the splurge of color in the sporadic yellow blooms. He understood instantly that the tiny church they were planting in this concrete land would come up and shine like this yellow flower. This church would bring hope to many thousands in the region. New life was coming soon, and now he understood. God had spoken to him through the dead ground.[88]

It would not be easy, but God was in charge of their project in the midst of this desert hardship and imminent warfare. Shrewd as serpents they had come, but gentle as doves they would now minister Grace in this hateful geography. Death would face them daily, and ISIS walked through open doors to move into the region.

ISIS would shake this land with their swords and knives—raping women and beheading the men who refused to recant their new faith in Jesus. But God's Sword would cut much deeper into their hearts, cutting much deeper than any jugular. His Sword would cut between the joints and the marrow, revealing the hidden motives of the heart.

As I heard this father's story, I remembered that we too had left our equivalent of the Syrian concrete soil, abandoning the one hundred twenty-miles of caliche-plateau in West Texas to come to the unlikely glacier-prairie of New England. Though this land in Massachusetts is green and full of houses and commerce, spiritually, it was like the surface of Mars. The wild storms of Mars were coming from every direction at once.

God's great Gospel plow had long ago cut through this dry land, but we arrived to seek a new crop of His yellow flowers in the broken hearts and unquenched thirst that waited in the region. In national surveys, Providence had gained the sad reputation as being the most negative toward the Gospel in the country, with Boston coming in 3rd in that same poll prior to 2014.[89]

Religions proliferated, but the people had not heard the Gospel of Christ. With sixty universities in the region, education was the god for many. Emptiness and fear don't subside where arrogance rises, and heroin had become the religion of oblivion for many. Sin hid behind these duck-blinds of self-salvation. Hope was not a language spoken by many of the citizens of Southern New England.

I remembered that God had sent His Son into a region where important and educated men could offer no hope. He spoke life into a region where there was no justice or mercy, and no faithfulness even among the religious teachers. Jesus showed them a better Way. He showed them the Way of the servant. He demonstrated the Way of love and forgiveness from the Cross.

These cities initially represented the extent of our tent pegs driven into this dry terrain,[90] stretched for around seventy miles. Our desert region was almost as dry as that in Syria, yet God would bring fruitful life within a few years, with Boston and Providence losing their top

Myopic Me!

spots in this very negative poll. Cities like Portland, Seattle, Rochester, and Troy, NY moved up in the polls into those negative spots.[91]

When we knew our time in Texas had ended, God said, "Where do you want your bodies to go?" We said, "Attleboro, Massachusetts!" And we were transported to a land we had never heard of, just as we had gone to Midland, Texas, having no previous knowledge of that city either. We had never heard of Midland before we left North Carolina. Now, we found ourselves going to Attleboro, a small city founded by the Pilgrims' offspring in the 1600s.

We were met in Norton by the neighborhood drunk who was horrified by our giant moving van invading his narrow streets. We would later realize that we were living in the land of addiction—to alcohol and to opiates of all types. Met by the very embodiment of addiction, this Colonial condo village had announced to us that we were entering the land of death through a very present plague.

We would eventually witness the routine deaths of young men and women from overdoses—typically laced with Chinese Fentanyl. We would spend good years at one church before we found a small church near Attleboro where a visionary young preacher was leading a small flock of one hundred people.

Tim Hatch arrived in North Attleboro from Norwood, where his father-in-law came as a missionary from South Africa twenty years before. Tim's mission is evangelism, preaching the Gospel, while allowing the prophetic voice of Christ speak into an age of secularism and empty religion.

From Brown University to Harvard in Cambridge, the day of faith had passed the region by, leaving the ground cold to the message of the Cross. Jesus was anathema in those two famous universities. With around sixty universities in the region, rationalism had become the new god.

Fifteen years later there are more than two-thousand attending Waters Church on special weekends, with an average of around fifteen-hundred. There are campuses in Woonsocket, Fall River, Apollo Bay Florida, Guatemala, and soon in Peru. There was a time I didn't understand growth, and numbers like these. I thought this expansion was an evil thing.

"Focus on the local church body, and keep it small and intimate!" I can now affirm that small groups make the church small and intimate,

The Syrian Desert Flower.

full of love and prayers, focusing on the weekend message, worshiping the Lamb who was slain for us.

"Our Father, pour out your presence in our midst, and receive our praise and thanksgiving for new life, hope, and healing." While the large room is full of worshipers bring forth vibrant and exciting demonstrations of the spiritual life of God in the community. Bring forth workers for the Harvest that is coming even before this Pandemic ends—and thank you for salvations and baptisms throughout this time of Covid-19 restrictions.

The church has progressed through four different buildings, with the building-size continuing to change to keep up with the spiritual hunger which God has brought into this area. He does not make people hungry for Christ where the Word of God is not preached. He lets those churches die a slow death instead. Our latest building is one hundred-thousand square feet—a former factory for gold and silver products.

Now the building is used to bring forth the spiritual gold in people's lives through the power and authority of Jesus' name. Even during the Covid restrictions, with masks and spacing, there are around a thousand people in three services each weekend. In one service at Christmas time, a group of people got up and left during the sermon. When informed afterward why they had left: "Because you were preaching too much about Jesus!"

We have come to understand that God's harvest always comes out of this dead ground where Jesus' name had not been heard for centuries. These were the walking dead until that same Jesus could redeem them, No matter which nation we call our own, no matter where our rituals take us, we are spiritually dead until Jesus enlivens us through the Holy Spirit, leading us through the only Door: The Cross of Jesus Christ.

We are continuing to learn to recognize the tiny yellow flowers popping up through the parched landscape, and God is expanding our vision to move far beyond North Attleboro, to the uttermost corners of the earth. God is taking us to the distant islands and to the mountain tops around the earth. We have become His sweet perfume, the scent of Christ, sharing this profound hope in Him.

6

Shadow of the Baptist Church.

"You must not covet [want, crave, hanker, desire] your neighbor's house. You must not covet your neighbor's wife, male or female servant, ox or donkey, or anything else that belongs to your neighbor."[92]

Then David sent messengers to get her [Bathsheba, the wife of Uriah the Hittite]; and when she came to the palace, he slept with her . . . So the next morning David wrote a letter to Joab and gave it to Uriah to deliver. The letter instructed Joab, "Station Uriah on the front lines where the battle is fiercest. Then pull back so that he will be killed."[93]

When our friend in North Carolina wrecked his motorcycle, he said that his Triumph 650 had run off the road where his neck was met with a rigid guy wire. He said that the near-death experience scared him so much he never wanted to ride the motorcycle again. He offered the bike to me for a reasonable price. I agreed to take a test drive on a one-third mile strip of road where we lived, while he and Ann waited for my return.

That road intersected a larger thoroughfare at a T, where a white wooden Baptist Church building waited across the road with heavy wooden doors at the front entrance. "This is the brake near your right foot; here is the accelerator on this right handlebar. The shifter is under

Myopic Me!

the other foot and the left handle bar." I had never ridden a motorcycle in my life, and I received this thirty-second primer before I gently gunned the bike up the slight hill.

I knew I was in trouble instantly when the accelerator had no effect, while the bike surged hard, nearly throwing me off the back. The accelerator was stuck in the wide open position as soon as I departed. Fifty, sixty, eighty-five miles per hour, I flew in a straight line, trying not to cause a loss of balance. In a few moments, I would fly across the road at more than a hundred miles per hour into the front door of that Baptist Church.

I tried the brake, twisting the accelerator back and forth, but the powerful surge was not abated. I remembered the shifter, but had no idea whether it would work at this speed, or if it would cause a crash trying to disengage it. My heart was beating hard, but I could not allow that thumping to distract me, for I would surely die. The options were few, knowing little about this homicidal machine.

I had no choice, and I realized that I had to try anything, everything, or I would explode against the front doors of the Baptist Church building ahead. That specter hung heavily inside my competing thoughts. I kicked with my foot [I don't actually remember what I did] until the gears switched into neutral, the engine whined, reaching the maximum revolutions before dropping back to idle. The bike slowed down rapidly, and I applied the brakes without wrecking the bike.

Quickly, the speed was reduced to nearly zero. I was alive! I did not die crashing the heavy double doors of the Baptist Church that waited across that road. I would not learn how it felt to die, torn to pieces, flying over the wood pile at a hundred miles per hour. That bicycle ride into the Nutt's wood pile in the woods at age eight had not come back to finish me upon the Baptists' thick front doors.

I did not fly over those handle bars as I had that day, when I was bruised but not broken, lying in the stickers and pine needles that were waiting for me in the woods a hundred feet from their ranch house. George and Donna Mae, Johnny, Richard, and little George, had not rushed out to find me crumpled in their woods.

And I managed to turn that six-hundred fifty cubic inch bike around, rolling it back down the hill with little or no confidence after my near-death experience. The owner of the motorcycle was there, staring at me,

Shadow of the Baptist Church.

bewildered at my returning. He and Ann had waited, side by side, to hear what I would tell them about my little test drive into the valley of the shadow of the Baptist Church.

I got the strange feeling that he already knew what happened. He had watched me accelerate, and he knew the cable had been captured wide open. He understood by some secret knowledge that only the owner possesses, that this bike would not come back the same way it had left.

I dumped the bike at his feet, unable to prevent its fall, as the great weight over-shifted, ripping it out of my hands. It fell in a self-made gravitational arc, cranking down at his feet where it belonged. I told him, "The accelerator stuck wide open. I will never ride a motorcycle again. Keep your bike—I don't want anything to do with it." He just looked at the bike as if he really didn't want it any more either. He didn't seem surprised that I had nearly died.

I headed for the apartment a short distance away. I was badly shaken by the experience, but I was exhilarated and full of life now—having avoided the jaws of death. I felt powerful, even though I had come to the end of me on that valley of the shadow of the Baptist Church. It never crossed my mind that this might not have been an accident, that Satan wanted me dead.

Was it at that moment that I realized I was not doomed? God had protected me, and now I had an increased feeling of alienation from my friend, hardly understanding why. I was pulling away from him, and there was nothing anyone could do to stop it. I remembered the day he had looked at me in the front seat of my parked 1969 Camaro. He was holding his bottle of Boone's Farm Apple Wine in a brown bag. "We are doomed," he declared to me. I said nothing, but spoke emphatically in my mind, "I am not doomed!"

I was certain of God's love, though my personal behavior during this interregnum was spotty at best. God spoke to me, saying, "You belong to Me! My Son has secured your freedom. You are free from such hopelessness. I have saved you."

Two voices were speaking in that car with the sickening smell of that apple wine in a bag. I realized that our cigarette smoke was choking me. It was not pleasant any more after five years of waking up with tar in my throat. It seemed, for the second time in my life, toxic. I had started back smoking while I was in the Air Force—"Smoke 'em if you've got 'em."

Myopic Me!

When I heard my friend's voice in the haze in that car, his dark sentiments seemed strangely convincing, but paled before the affirmation of God's voice in my spirit. "Smoke 'em if you've got 'em" had lost its deadly grip on my life. I realized for the first time that we were different—my friend and I. We were co-conspirators no longer.

We were in the same company, in the same car, and sometimes in the same mood; but we were living in a very different spiritual reality. What fellowship does light have with darkness? It is not a question of me being better than he was. It was a matter of pure Grace. To whom were we giving our hearts and bodies? To whose voice were we attending with our trust and obedience? Max Lucado clarifies this incredible divide in the murky waters of life.

> Christmas begins what Easter celebrates. The child in the cradle became the king on the cross. And because he did, there are no marks on my record. Just grace. His offer has no fine print. He didn't tell me, "Clean up before you come in." He offered, "Come in, and I'll clean you up." It's not my grip on him that matters but his grip on me. And his grip is sure. So is his presence in my life. God is always near us—always for us—always in us. We may forget him, but God will never forget us. We're forever on his mind and in his plans. He called himself "'Immanuel' (which means 'God with us')" (Matt. 1:23).[94]

I listened to God most of the time, but my friend listened to the spirit of witchcraft always whispering into his life—Ouija boards, Tarot cards, and rebellion. His vasectomy had made him a good candidate for women who were looking for a safe way to have sex. Even his dark complexion and thin lips might have steered me clear of this dangerous friendship.

His inner voice said emphatically, "I am doomed!" Mine said, "I am loved by God." It is not even a matter of God loving him, for He loves each of us. But my insubstantial friend believed in nothing or in everything. He had no discrimination about spiritual matters, manipulating every situation for his own gain. He was in the camp of the amoral.

Under this spiritual sway, he had become arrogant, contemptuous of God, cynical; and yes, he was doomed, not believing in the Son God sent to save him.

I learned far too much from his dark spirit of Cain, yielding to my flesh's unhealthy desires far too many times along the way; but I knew that I was not doomed. He was cursed, like Cain, and a wanderer through life. But God had adopted me, and I knew it. I couldn't articulate it very well since I still had not read the Bible; and no one had taught me. I knew God's word by faith, and through the confirmation of His Counsel coming from the "Faith-Time Continuum."[95]

God had told me at age twelve that He was God. He explained what that meant. My actions could not negate that truth Jesus had spoken into my heart. "Be still, and know that I am God; I will be exalted among the nations, I will be exalted in the earth."[96] That day in the car, I found myself exalting His beautiful name, not fully acknowledging him before men.

The Lord Almighty is with us; the God of Jacob is our fortress. The God of Jacob had met me in that car, in spite of the Boone's Farm Apple Wine in a brown bag. God loved me, and I knew it. I might go into that famous box canyon with no way out, but I would not miss what God's Son had purchased with His blood. The One Who made me would not stop guiding me through dark valleys and every shadow of death.

When I flew into that dark interface with the physical Baptist Church, He was with me. Then, and now, His rod and staff comforted me. He was there to show me what to do, to help me flip the gears to neutral so that I would survive to finish the Good Works He had Prepared for me to perform!

That scheme of the devil to take me out of this race, to knock me off the track—that scheme failed when God said, "You will not take his life! But you can twist him like a pretzel in the wind into the shadows of that Baptist Church." He told Satan that I would soon declare, "Christ is my God, and Him alone!" He would entirely separate my family from former alliances with friends who mocked or scoffed at the Light.

Soon, I would join the others in Winston-Salem at the church named after Stephen, who died witnessing the glory of the risen Christ. Saul stoned him to death, but Stephen knew the Lord. Now, we were creating the banners from felt which declared, **"Jesus is Lord."**

Myopic Me!

    I would look at that banner with the deepest reverence for those three incredible words! Little more than arts and crafts, the words, "Jesus is Lord," struck me with a conviction exceeding the dread of that impact with the Baptist Church's front door.
    The same God who saved me that day in the shadow of the Baptist Church has always held the exact moment when I will depart this world, and nothing, and no one, can edit that time and destination in His supernatural SpaceTime. Will His Son return in glory to call me into the air along with the rest of His Church?
    "His Church," not "my church," will be called from these shadows into His full Lightness when the Archangel shouts, and Trumpet blast splits the heavens apart. Will I be called into the air when I hear the Good Shepherd's voice saying, "Come! Come to me, My Bride!" His finger always moves us to safety, according to His perfect will, until that time when His final assent brings us to Himself.
    I am the worst of all sinners when it comes to mis-imagining this moment, misconstruing it as a tragedy. But Death, where is your sting? Is that sting of death absorbed into the body of Christ, defused by the Lamb of God who took upon Himself the sins of the world?
    That death-stinger was removed when He said, "Father, forgive my servant John, for he did not know what he was doing. Though his sins were as scarlet, now wash him as white as the new fallen snow in New England [before the snowplows and dirty sand and salt flies everywhere]."

> "I can never escape from your Spirit!
>   I can never get away from your presence!
> If I go up to heaven, you are there;
>   if I go down to the grave, you are there.
> If I ride the wings of the morning,
>   if I dwell by the farthest oceans,
> even there your hand will guide me,
>   and your strength will support me."[97]

    "When my borrowed bike tries to *Triumph* over me; even then, You will guard my life!"

7

Beautiful Woman with Potato Chips.

> For you have been called to live in freedom, my brothers and sisters. But don't use your freedom to satisfy your sinful nature. Instead, use your freedom to serve one another in love.[98]
>
> It might not be a matter of conscience for you, but it is for the other person. For why should my freedom be limited by what someone else thinks?[99]

She is beautiful as she opens the bag, removing a single perfect chip with her thumb and forefinger. She moves the chip steadily toward her perfect red lips, and her mouth parts just wide enough to insert the delicacy inside—I watched as it came to rest on her pink tongue. I could almost taste the salty goodness, nearly able to hear the crunch of this irresistible delight.[100]

Many more chips would follow, of course, but they would be devoured after the cameras were turned off and stored away in their protective bags. The beautiful young woman would still be sitting there in her mock kitchen backdrop. She would by now have fallen victim to that open bag and that irreducible memory of those perfect chips waiting inside. The bag would lie there, her mouth still parted, chips spilling right out at the edge of the opening.

Her fingers would move faster and faster from bag to mouth, and back again. Nearly empty now, she would rise from the beautiful set to walk away—Had she escaped so easily from her sensory rush? She wished that she had heard "quiet on the set—light—camera—action" a hundred more times. Each chip arrived on her palette like the purest pleasure.

The ashtray, always full of butts, sat on my desk during that earlier time, and the Pall Malls were burning a hole in my left shirt pocket. Shirts had pockets during that blind, deaf, and dumb time when the ash tray held a familiar place in every social interface.

The phone rang at work, and I slapped my pocket to find that familiar friend, the beautiful pack of twenty cigarettes waiting there—waiting for the fire from my **gold** Zippo lighter. The resulting pungent odor hung in every major gathering place, stoked by the smoke from a pack a day.

In my family home, the sprawling trays became central fixtures built into the decor of the room, and they were often full of Lucky Strike butts. The malodorous stale air of the crematorium filled the room on a typical day.

I had watched the smoke rise from my father's head—following me from room to room as I followed Pop everywhere—from setting stones in the yard to grading papers in his pine-paneled-office with the Japanese sword on the wall and the picture of my uncle with the press-camera he reached for when the German bomb obliterated his ship in the western edge of the Mediterranean Sea.

Once I sat in the front of his classroom as he taught twenty future soldiers the deep meaning of *Childe Harold*, the young man weary of never-ending wars. No one knew the difference back then, when the deadly smoke rose from the red tip, settling in the hair of the one who loved the white tubular smokes. No one had that clear warning about the damage done to the body when that tar and nicotine merged with the cilia in the lungs, and with the blood in the capillaries.

But during this year, tens of thousands will die a horrible death because of this beloved smoke curling around their nostrils under a pretty blue sky on a wonderful sunny day. The anti-smoking ads on TV, show the destructive effects on the body, with the breathing tube, the deformed face, and the rasping sound of a partial lung.

The moguls actively covered up the truth with seductive ads in the 1950s. They secretly destroyed the lungs of millions before anyone got wind of the truth that the wonderful smoke would kill them in a few years. The potato chip ad also disguises a long-term consequence quite similar to consequence of smoking Lucky Strikes, Camels, or becoming the Marlboro Man on a powerful horse!

The healthiest and happiest people in the world held cigarettes between their fingers, while the good life smothered them with two-thousand chemicals summoned into every toxic breath. These kinds of Ads on TV always exploit the Body's affinity for pleasure—and the ad for Lays Potato Chips effectively focused our eyes and appetites on her beautiful mouth as the destination for every delicious salty chips from her perfectly vacuum-sealed bag.[101]

You may wonder why this represents exploitation, but you can easily see with your own eyes that it is seductive in the same way that the young girl on that stage in Charleston was seductive when her clothes dropped around her ankles in front of five-hundred cadets.

The beautiful woman with the potato chip is intentionally attracting the eye—in the same way that the north pole locks on to the south pole of a second magnet. The lips of the beautiful model becomes the visual force-field, requiring the viewer's eye to "Focus!" attention on the depths where she places the perfect potato chip. She shows us that, "It is okay for you to love this new addiction, for I am beautiful, and you will be beautiful!"

This seduction comes to entice the hand of the beholder into the monkey trap with the one-way opening. Once the hand is inside, the fist-full of potato chips cannot be retracted. She is captured with her first bite. She is seduced with the taste and smell, which is by-design, intending to hook another million innocent victims.

The animal fat, the salt, and the divine crunch are tuned for a maximal sensory-capture for each defenseless visitor to this snack-trap. Knowing its effects on this woman, I imagine her reaching into the strong cellophane bag nearly ten years later.

Sitting in her bed clothes, her bag of chips disguised by the covers, that beautiful girl [one of us] is now one-hundred pounds overweight. Her blood pressure is hovering just below a stroke while she watches a reality TV show about a family starving to death in Los Angeles.

She has disappeared down the rabbit hole into the bowels of her private Wonderland! Her body will ingest the magic mushrooms to help

Myopic Me!

her fit through the tiny doors into Alice's haunts, passing the caterpillar at the entrance.

In Wonderland, her body will be targeted for every potential dollar that can be extracted from her dying fingers. Like the hookah, puffing blue smoke, she will be sucked until there is nothing more to be sucked out of her. Obsessive-compulsive is what the psychiatrists call it, but she calls it her "comfort food."

This half-truth is not what God has intended for us, for Paul showed us that our bodies are to be a living sacrifice, reflective of our true worship. The half-truths we buy about our bodies are fully lies. Satan makes most of his considerable income in our half-truths.

We are exhorted to leave behind the patterns of this world which have no good intentions for us.[102] Those good old days of the 1950s projected the happy, healthy people with smoke coming out of their mouths and noses, as if they were the healthiest folks on planet earth!

To be happy like that, we bought into this wonderful imagery of the smoke (Corporate Profits $$$) curling around our nostrils. I should know, for I lived right down the street in Winston Salem on the eighteenth floor of the Nissen Building where I smoked for four years.

Roger and I would drive down that frozen canyon of West Fourth Street once a month to purchase their salvaged electronics, transformers, fixtures, and discarded transistor boards—the air was frequently heavy-laden with the smell of raw tobacco wafting into our nostrils.

For me, those seductive, or nauseating, images come back to remind me of my father dying in his bed, barely able to sit up, gagging with the nausea, his body in constant pain, while one of his former students stood there in the room, looking for words to say. They came from different geographic areas, coordinating their arrival, hoping to celebrate their heady success as authors and newspaper editors. They came hoping to visit their beloved professor after many years had passed.

Now, Pop weighed eighty-five pounds, having lost one hundred pounds in less than three months. Only the opium made his journey through this pain possible. Ironic that opium should be his helper for his final days. That famous drug helped him die peacefully after the deadly conclusion from another addictive drug—the cigarette's tar and nicotine containing toxic chemicals.

Beautiful Woman with Potato Chips.

On my wife's side of the family, my last mental picture of her mother is very similar. Her body was so thin! Her arm was not much thicker than the cigarette she held unlit between her fingers. She was lying in a Duke Hospital bed, where she died a week later. She had spent her life killing herself and exposing her daughter to her second-hand smoke.

There is selfishness in this addiction of smoking which is deeply rooted, and the addict can become like a cornered and wounded animal, defending itself to the death. Those who smoke have staked out their entitlement to their addiction as if it were a legal deed for property, a legal writ for a great estate, or a sacrosanct title for a sentimental family homestead.

This, in no way, takes away from my compassion for the people who are addicted and trying to quit. What I hate is arrogance and suicide rolled up like a box of Valentine's candy. Addicts deserve every help and every support, but to those arrogant, angry folks who still believe it is their right to envelop their friends and family in their second-hand smoke, I say, "Read the handwriting on your own wall!"

When my father died from lung cancer, it was terrible. My brother's death from throat cancer was traumatic and deeply saddening. His wife had died in his arms of a massive heart attack likely caused by cigarette smoking for many years. My brother spent his considerable savings trying to save her as she smoked to the very end. His house smelled like an abandoned ashtray.

You may survive the years of smoking two packs a day at a cost of $10,000 per year, but your child or spouse, or neighbor, may not be so fortunate. Neither is that money yours alone. It belongs to your family! You are stealing it from them! Matthew 25 shows us a better way, feeding the hungry man right in front of our eyes. The money belongs to God, and He does not sustain addictions; He sets captives free.

My body, I am learning, has a new eye tuned to God's grace. The people of Jerusalem and Boston are "like sheep without a shepherd, confused and bewildered." Yet I know that Jesus wants to spread His wings over them like a mother hen to guard them from the snapping blades of utter futility.

For me: Too much salt and sugar; too little exercise; squandering of money; wasting time on fruitless things; obsessive-compulsive predilections, and stupid superstitions; avoiding the Word of God in favor

Myopic Me!

of sitcoms and movies; forgetting to pray on good days; walking by too many opportunities to serve the one who is without—these are the pitfalls of the flesh.

But God does not condemn me still, and I know that God did not give me a spirit of fear. He gives me Jesus' authority that was bought at a great price. I know that I cannot change myself, but Paul said the living sacrifice of my body will separate me from the patterns of the world which I still reach for—including vague addictions and health patterns that are destructive.

The Holy Spirit breaks the dominance of bad rituals in my body. I have been forced to apprehend these things because of my own health breakdowns from past abuses. Even then, it is impossible to change without God's initiative and power. I have identified three big enemies working against and within my own body, sometimes preventing the health which God intends for me.

- Appetites, amplified by the five senses
- Culturally approved patterns that are harmful
- Spiritual Stunts: Demons despising faith

The prophet Isaiah describes our Jesus before He moved into our neighborhood. This description is so important for every Christian to understand. It describes a place in the spiritual realm and in the earthly realm in which we now live by confidence and faith in Him, and in His promise to eradicate the wall of hostility that keeps us from God's great provision.

> Yet it was our weaknesses he carried;
> > it was our sorrows that weighed him down.
> And we thought his troubles were a punishment from
> God, a punishment for his own sins!
> But he was pierced for our rebellion,
> > crushed for our sins.
> He was beaten so we could be whole.
> > He was whipped so we could be healed.[103]

8

The Body Speaks.

> Do not let any part of your body become an instrument of evil to serve sin. Instead, give yourselves completely to God, for you were dead, but now you have new life. So use your whole body as an instrument to do what is right for the glory of God.[104]
>
> The law of Moses was unable to save us because of the weakness of our sinful nature. So God did what the law could not do. He sent his own Son in a body like the bodies we sinners have. And in that body God declared an end to sin's control over us by giving his Son as a sacrifice for our sins.[105]

I could see that it is always about the body's form, its fit, and its function in the world of men. The business card of the missionary from my church denomination at that time was lying in the ashtray on the 34th floor of the Amari Hotel in Bangkok where I was staying.

After visiting the city's famous Temple, the filthy river, and the sad shopping among the boat people at the edges of the river gardens, I suddenly lost confidence in the motives of every hired cabby who had taken us to places we had never seen—I wondered if we would ever come back alive from those cabs. Later, we encountered the bodies of men and women on that famous strip in Pattaya, the transsexual boulevard where no one could discern the original gender.

It all seemed a curiosity until we saw it up close. Our guides took us there to see this extreme and disturbing transmogrification of the bodies of men and women. Their bodies had fallen prey to many monetary and sexual motivations, while plunging their souls into a litany of unsettling distortions!

This is nothing new, for Jonathan Swift the satirist saw these traps set for the body more than two centuries ago. His character, Gulliver, understands how difficult it is to return from Brobdingnagg or Lilliput to the real world. It is hard to trump the Houyhnhnms once you have spent time with these horse-like creatures of seemingly divine character. Gulliver tries to conform his body among the tiny Lilliputians, adjusting as well to the colossal Brobdingnagians.

But Gulliver is always aware of the trap which is being set for his body in these extremes which he discovers on his voyages: from the giant maids who tend to him as if he were a doll, to the twelve-year old Yahoo girl who couldn't get close enough to him. His body is vulnerable everywhere he goes.

Paul the Apostle, who at one point in the Book of Romans cries out, as Gulliver must have, "Wretched and miserable man that I am! Who will rescue me and set me free from this body of death, this corrupt, mortal existence?"[106] Paul discovered that he had, in some ancient time, drunk the intoxicating liquor of coveting.

Today, **Myopic Me!** is convinced, with Paul and Gulliver, "There must be a million eyes looking at my latest post." Like Gulliver in the maid's hands in Brobdingnagg, body language becomes very important to communicate true feelings.

Posture and Tone deliver ninety-three percent of the total messaging with those giant teenagers.[107] Only Seven percent of the message is derived from the words Gulliver utters, and it is not a function of his tiny larynx. Without the tone of voice and body language, it is impossible to really know what the other party is saying, or meaning.

The movie "Elegy"[108] pushes the envelope for "body language," and Penelope Cruz's body is the focus for much of this language. Though I have typically used the Parental Guide to help me evaluate films, reading about the naked, the naughty, the foul-mouthed, and the negative leaves me with very few movies I should watch. They have too much sexual content, too much obscene language and violence, and too much political ax to grind in nearly every one.

The Body Speaks.

Paul reveals that **everything is permissible** [Parental Guide], **but not everything is edifying** [Can anything good come out of Hollywood].[109] I can't sit through two hours of obscene language and be unaffected. I can't watch people having explicit sex on the screen, and call it a good use of my time.

In the **vast majority** of Hollywood offerings, edification is thrown out the window. You have to decide for yourself, while Paul jerks the reigns with two explicit guidelines: Edification & Worthy of Praise.

> Fix your thoughts on what is true, and honorable, and right, and pure, and lovely, and admirable. Think about things that are excellent and worthy of praise.[110]

This freedom places a great responsibility on our sensitivity to the Holy Spirit, rather than our implicit trust of the pundits from Major News or from Hollywood. The Holy Spirit knows what we can handle, and He knows what will destroy our souls and bodies. Movies coming from the cinematic factories in Wonderland can score a 10 for sexual situations, violence, or offensive language, and people will flock to the theaters for this bombardment.

Love is something different from these, and there really is a good "Love" in the world, in spite of the bad love we see on the screens we watch for nine hours a day. This quote from philosopher Erich Fromm may be useful. During this present Epoch of the Hyper-Tolerant Police State, Fromm has a point of view worth considering.

> "If other people do not understand our behavior—so what? Their request that we must only do what they understand is an attempt to dictate to us. If this is being "asocial" or "irrational" in their eyes, so be it. Mostly they resent our freedom and our courage to be ourselves. We owe nobody an explanation or an accounting, as long as our acts do not hurt or infringe on them. How many lives have been ruined by this need to "explain," which usually implies that the explanation be "understood," i.e. approved."[111]

Myopic Me!

Erich Fromm's encouragement is mostly biblical—but Paul has called us to bring edification everywhere we go, and we are accountable to God, and to our neighbors, as well as to ourselves. We the People apparently prefer violence, sexual situations, and nonstop offensive language in our entertainment. The box office success for movies is always highest when Narcissism is sizzling, and profanity is selling tickets; where sex and nudity have become the default queens.

Edification is always an issue when selecting a movie, and Ben Kingsley's "Elegy" pushes to the edge of credulity. God's Love is edifying! Man's love is exploitative. Buyer beware. Every movie is not edifying for you. You might need to stop after my review, rather than actually watching "Elegy."[112]

Though it is fairly low-scoring on many of the parental parameters, it features the life of a tenured soft-core sexual predator at a famous university who intercepts beautiful young women shortly after her semester in his classroom is concluded. He meets them in the intimacy of his famous afterparties where every pretext of professional distance is discarded.[113]

My review of "Elegy" simply focuses on the way the body can entice and disturb the soul of man, creating incongruous hostilities in every beguilement. I am not commending "Elegy" for your family, for this film speaks to the seductive aspects of the sometime beautiful human form.[114] Do not allow the enemy to entice you where you should not go.

This wrenching story stars Penelope Cruz as a naive young woman who is looking for love with this older, famous man. Her fling leverages visual and emotional intimacy as they face the parallel experiences of their dying bodies. Each character faces death in vivid and personal ways.[115]

The curse of her breast cancer arrives grimly from stage left. That deadly scourge effectively upstages any prior objectification of her body. The professor, and the viewer, are captured by the tractor-beam of this ruinous news. The breast Cancer shows no favoritism, seizing Penelope's museum-quality figure.[116]

Herbie Hancock has a relevant lyric in his jazz album concerning his gal's body: "I'm obsessed—what a mess."[117] An Ed Sheeran hit song declares, "I'm in love with your body."[118] There are many others from Hip-Hop and Pop with similar lyrics, but all of them admit to the

The Body Speaks.

preoccupation with the hypnotizing shape, form, and fit of the female body: God's perfect design, with the Serpent's seductive twisting.

"What a mess!" The plot of "Elegy" begins with appreciation and attraction, but it slithers into intoxication and obsession. In the theology of sin, this is Garden Party idolatry, objectification, distracting sleight of hand, arriving at an idol for worship—installed in all the viewing areas of the heart!

Our minds perform the photoshopping until the imperfect becomes perfect. The worship reserved for our Creator is siphoned off by the disproportionate affection for the created thing. The body is placed between the knees, posed in the video, or captured in the Selfies—leaving us breathless.

We should have poured out our worship and love into the body of Christ, into Jesus Himself, for the will of God our Father in Heaven calls us out of this idol-making frenzy—into Adoration—of Himself! In "Elegy,"[119] we find that Sin's toxic chemistry has been secreted into the perfect Garden we have made for ourselves, corrupting our Paradise, and sending us East of Eden with our fearful dirge. "Fear not!" Jesus reminds us.

Sin is death. Sin is a terminus with no rest. Sin is cold, lonely, and terrifying. Unprepared for this surprise attack upon his beautiful young woman, watching this genetic chaos burst their dream, the professor watches the dung-eating grin of Death climb into their bed. He hears the worst, "Come, little daughter of ruin. Follow me!"

> You are proud of your fertile valleys, but they will soon be ruined. You trusted in your wealth, you rebellious daughter, and thought no one could ever harm you.[120]

Death's stinger slides into her flesh, ruining her defective love story—for both characters will now have to face their humanity, their own imminent deaths. Her unbeautiful death heralds his own slow demise, as we arrive with each of them, looking into our own personal mirrors.

Eternity usurps the foreground shot as the camera zooms wide to leave you and me, still alone, staring at that empty stage. Our past blurs with our future, and we die alongside the cast and the crew. Time blurs, and our lives are now flashing across a private screen.

Myopic Me!

We have to step out of that ominous future, or die. We hear the nearly arrogant voices speaking: "For us physicists, the distinction between past, present, and future is only an illusion."[121] We realize this is true for them, until one of them hears the doctor say, "It's cancer." Even the physicist can't find an escape route from that verb tense.

> But when they went out to bury [Jezebel], they found only her skull, her feet, and her hands. When they returned and told Jehu, he stated, "This fulfills the message from the Lord, which he spoke through his servant Elijah from Tishbe: 'At the plot of land in Jezreel, dogs will eat Jezebel's body. Her remains will be scattered like dung on the plot of land in Jezreel, so that no one will be able to recognize her.'"[122]

Meanwhile, Penelope Cruz's character, no Jezebel, becomes scattered across the land, fed to us dogs, but preserved as an inanimate museum piece in polyvinyl chloride, eternally captured in a time-capsule memorializing her body: "Forever thirty-four."

She is captured in her Plexiglas display playing on a loop. She will be admired and worshiped for every symmetrical curve, and for her beauty and gentle demeanor.[123] Fondled cruelly by breast cancer, she is brought to life again and again in the floating mirage emulating life.

"Do you like it?"[124] she asks her lover. The professor's answer, not knowing for sure what she is asking, is, "Yes. Yes, I like it." Though God's heaven is superior in every way to this disturbing walk through Elegy's museum, the poet and the professor, the long-time colleagues and co-conspirators with young women, are forever trapped in their Blu-ray expose of their shallow lives. By Grace we are saved, and not by good works, for no one can boast. It is God's favor, undeserved.

These two raconteurs commiserate, with no Gospel allowed in their thin world. They realize that they have to make a change, finding something real to cling to, rather than these temporary girls from their classrooms. Receiving no granite statues or plaques for their shadowy exploits, these professors face several unsatisfactory endings, pixels flickering for forever, Amen.

The Body Speaks.

Elegy means, "Dirge." Without God's grace, life is a Dirge. Dirge means Lament. The professors lamented they had squandered their lives. When a visiting speaker came to Waters Church several years ago, he lamented his own shocking sexual history.

No professor at a major university, Stephen unleashed his testimony of redemption from the slave pits of Egypt—from the idolatry of the Nile River Delta. If the professors' stories were shameful, then Stephen's stories were far worse. But Grace had performed a miracle upon his script in Provincetown.

The camera zooms in from outer-space, coming to rest in the apartment of a homosexual man living in the welcoming habitat of Provincetown, Massachusetts. We find him trapped in the lifestyle that includes sexual and chemical dependencies, and aberrations of all kinds. But somehow, this amazing Grace story flips as Stephen discovers an exit door from hell that had in a few years nearly killed him.[125]

Stephen did not preach so much as he shared his painful odyssey in graphic fashion. Those who got up from the theater in a huff to leave, failed to hear his profound and universal insights into God chasing him as the Hound of Heaven. It was surely amazing grace, but it was also a miracle of God's love.

Swept into drug addiction during the few years he lived in Provincetown, his deep dive into sexual profligacy became the crumbling taco shell of his nearly accidental lifestyle. He described how others convinced him that he was gay, and gradually he found himself seduced by everything inside of that world.

God finally awakened him from his nightmare to lead him out if he was willing to go. His escape came after a persistent visitor loved him enough to ignore his very negative responses to her visits. She helped him see the One doorway to freedom.

She persistently shared the scriptures which opened his heart to faith and hope.[126] After her repeated visits, bringing the Word of God each trip, she encouraged him to leave by the front door—Stephen began seeing a lighted way out of his wretched narrative. But it would be hard to leave.

Though he was told daily by his friends that he had no choice about his sexual orientation, he discovered a previously hidden pathway. He discovered there was an alternative, though he had dug the hole and

Myopic Me!

buried himself barely alive in it! The promised way out faithfully changed the course of his life.

Though he could not repair his former history, God's Son showed him a new narrative for the next chapter of his personal story! He found his specific prison of sin listed in plain English in Paul's letter to the Corinthian church. The verses started with the warning which he had already understood. His irredeemable lifestyle could be redeemed, and a miracle journey rose to replace his sexual history.[127]

> Don't you realize that those who do wrong will not inherit the Kingdom of God? Don't fool yourselves. Those who indulge in sexual sin, or who worship idols, or commit adultery, or are male prostitutes, or practice homosexuality, or are thieves, or greedy people, or drunkards, or are abusive, or cheat people—none of these will inherit the Kingdom of God. Some of you were once like that. But you were cleansed; you were made holy; you were made right with God by calling on the name of the Lord Jesus Christ and by the Spirit of our God.[128]

He already knew he was doomed according to the first part of this message, but he found the Good News Paul presented so faithfully concerning the cleansing. He could be made holy. He knew that it was the day of his salvation. When he got married, he also understood that narrow-mindedness would fill the air around his wife and family, unrelenting to the present day.

> For a time is coming when people will no longer listen to sound and wholesome teaching. They will follow their own desires and will look for teachers who will tell them whatever their itching ears want to hear.[129]

The political activists have threatened his life more than once. Yes, he got married and has children of his own. He speaks around the world about his miraculous deliverance from homosexuality. The strongman has followed him everywhere he goes with the whirling razor wire of

The Body Speaks.

entitlement from the deepest rootings in hell. Intolerance has come at him like those locusts into the harvest field.

Several years later, I looked at the old internet reviews for that message which has been streamed on YouTube. There were many hateful comments directed against him personally. I cannot reprint them here because they contain such profanity and contempt for him and his family. Hatred has no face, but hides in shadows making vile threats.

The comments read like the dialogue from Sodom and Gibeah, with those conversational details captured in Genesis 19 and Judges 19. The hatred expressed toward his personal redemption offers the very face of hell coming down to the earth. Hatred can wear various disguises, but these come like those crowns of thorns that were jammed down on Jesus' head. They are full of cruelty, stupidity, and hatred.

Stephen has received many death-threats in recent years from murderers whose hatred cannot bear to listen to his honest story.[130] Jesus' words from the Sermon on the Mount promises Stephen and his family a blessing for being persecuted for their testimony of Christ.

> "God blesses those who are persecuted for doing right, for the Kingdom of Heaven is theirs. God blesses you when people mock you and persecute you and lie about you and say all sorts of evil things against you because you are my followers. Be happy about it! Be very glad! For a great reward awaits you in heaven. And remember, the ancient prophets were persecuted in the same way."[131]

His new day arrived on that night when Stephen took God's Word seriously. Stephen told the crowd at church that night that Paul's catalog of sinners became a potent message of hope for him. He had not imagined that he could be set free of his sexual despair, that he could actually change.

A way out of the black widow's crackled web had been revealed by Paul's Holy Spirit inspired reference to some who would be hearing his letter read out loud in the Corinthian church services. He found deep comfort as the Spirit spoke clearly to him that the same redemptive path would lead him out of his storm as well.[132]

Myopic Me!

> **Some of you were once like that** [male prostitutes, or practice homosexuality]. But you were cleansed; you were made holy; you were made right with God by calling on the name of the Lord Jesus Christ and by the Spirit of our God.[133]

He described how he had left his male partner in the bed to visit their master bathroom. He fell to his knees to pray beside that ceramic throne—why do we pray when we are crushed by the stuff of life? Why do we pray beside toilets? We pray there, or anywhere, because our problems are far bigger than our souls can bear. God makes the place holy.[134]

On the occasion of this true-heart's cry, God heard Stephen's repentance, him now sincerely willing to leave that former life behind, that life that had gone off the rails. For he no longer had any question about his desire to be free. God would soon wash and transform him, as Stephen increasingly trusted Him.[135]

His confession speaks of this democracy of sin which Paul described in his letter. Though we may not fully understand this revealed truth, we will eventually find ourselves listed in that catalog of infamy.[136] Each of us has that same divine invitation into holiness, into a deepening trust in God, believing the Son whom He sent.

Each of us will say, "I see my name there—abusive drunk, greedy man, indulger in sexual sins. And I see there is a way out of that slavery! Lead me out Lord! You are the Way, Truth, and Life. Show me your hands and feet, the crown of thorns on Your head, and the spear through Your side, and I will believe!"

The grammar of sin is the feast of the Pharisees, ancient and modern versions, who despise the Way of Grace. These elder-brothers are famous for their jealous rules for family, cramming their self-righteous expectations down our throats, while the love of God never penetrates them. But a few discover, with Paul, that no one is good—but the Father.

Along with us, they have come to see that we all find our heritage among the drunks, the abusive-tongued shepherds, the cheaters, and the inveterate liars. It turns out we were gluttons who could not stop eating until our cellophane bag is empty. Our favorite food is our drug of choice, and our escape is found at the bottom of every empty bottle.

The Body Speaks.

These dark Lords have ruled us, lied to us, and extorted us, with their detailed records of our ugly sins.

We have lived our lives in perpetual entitlement, leaving friends waiting in the foyer of our selfishness. Paralyzed with fear, we no longer attend church services, keeping our rooms dark and our doors closed to visitors. We recoil when God asks, "Where is your body now? Where is the body of Christ now?" When He reminds you to, "Make your bodies a living sacrifice, wholly acceptable and pleasing to God?" you get very quiet, hiding inside your most audacious new clothes:

> "And so, dear brothers and sisters, I plead with you to give your bodies to God because of all he has done for you. Let them be a living and holy sacrifice—the kind he will find acceptable. This is truly the way to worship him."[137]

Life is worship. Worship is life. What does your body worship these days? My professor emeritus father realized years ago that his body's worship was coming to an end. He could not keep his aging body as if it were his decision. Ever forthright with his students and with me, he included his great sense of humor in every conversation, though he was a very serious man.

He was spinning no fable when he soberly recounted his out-of-body experience in the operating room in Anderson South Carolina, eighteen miles from our fieldstone house in Clemson. With blinding cataracts in his eyes, he was there for this eye surgery years before this procedure became fairly routine.

He found "himself" floating above the operating room table. He was looking down on his own body below him. The doctors and nurses were frantically working to keep him alive. With extremely high blood pressure, his body was failing, and he casually watched as if the actions below had nothing to do with him.

Detached, above their desperate actions, he could see the stress they were experiencing as they tried to bring him back from the tunnel of death. He had never shared such personal stories with me, though he would recapitulate his trips to the Southwest and to Mexico with the slightest nudge. Now, he was sharing about his death, as if it were

Myopic Me!

something valuable—as if he were presenting me with gold coins from his locked cabinets in his office.

My friend is in the hospital at Mass General in Boston as I edit this paragraph. He might have a tumor on his brain, him having been there for many days during this Covid Crisis. For a whole day they had to leave him in a hallway for lack of a place to put him. Postscript, he joined our small group online via Zoom and we all prayed for his healing. He is home now, no cancer after a biopsy of his brain. To God be the glory.

Meanwhile, my father's body belonged to those frantic doctors, and there was no Covid crisis in that hospital in the 1950s. Their antiquated methods pale in comparison to the techniques employed at Mass General today, but Pop had escaped the tie-down straps of this life with no fear whatsoever. He had left his body, died, and lived to tell about it.

On that day, sixty-five years ago, Pop's aerial escapades refined his primitive perception of the body's role in this life—He observed his body, while perching on the soul's perspective. His out-of-body viewing altered his understanding of what it means to die! Before that experience, everything was academic, rationalistic; but now it seemed vivid and confident.

His career as a classroom teacher had come to an end, for his eyes were destroyed in the surgery. He had to retire from the daily pursuit of revelations and relationships. He loved teaching, and the professor was now teaching me about the day when his body's anchor broke free for one hour. He wanted me to see that he had no fear of dying.

God alone offers every *Myopic Me!* a Way out of the terrible I-disease called sin. His eye surgery is only performed at the Cross where the Centurion's spear confirmed that Jesus died of asphyxiation. He had to be standing at the Cross of Jesus Christ, King of the Jews, for no other cross would heal him.

Today, we are waiting for our appointment for the Covid vaccine, and we can only get the vaccination at Gillette Stadium. We have to go there, and get into that long line, and wait for the healing syringe to pierce our shoulders. For Pop, and for the Roman Soldier, witnessing the death of a Jewish Rabbi alone could heal their eyes. Of course, the same is true for Ann and me.

The Body Speaks.

The Centurion had watched hundreds suffer and die in this pragmatic Roman cruelty. With the thrusting of his spear one more time, this unique blood and water from Jesus' side sprayed his eyes, and a soldier's blindness was forever washed away.

No longer standing tall in his oak-lined classroom exhorting his students with poetry and songs, he had retired from teaching. In his familiar classroom in Tillman Hall, he twirled Shakespeare's best scenes together with the verses from Job, the Gospels, and from Ecclesiastes like cotton candy. Now, his eyes were opened wide to perceive the meaning of the Cross.

The dullest students loved his one hour dives into literature and life, reminiscing about his days in front of the bag at first base with black players before they were allowed onto the field of dreams in their first big league games. He whirled together the poet's common struggle with their own painful life experiences.

Professor Lane warned his students about the fantasies that would become scales over their eyes in a world where truth is spelled with a little letter, and Honor is exchanged for Entitlement. "***Myopic Me!*** [my term, not his] will try to replace empathy with the selfish lens!"

> We have a priceless inheritance—an inheritance that is kept in heaven for you, pure and undefiled, beyond the reach of change and decay.[138]

On that operating room table, Pop had watched the arrival of that out-of-body flight into the unknown which he described to me. Like that sudden bankruptcy of Penelope's body in "Elegy," or Stephen's dramatic ejection from Provincetown, Paul's question also invites our rapt attention:

"Who can save me from this body of death?"[139]

> For we know that when this earthly tent we live in is taken down (that is, when we die and leave this earthly body), we will have a house in heaven, an eternal body made for us by God himself and not by human hands.[140]

Myopic Me!

This new body is freed from medical bills, or various compulsions in Provincetown, or even the urge to read this chapter. This new body is the final inheritance, conveyed by Love across the barriers of Time and Decay.

While our natural inheritance transfers lands, houses, and money, this eternal inheritance delivers God's Goodness—beyond the reach of thieves, moths, and rust—beyond the reach of sin, pain, and especially Death.[141]

> Store your treasures in heaven, where moths and rust cannot destroy, and thieves do not break in and steal.[142]

9

The War in the Womb.

> So God abandoned them to do whatever shameful things their hearts desired. As a result, they did vile and degrading things with each other's bodies.[143]

> "The people of Samaria must bear the consequences of their guilt because they rebelled against their God. They will be killed by an invading army, their little ones dashed to death against the ground, their pregnant women ripped open by swords."[144]

A Life Magazine spread by photojournalist Michael Clancy is now famous, circa 1999. His photograph showed the tiny hand of a baby reaching through the incision in the womb of its mother. Four months later the baby was named Samuel Armas, but on that day, the boy's spina bifida deformity was being surgically repaired in his mother's womb.[145]

When the baby grasped the doctor's forefinger with a strong grip, the astonished pro-abortion doctor realized this baby had become a person, a boy in fact, and no longer was he a fetus! The reality of life at conception struck him full force, and he would never be the same, becoming an advocate for protecting every miracle in the womb.[146]

The prophetic images from the prophet Hosea fits our time far too well: Soldiers arrived to cut open the wombs of the pregnant women in Israel, destroying their babies before they could grow into soldiers. This methodical strategy would control the populations of the future army born in Israel.[147]

Myopic Me!

In modern times, this eugenics strategy mostly applies to a large population of black babies born out of wedlock. Fueled primarily by liberal lawmakers, and funded with federal tax revenues, more than sixty-million babies have been targeted in the wombs of young women. This eugenics methodology assures the reduction of poor black children on the dole in Washington D.C. and in every major city. With a billion dollars going to India and China, this effort is expensive in more ways than one.[148]

Who is it that kills the babies? Where does the motivation come from? It is Mayors, Governors, Senators, and even Presidents who promote these policies in large cities on either coast in America the Beautiful.

It all started when the Supreme Court Judges ruled on a woman's case in Texas when she decided not to raise one more baby. Behind her came the enthusiastic millions of girls and women who did not want their babies to interfere with their lives. They were encouraged by the news that babies really weren't alive until birth anyway.

> Clearly, life begins when you draw your first breath. That is when God places your soul in your body. Your soul enters your body with your first breath and it leaves with your last. The body is just a vessel — your being, your humanity, is your immortal soul. That's what the Bible says, and for the life of me I cannot understand why so many people, especially supposedly religious people, get this wrong. There is no question, no moral ambiguity. Abortion destroys an empty vessel, it does not kill a human being.[149]

In Hosea's warning from God, the soldiers were employed in the abortion mill of their commanders to destroy the future army of their enemy. They slaughtered these future soldiers while they were still in their mother's wombs with their tiny, invisible fists, hidden inside their mothers nurturing bellies.[150]

That future army was neutralized before the sword or spear or shield could be lifted by their muscular hands. The landscape was strewn with

The War in the Womb.

the perfect bodies of the battalions who would never string a bow or toss a spear.

Today, we celebrate murder, sexual perversion, covenants made in the dark, sexual slavery, and pornography of every kind. We export evil around the world, especially sexual evil. We kill millions of babies in the womb, and the world's newspapers report that it is okay. Therefore, why would any girl facing this trouble not abort her own baby? David gives us the explanation, and his words are life.

> You watched me as I was being formed in utter seclusion, as I was woven together in the dark of the womb.
> You saw me before I was born.
> Every day of my life was recorded in your book.
> Every moment was laid out
> **before a single day had passed.**[151]

During the Covid Pandemic, you can't take off your mask in a public place, but you can kill your baby in the womb. You can bloody a Conservative or a Christian, but you can't protect your own property with a gun when the mob arrives to burn your house down.

The world is upside down, and evil is promoted openly as the good. The good is mocked on social media and in the news, and LGBT is a fixture on the sitcoms. The identity of every human person is perverted by the view through Alice's Looking Glass, [152]distorting and corrupting what God first intended.

When the writer in the *Baltimore Sun* says that it is obvious when life begins, he speaks without examining every message of life from the Scriptures. He misconstrued the fact that Adam alone received the breath from the Father's mouth into his lungs. Through him, God breathed into everyone of us. Through the DNA He made each one of us from the dust of the ground. But take note of this.

Even Eve was made from the DNA which God took from Adam's rib. All the babies born of woman have come directly from that initial dose of divinely appointed DNA. We are made in His image, and in his image. Thereafter, every "breath" came into our bodies through the divine umbilical of our mother Eve, whose progeny made possible our mother's dream of a good life for us.

Myopic Me!

Our mother's blood streaming through that temporary umbilical cord [nine months +/-]. DNA, proteins, antibodies, and oxygen traveled first into Cain and Abel's circulatory systems from our Great Great grandmother Eve's umbilical, from her blood stream, oxygenating their bodies with the single breath of God. She was alive, made from bone marrow, and her baby was alive, made from the egg, the sperm, and the combined DNA.

As for the soul only entering a man when God breathes, the soul is there from conception, for life begins at conception with the blood and the DNA. That first breath of life into Adam's dusty lungs has been translated into every baby through the miraculous conveyance of the mother's bloodstream, and Eve has made Adam the father of many sons and daughters.

> So the Lord God caused the man to fall into a deep sleep. While the man slept, the Lord God took out one of the man's ribs [source of DNA] and closed up the opening. Then the Lord God made a woman from the rib [no breath of God required], and he brought her to the man.[153]

When Jesus was alive in Mary's womb, begotten, not made, Jesus was touched with the divine nature to go with His entirely human nature in a body like ours. The Holy Spirit had touched Mary's womb, and from that miraculous conception Jesus was born the son of man, and the Son of God. As if to prove this, the baby leaped in Elizabeth's womb when Jesus passed by, though He was still inside Mary's womb. There is no question that He was alive by the Spirit of God in Mary's womb.

> [Mary] entered the house and greeted Elizabeth. At the sound of Mary's greeting, Elizabeth's child leaped within her, and Elizabeth was filled with the Holy Spirit. Elizabeth gave a glad cry and exclaimed to Mary, "God has blessed you above all women, and your child is blessed.[154]

The War in the Womb.

Photographer Michael Clancy captured the moment when the gifted surgeon witnessed the baby's four tiny fingers grasping his forefinger. The baby reached through the incision in the womb to grab that famous finger. The surgeon transitioned from pro-abortion, saying, "I know that abortion is wrong now—it is absolutely wrong."

Samuel Armas was born a few months later, and he was given that name that has come to mean life for so many.[155] Samuel's biblical antecedent was Hannah's son, whom she gave to God, after she had asked God to end her barren womb by giving her a son. "Samuel" means "son of God."[156]

Samuel was the boy sleeping near the Ark of the Covenant on the night when God spoke to him. Hannah, Samuel's mother, had delivered him as she promised, dedicating him for the work and will of God. Samuel became the one who listened to God's voice, doing everything He instructed.[157] Eli, the elder prophet, was removed for his failure as a father and as a keeper of God's holy rituals.

> "I am about to do a shocking thing in Israel. I am going to carry out all my threats against Eli and his family, from beginning to end. I have warned him that judgment is coming upon his family forever, because his sons are blaspheming God and he hasn't disciplined them. So I have vowed that the sins of Eli and his sons will never be forgiven by sacrifices or offerings."[158]

God's wrath opposed the profligate family that was reducing His house to a house of prostitution. Since Eli did not discipline his sons, the wrath fell on him. Though he was in charge of the worship in Israel, he died for his failure to cast out the evil from his own household.

Samuel Armas became that boy sleeping beside the Ark of the Covenant. He became that prophetic boy, reaching out of his mother's womb to speak a potent message to the sophisticated medical world: "I am a living boy! Don't molest me!"

Abortion is nothing more or less than the ripping of the living boy or girl from the womb! When the doctor worked on him, still inside his mother, this baby would be surgically repaired for a life yet to come.

Myopic Me!

He was able to establish a relationship with the doctor who lived in a world his mother understood.

By gripping the surgeon's finger, a doctor's heart was healed. The inscrutable secrecy of the womb became scrutable when photojournalist Clancy captured that moment of compassion and empathy for the living being who connected with him. That tiny and perfect hand reached out of the mother, touching many millions who saw that photo on the Life Magazine cover.[159]

This tiny child was permitted, by rare circumstances, to make contact with the world of man, beyond the protective boundaries of his mother's enveloping orifice. The tiny object of wrath in the Roe vs. Wade interregnum had reached all the way into a brilliant surgeon's heart.[160]

There is no priority, as it relates to government-entangled issues, which is more important than the issue of "abortion on demand." I do not come to this position because of my own goodness. I come to this provocative and emotionally tearing issue out of compassion that God has placed inside of me that cannot be silenced.

No one is good, but I can try to empathize with the woman's trauma when her womb is filling up with life, and she can no longer be at work daily to pay her bills. Living alone, she is trapped in an economic nightmare which no man can fully appreciate. He will release his sperm with a rise of hormones that will make him feel wonderful.

He will put on his jeans and head home, but she will stare at her bulging tummy with a growing realization that she will soon lose her job, her husband, or her family. She will too often choose to lose the baby instead of her job. The baby will be murdered to solve her nightmare—allowing her to breathe again. She chooses the lesser of two evils—or does she?

I have continued, for many years, to believe that abortion is a heinous crime, being committed by a great nation against those who have no voice and no capacity to defend themselves—sixty-two million babies have died, defenseless against the selfish will of man. I am enough of a student of history, particularly biblical history, to know that God does not put up with nations who mistreat the defenseless ones.

If there has ever been a creature who cannot defend itself, it is the baby in the mother's womb. It is powerless, helpless, without a voice, and with few defenders. You may quickly rage against the Light when

The War in the Womb.

you hear this perspective, but I am very much on your side! I don't want you to be a victim of the trauma which sometimes takes seven years to visit you.

I am concerned about your welfare—not governmental welfare—but your spiritual, physical, and psychological wellbeing. The one who willingly gives her baby over to these cold medical instruments is often deeply scarred years later. Many cannot forgive themselves. They fall into self-hating behaviors, sexual and chemical deviancy, and self-destruction. They carry a deep scar in their souls that haunts them when no one else is around to encourage them.[161]

Sexual intercourse defines the primary launch pad for all of these discussions, but accountability brings us to the crosshairs of the present surge of genocide. No one takes any responsibility for their actions, or failure to act. Their comfort comes from a Supreme Court decision called Roe vs. Wade in 1973.[162] That case is always unfurled for its apparent approval of absolute and legally protected sexual or reproductive freedom.

More than 99% of the time,[163] abortion is an action to protect the mother from any external losses which pregnancy will bring on the woman like a flood—financial, physical freedom, sexual freedom, and career opportunities, are among the most significant—but shame and humiliation is another. Many will be furious over her pregnancy—and its impingement upon their freedoms! These are real issues, and they need to be addressed by organizations who can support the pregnant woman or the pregnant girl.

Parents may not always be the most helpful, but they may be the most important of all. The abortion mill will merely recommend the expulsion of the dead baby [the insignificant fetus]. Abortion, the shame of a nation, is driven by those who profit from the death of an early term or even full-term baby. Even the body parts were being sold to the highest bidder. Full term babies were left on counters to expire without the mother's touch or awareness of the cruelty to the boy or girl who already looks like the father or mother.[164]

Though the mother might be disguising her unwitting pregnancy from her father, or from her boyfriend, or from her friends and teachers, she is not the primary causal factor in this holocaust. The primary reason for an abortion is a nation's convenience.

Myopic Me!

The nation is shielding itself from the cost, shame, and responsibility of proliferating a population of unwanted babies into the care of unprepared mothers who have no jobs, no future, and no desire to raise their children in a way that will benefit the nation.

The baby, and the mother, become the burden falling upon the State. The State taxes the populous to raise the revenue to care for the babies out of marriage, and the babies grow up hating the very State and people who took care of them in this impersonal way. We become the people who are entitled by several twisted truths of the age.

Erich Fromm, American philosopher and psychoanalyst said, "Selfish persons are incapable of loving others, but they are not capable of loving themselves either." As Shakespeare said, "Ah, there's the rub!" The rub is the PTSD that comes for many who act against the life that is within them. "If a person loves only one other person and is indifferent to all others, his love is not love but a symbiotic attachment, or an enlarged egotism."[165]

Myopic Me! says, "It's my body!" But biologically, we know that life trumps all such arguments. Conception occurs when the sperm excites the egg in the womb, triggering a domino effect in the assembly of cells that results in the formation of a human being. You can say what you will about this process, but the human being is "fully formed" at the moment of conception because of the miracle of the DNA instructions which are deployed.

The single strand of DNA from a human cell contains the information which would be stored in a thousand hardback volumes. Have you read them all? I have not. Yet this DNA defines the complete human.[166] Every rule for assembly is established at that moment.

The unique human being, with inheritance and race and sex are activated. DNA is energized to launch the creation of a full person to be delivered from the womb to the mother's arms in approximately nine months. This process is predictable, yet miraculous. Every baby is different in many specific ways. Each is unique.

In David's wonderful song, or Psalm, he proclaims that God knows everything about us. He knows our every thought and word, our every motive and inclination. He knows our whereabouts and our attempts to hide from Him, but He loves us in spite of this wonderful knowledge. He made us. He protects us, and He provides for our every need.

The War in the Womb.

> O Lord, you have examined my heart
> and know everything about me.
> You know when I sit down or stand up.
> You know my thoughts even when I'm far away.[167]

You may not understand this reality any more than David did, or I do, and you may reject God altogether. If you do reject Him, then we are left with science and vague moral principles to guide us in decisions about life and revenge. We may not be able to come to agreement on any of this. Yet, we may be able to agree on basic concepts like "biological death" and the powerful religion of "convenience."

> I can never escape from your Spirit!
> I can never get away from your presence!
> If I go up to heaven, you are there;
> if I go down to the grave, you are there.[168]

This song acknowledges the predictable pattern of men and women who try to hide from God. Adam and Eve did this in the Garden when their faces were flushed with shame over their nakedness. They violated God's one rule in Paradise—don't eat the fruit from the tree of the knowledge of good and evil.

"Don't choose death! Choose life!" This was essentially what God instructed them to do. They tried to hide from God because they knew that they had disobeyed. They willfully chose death rather than life. The Tree of Life remained untouched, ignored. ***Myopic Me!*** always chooses death, ignoring the silent cry of the baby in the would-be safety of the mother's womb.

An interesting thing happened when God asked Adam and Eve what they had done. They started blaming each other! They even blamed Him. That pattern continues to the present day. We refuse to be held accountable for our own actions. We all know, with no coaching, that we have yielded our appetites to the temptations which come our way daily!

"Sanity" is a term the psychologists bandy about, but even these ideas are in jeopardy in our day when a daughter can sue her parents for default on payment of her college expenses.[169] We live in a day when the steel Cross was briefly forbidden at "Ground Zero," while a Muslim

Myopic Me!

Mosque was installed, before permitting a statue of Buddha among the memorial artifacts assembled.[170]

What we include, and what we exclude, define who we are, and who we are becoming. When we exclude Creator God, then we are sealing our fate as a nation. We live in a day which discriminates against Light and Life—while calling down all kinds of evil upon our families. Right is wrong, and evil is good in the day when atheists insist that a statue of Satan has to be positioned next to the Ten Commandments in our court buildings.

The fundamental war between Satan and the Christ of God is made moot because Satan, the created being, is doomed to the Bottomless Pit and the Lake of Fire. In a day when half the people you talk to have used heroin or cocaine, we may need to admit there is no common ground. What fellowship does Light have with darkness? A house divided cannot stand. In a time when marriage is no longer a covenant made before God, [Who?] we will likely end up wrangling over various prenuptial torts. But God remains on the throne, and our arguments are moot, for there is sin, righteousness, and judgment. These do not await our agreement.

> Then the Lord God made a woman from the rib, and he brought her to the man.
>
> "At last!" the man exclaimed. "This one is bone from my bone, and flesh from my flesh! She will be called 'woman,' because she was taken from 'man.'"
>
> This explains why a man leaves his father and mother and is joined to his wife, and the two are united into one.[171]

Adam had tried to find a help-mate when he named the animals, but could find none. Neither buffalo nor bear, tree-frog nor hare, could meet his need for a mate. Men and women are still looking in the wrong places trying to find a mate other than the one God made for us.

There is increasing push-back against God's design and intentions for our lives. Paul put it this way, this war against the Creator, whom we reject with our foolish and arrogant philosophies and false gods:

The War in the Womb.

> They know the truth about God because he has made it obvious to them. For ever since the world was created, people have seen the earth and sky. Through everything God made, they can clearly see his invisible qualities—his eternal power and divine nature. So they have no excuse for not knowing God.[172]

The complexity and beauty of the Human Genome has not yet opened every eye to see the design protocols of the Holy God. They look at the DNA, I suppose, and declare that this intricate, beautiful system of assembling life is simply a random accident. This is arrogance for a country that is behind Swaziland in math scores. Before we boast in our superior intellect, we should study to become masters.

Since we cannot resist God's wisdom, nor explain where He got the material that He would use to form the universe of an octillion stars, then how can we tell Him that life does not begin in the womb? Fetus is a Latin word which means offspring, young one, or little child. It is scientifically improper to say that a fetus is not human, when in fact it is accurately an early stage of human life.[173]

Carl Sagan was fatally biased when he stated there is no difference between the sperm and the egg when these are compared to the fetus or the embryo. A geneticist can quickly distinguish between the human fetus and the chimpanzee fetus at its earliest stages, since the DNA for the human is so obvious.[174]

More than sixty-million babies have been killed since 1973 (Roe vs. Wade), in which the mother has since testified that she misrepresented what really happened in her case.[175] Dr. Warren Hern, who teaches doctors to perform abortions for the seventeen week old fetus, provides this procedure for them to follow:[176]

> "Then I insert my forceps into the uterus and applied them to the head of the fetus, which was still alive, since fetal injection is not done at that stage of pregnancy. I closed the forceps, crushing the skull of the fetus, and withdrew the forceps. The fetus [human being], now dead, slid out more or less intact."[177]

Myopic Me!

In 2004, the "Unborn Victims of Violence Act" was passed in congress. This law protects the unborn from being intentionally killed. The fetus is protected as a human being inside the womb. Anyone who perpetrates this crime will be prosecuted for murder. But look at the double standard in the same legal system! That same baby could have been executed by an abortion doctor who was paid a significant fee for killing the child![178]

People would march in the streets if you got too close to the abortion center during that same execution demanding protection for this doctor! They would be siding with the mother and her inalienable right to kill her own baby, though no one else on earth would be permitted to kill that baby upon penalty of death or life imprisonment out there beyond the abortion mill!

Technology sometimes helps us see. Sonograms have performed that function for an increasing number of pregnant mothers. The new technology has greatly improved clarity and 3-dimensionality so that the mother can see her child's actual progress in her womb. The mothers who intend to abort their babies but see these sonograms change their minds nearly 90 percent of the times: They refuse to abort their own beautiful baby.[179]

> Don't speak evil against each other, dear brothers and sisters. If you criticize and judge each other, then you are criticizing and judging God's law. But your job is to obey the law, not to judge whether it applies to you. God alone, who gave the law, is the Judge. He alone has the power to save or to destroy. So what right do you have to judge your neighbor?[180]

For those of you who understand probability theory, the probability of a fetus becoming a human being is One [barring some medical, accidental, or intentional intervention which kills the baby]. The body of the aborted baby includes fingers and hands, arms and legs, torso and head, a human being protected by the laws established for a civilized Republic.

Lest you think I am speaking out of turn, a **feminist** group has stated: ". . .if unborn children are not safe, no one is safe."[181] The same group stated that discrimination of human rights should assure protection for the baby in the womb.

> "without consideration for race, gender, disability, age, stage of development, state of dependency, place of residency, or amount of property ownership."[182]

Rosmary Bottcher argues that the feminist movement has degraded women, demeaning them, and depicting them as unable to handle the stresses of childbirth and child rearing.

> "The anti-abortion laws that early feminists worked so hard to enact to protect women and children, were the very ones destroyed by the Roe vs. Wade decision 100 years later" [Serrin Foster, president of Feminists for Life].[183]

This family planning increases the potential for teenagers to get abortions without notifying their family members. Some high governmental officials think this is a good thing. This policy hides the truth from parents concerning their daughter during what is possibly the most traumatic event of her life. They may be excluded entirely.[184]

As for the demographic and statistics concerning abortions around the world, it is well known that unwanted females are eliminated by the abortionist's forceps, hooks, or injections with horrifying frequencies. In India, the population of several villages totaled 10,000, with only fifty being girls. In Mumbai, when 8000 tests indicated female fetuses, all but one of the girls was killed by the abortionists.[185]

In China, two-thirds of children born are male, with a four-to-one ratio for boys in the rural areas (this information circa 2000). In one American case study, the amniocentesis testing of ninety-nine mothers indicated equal numbers of male and female fetuses: Only one boy was killed in the womb; twenty-nine girls were killed![186]

Studies indicate that the mother who goes through with an abortion will have much difficulty later on with PTSD-Post Traumatic Stress Disorder—manifesting in drug abuse and addictions, promiscuity, depression and self-abuse, child-abuse, and the transport of shame

Myopic Me!

and guilt everywhere she goes. She will not be able to outrun what she has done![187]

The Choice, as it is defined by Abortion Rights people, is all about child-killing as a kind of proof-text for women's freedom in a world which has abused women for centuries. This pattern of abuse, throughout history, regardless of culture or nation, is reprehensible.

Yet, Pro-Life advocates would never begrudge a woman's inalienable right to seek her own freedom and fulfillment as a woman, mother, wife, stockbroker, lawyer, or company president. The only priority they would seek for her is the ultimate authority of the Word of God, which is Christ Himself: Way, Truth, and Life.[188]

Still, there has to be a way to help her achieve those things without killing her baby. Our society is imploding because of our terrible management of this moral, legal, spiritual and societal dilemma. Pre-marital sex, adultery, and fornication have consequences—there is science behind those consequences. There is a biological imperative that will not yield to passion or corrupted motives.

The joining of sperm and egg, accidental or intentional, will produce a human being. From that moment on, the entire blueprint in the DNA is executed like a high-speed train heading into the distant station.[189] The mature human being, with all her features, and even many of her strengths and weaknesses, will be completed in that short journey of nine months. Dietrich Bonhoeffer spoke of this life journey before Adolf Hitler hung him in 1945, and his words bring great clarity to the subject.

> Destruction of the embryo in the mother's womb is a violation of the right to live which God has bestowed upon this nascent life. To raise the question whether we are here concerned already with a human being or not is merely to confuse the issue. The simple fact is that God certainly intended to create a human being and that this nascent human being has been deliberately deprived of his life. And that is nothing but murder.[190]

The question for us nascent human beings is this: What do compassionate and lawful people do to accomplish the best possible outcome? C. Everett Koop stated that there was never a reason in his thirty-six years

The War in the Womb.

as a physician where it was necessary to perform an abortion to save a mother's life. He became the Surgeon General of the United States. He said the use of this medical argument is simply a "smoke screen."

Dr. Landrum Shettles agreed, saying that less than 1% of abortions are performed to save the mother's life.[191] Norma McCorvey, a.k.a. Roe vs Wade, claimed that she was raped and that her case should not have happened in the first place. She later recanted her story, saying she was looking for sympathy from the court when she offered the "rape card."[192] She most recently was among the marchers at an anti-abortion march at Notre Dame University during President Obama's visit there.[193]

There are many medical side-effects, or risks, that come with the terrible abortion processes that have proliferated over the years since her 1973 case. Risks of cervical cancer, placenta previa, ovarian and liver cancer, and breast cancer go up dramatically for one abortion, and go even higher for those who have multiple abortions.

Mortality rates for full-term mothers who previously had abortions is more than three times as high as those who never had an abortion.[194] Reportings are low for these deaths since the abortion victim often dies months after delivery of her child due to complications (predictable consequences) which result in her death. These deaths are rarely reported as abortion deaths.[195]

More than one woman who was raped has gone full term to have her baby. Some have given their child up for adoption. In most of those cases, the mother did not regret the decision, and loved the child as her own precious baby.[196]

One dramatic, inflammatory argument of Pro-Choice activists is the issue of child abuse. Has child abuse been reduced as rates of abortion have been dramatically increased—as had been predicted? The premise is that fewer unwanted babies in the house would precipitate rapidly decreasing child abuse cases.

Since 1973 the number of abused children has increased 540%, from 167,000 to 903,000. Why? The judgment of Pro-abortion experts was entirely flawed. Child killing and abuse cases have increased exponentially![197] One explanation is this: As the child becomes the object of a nation's wrath, the abuse is exacerbated, with more scapegoating of the child for every problem between parents and with the broader world.

Myopic Me!

Mother Teresa made an emotional and personal offer to any pregnant woman. She spoke for many who had been through the eye of the needle we call adoption. The process is challenging and expensive, with extreme requirements and legal scrutiny, but the labor can also bring life and hope.

> "Please don't kill the child. I want the child. Please give me the child. I am willing to accept any child who would be aborted, and to give that child to a married couple who will love the child, and be loved by the child."[198]

A radio talk show host told Randy Alcorn, author of *Pro-Life Answers*, that she was offended when people called her pro-abortion instead of pro-choice. Randy asked her if she thought there was something wrong with abortion? She said, "Abortion is tough." He asked her, "Why 'tough?'" She said, "Well, you know, it's a tough thing to kill your baby!"[199] Forgiving herself will be the most difficult challenge of her life.

Compassion for her is a deep and unanswered need in our American Wasteland. Though the world is broken because of sin, God has the perfect plan to deal with any sin we have committed and any mistake we live to regret, no matter what it is. There is no condemnation for those who are in Christ!

He heals us through a relationship with the King of kings. Being a Christian is a relationship with God through His Son Jesus who walked the earth as both man and God. He experienced appetites, temptations, and pain, just as we do. He understands our suffering.

> Our Father, change our hearts toward your plans for our lives. Change our hearts toward the fate of the unborn. Bring us as a nation to repentance for our 60+ million murders. As a nation, we have done this. No one can claim to have completely clean hands, though many brave people have fought to end this for years. Only as our hearts are changed can we alter this path to destruction. Whereas, Adam and Eve ruined their future by one act of disobedience, we are destroying our nation

The War in the Womb.

by one decision to allow abortion on demand. All of us will pay for that mistake. All of us will be held accountable for what we do or fail to do. Give your peace to those who have taken life, the mothers, the doctors, the abortionists and the charlatans. Forgive all of our sins, in Jesus' name, Amen.

10

Medium Security Prison.

Don't you realize that those who do wrong will not inherit the Kingdom of God?. . . Some of you were once like that. But you were cleansed; you were made holy; you were made right with God by calling on the name of the Lord Jesus Christ and by the Spirit of our God [*Cancel Culture* would never allow this to stand, this redemption, this forgiveness, this sanctification; and there are a lot of elder-brother christians who would agree with *Cancel Culture*].[200]

But Moses and Aaron fell face down on the ground. "Oh God," they pleaded, "you are the God who gives breath to all creatures. Must you be angry with all the people when only one man sins?". . . And Moses said, "But if the Lord does something entirely new and the ground opens its mouth and swallows them and all their belongings, and they go down alive into the grave, then you will know that these men have shown contempt for the Lord." He had hardly finished speaking the words when the ground suddenly split open beneath them. The earth opened its mouth and swallowed the men, along with their households and all their followers who were standing with them, and everything they owned. So they went down alive into the grave, along with all their belongings. The earth closed over them, and they all vanished from among the people of Israel.[201]

Myopic Me!

As we entered the prison grounds, passing through the first two gates, we vanished from among the living. I remembered that story of the ground opening up to swallow whole families with their possessions. I also recalled the Russian nesting dolls Rutherford [Rud] gave us when he returned from Moscow when I was growing up in South Carolina. We had surely entered the nesting doll to find that final tiny doll inside.

The Norfolk Medium Security Prison felt like that nesting doll, and the ground had surely opened up to swallow these incarcerated men who were housed behind its bars. The multiple walls and fences seemed to offer one more room inside every room we passed through. We had left our automobiles in the gathering darkness of the free world behind us, but we knew our strange mission was from Jesus' own words.[202]

Each of us had come freely from that peculiar kingdom where many are slaves to sin, and many more are breaking out of the razor wire of their empty and meaningless lives. Prisoners inside or outside still struggle with the thick walls of interpersonal hostility while they hide inside their nesting dolls of unforgiveness.

The outer walls of Norfolk are forty feet high with multiple high voltage wires that run the perimeter along Route 1A. As we continued through the first few layers, following thirty minutes of delay, we entered into an open-air zone in the dark of night deep inside the complex. This open area was off-limits to prisoners, being monitored by guards with automatic weapons.

We chose to enter the prison compound in order to spend time with brothers in Christ whose crimes brought them into this impenetrable prison. Four of us from Waters Church were entering with the Chaplain who had developed a mentoring role with around thirty incarcerated men. His weekly meetings with them had led to this invitation to gather in their inner auditorium for worship and preaching by the Senior Pastor.

The chaplain had shared a series of messages from our church library, entitled, "Bitter or Better?" Whether inside or outside, the issue of bitterness is an important prison topic. Our Senior Pastor had presented these messages months earlier to the local church and online though our YouTube channel. The urgency was obvious for these men incarcerated with years away from the freedoms of civilian life—away from families and friends.

Medium Security Prison.

The prison bars of this medium security prison could be despised when seen through this lens of bitterness, but a few of these men were grateful, seeing the bars as the grace of God healing their lives. They understood that Jesus has given all of His disciples—in prison or out—the same power, authority, and gifts which He demonstrated in the earth during the three years of His ministry.

He said that we would do even greater things than He had done. After watching Tim's video messages on bitterness, these men were so excited to meet the preacher, and to hear and see him standing in their full gathering in the central auditorium.

For the Christians inside, this auditorium had become their Most Holy Place where the rare unity in the Holy Spirit awaited them. There, they could enter into God's good and perfect will, into His presence, even though they were incarcerated. That auditorium was our destination as we continued our processing through all the gates and barriers.

Tim Hatch would be with them in the Spirit as well as the flesh, and he would speak of the many prisons mentioned in the Bible where great works of God were accomplished. Tim would speak to them about the only true freedom available to their entire prison population. The Gospel was free, producing freedom, and hundreds would gather to hear the Good News in Jesus' name.

Through all the privileged doors we traveled, as we were instructed, adjusting ourselves with every set of bars, until we were reduced to nearly the size of these prisoners inside the sprawling facility. There was more stripping down, having to remove every item that could be construed as a weapon, passing one-by-one through familiar screening technologies.

When we arrived in the bowels of this facility, we had given up our identification papers, debit and insurance cards, keys to cars and houses, and our money to purchase bits of our lost freedom. There was nothing left but our meager clothing on our backs, and we were their prisoners now, locked away forever if they wanted to keep us there. We had decided to trust this system, and we had no certainty of how this would end. That aggressive security left us with a dwindling control of our future or past.

Those final layers inside this Medium Security Nesting Doll included more heavy steel bars and doors, delays, and signatures on

Myopic Me!

logbooks, until we finally saw a dark building in the center. It was a place of great freedom nestled inside the steel and concrete walls surrounding everything. From that building we heard a beautiful sound of worship rising to heaven.

It was powerful and moving, vibrating us as we shuddered with joy; and even though the words were still muffled in the darkness, we were drawn like heifers leaping, running into the green pastures of God's provision, drinking from the clear waters, gamboling into the Shepherd's wonderful presence as He touched us with His supernatural hand.

We looked at each other with wide eyes, like children, as we went through the final set of doors into the room where the joy of that worship filled us up. We were home, with family. I cannot fully put into words the astonishment and wonder of that homecoming with those men, who were strangers before, but had become brothers instantly in Christ's presence. They had come beside these still waters trusting their Shepherd.

Tears come to my eyes as I remember those sounds, the hugs, the joyful smiles, and the authentic shouts of praise to the One who loved us all. After that joyful welcoming, and when the embracing had finally subsided, we sat down near the front with the assemblage of men spreading out behind us.

A young man was leading their worship, and he started to speak, explaining how important it was for him to carefully choose God's words, not his own, for his opening remarks. He confessed his struggle to find the right words until he understood what God wanted him to declare.

He said that weakness was his only offering. He had nothing besides his own human weakness. He confessed that he could not be a better person through his own efforts. He could not choose the right words from that former pride and arrogance.

He could not be their strong leader, or do what was right through that former stuff that came with the broken territory of his life. He just confessed his weakness before us—his never ending need for Grace. All he could do on this night, or on any night, was to trust God to work through him. He quoted Paul's second letter written to the church at Corinth.

> That's why I take pleasure in my weaknesses, and
> in the insults, hardships, persecutions, and troubles

that I suffer for Christ. For when I am weak, then I am strong.[203]

These introductory words set the stage for Tim to stand and speak his much anticipated message which pointed to the reality that everybody close to God's grace in the Bible found themselves in jail or prison. In weakness, these men found God's purpose. God worked His salvation through them in prison, and spoke His words through them while they were held in jails across the Roman Empire.

In the Old Covenant, there was Joseph, whose time in jail led to his delivering Egypt, his brothers and father, and the known world from starvation during the famine which persisted for years. During his time in prison, he did not blame God for his troubles. Instead, his relationship with God grew stronger.

There was David who committed adultery and murder, yet he is referred to as a man after God's Own heart. He repented of his sins, acknowledging God as his Savior and King. The great king bowed down to the True King. Yet he suffered great loss for his sinful acts, losing his son Absalom.

Noah could not leave the confines of the Ark for nearly a year, but God signed a Covenant with his family to populate the whole earth. Gideon hid in a wine press for years, but God used him to win a great victory. Moses himself fled from Egypt to live for forty years as the shepherd for his father-in-law's sheep, living far away from the luxury of Egypt—he went into hiding with his own Hebrew people after killing an Egyptian foreman who was beating an Israelite slave.

The Israelites were imprisoned by Pharaoh, making his bricks with mud and straw for centuries before God sent Moses to Egypt to deliver them from another Pharaoh. In the New Covenant, Peter, Paul, and John were locked in prisons throughout the Roman Empire for various terms and times. One of the famous stories of the book of Acts describes Peter's escape when an Angel of God leads him past locked doors, guards, and to safety with the disciples.

Paul wrote much of the New Testament while in prison. John spent many of the latter years of his life in exile, after he had been boiled in oil, surviving, several years before he wrote the final book of the Bible,

Myopic Me!

Revelation. He was held as a prisoner on Patmos Island until his death by natural causes.

Dietrich Bonhoeffer spent two years in prison before being hanged by Adolf Hitler two weeks before World War II ended. His intercession for the church in Germany for a decade helped to bring down the dark evil of the Hitlerian empire that was expanding in all directions. Like Joseph in Egypt, Dietrich told the hangman that what the enemy meant for evil, God meant for great good. It was God's will for him to die in Germany.[204]

Charles (Chuck) Colson, of Watergate infamy in Washington, served the President, and yet found his true voice while he was in prison for a year. His greatest purpose in life came through his great weakness and time of shame. Colson had been President Nixon's advisor during the Watergate era in the early 1970s.

He had been prosecuted in an unprecedented televised trial, and he served time in prison for his part in the cover-up and lies related to the break-ins in the Watergate Hotel in Washington DC.[205] While in prison, Chuck Colson started Prison Fellowship and BreakPoint Ministries, and he wrote several books, including *Born Again*; *How Now Shall We Live?*; *The Faith*; *Loving God*.[206] In weakness, Chuck became strong, but it was no longer that strength he had been given as the President's Lieutenant.[207]

He found true freedom when his worldly freedom was taken away. While he was restricted in this prison environment, he discovered what he had never experienced during his time serving as President Nixon's #1 advisor. He discovered the true purpose for his life, and experienced a joy he had never known.[208]

Eric Metaxas, one of my favorite authors, describes Colson's book, *Loving God*, after he had become what his left wing friends referred to as, "knuckle-dragging enemies [born-again Christians]."[209]

> One of the memories I will treasure for the rest of my life is the feeling I got when I read the end of the first chapter—which I hope you will soon read—about the Jewish doctor in the Stalinist labor camp and the patient to whom he told his outrageous story. The feeling of reading the ultimate words of that chapter will be with

> me the rest of my life . . . destined to become a classic of the faith.[210]

These captive men in the auditorium were serving lengthy terms, and some will yet die in prison. But the mission of the God of heaven was greatly nurtured and encouraged on that night. Other volunteers would follow us to bring the Gospel to these men who were cut off from their families, and separated from all the sounds of freedom which we take for granted. Carl continues to go weekly, when Covid permits, and the Word of God is the Center of their time together.

Even though the access by outsiders is very restricted, and very few personal items can be brought into the prison by visitors, these men exemplify the freedom which the whole world needs so desperately. Anyone held captive in their fine houses and perfect neighborhoods could benefit from a night with these free men. They showed us the freedom of Christ that does not depend upon social class, but thrives because of the unity of the Holy Spirit.

Christians were serving in Nero's house in Rome while the Emperor was burning the Christians to light his Mamertine Prison. Paul was chained to guards who became believers while they listened to his testimony daily. The Full Armor of God[211] came from that vivid experience.

The man who hung Dietrich Bonhoeffer became a believer on the way to the gallows to hang him.[212] Peter preached upside down until his guards believed in the Christ, before the disciple of Jesus would give up his final breath on his upside-down cross.[213]

God's miraculous reconciliation brought unity to men whose former lives had reflected rage, hatred, and revenge. The razor and high voltage wires no longer separated these brothers from the freedoms of God's purposes. That hostility of sin is far more divisive than any razor wire. Through Christ, they experienced remission from that consequential Dividing Wall that completely cut them off from their Father in heaven.

When these brothers believed in Him, they exemplified for us the stunning power of the Gospel which does not depend on geography or architecture, freedom of egress, or the ability to point the family car toward the golf course or the ball game or the favorite restaurant.

No forty-foot high wall could come close to describing that terrible gulf which sin produces between God and man, which can only be

Myopic Me!

resolved by Jesus' blood shed on the Cross as the final Lamb's sacrifice. If you are a traditional Jew, your Messiah has already made a way for you. Receive His substitutionary and finished work!

While we learn to live in the relative freedom of a Covid-19 pandemic affecting the whole world, these prisoners are socially distancing, wearing masks, and avoiding dense gatherings. They have their own challenges, being chased by the Coronavirus into their cells and routines.

But they still watch as the sermons, podcasts, devotionals, and video-skits stream from the Waters Church YouTube site. So, their faith and love can continue to grow, like Paul in the Philippian jail, with the freedom to worship and minister Christ to all who come near: "If the Son sets you free, you are truly free."[214]

11

Chinese Orphanage.

God decided in advance to adopt us into his own family by bringing us to himself through Jesus Christ. This is what he wanted to do, and it gave him great pleasure.[215]

And we believers also groan, even though we have the Holy Spirit within us as a foretaste of future glory, for we long for our bodies to be released from sin and suffering. We, too, wait with eager hope for the day when God will give us our full rights as his adopted children, including the new bodies he has promised us.[216]

In Morgan's Mandarin classroom at Texas Tech, she had turned around to see the cowboys lined up across the back of the auditorium with their boots propped up on the desks in front of them. She was amused, knowing that she was the only Asian student in the class. She had sat down on the front row hoping to revisit a little more of her native Chinese language.

The young Asian instructor had already smiled at her, unaware of Morgan's ancient genealogy as the courageous Wei Wan.[217] In that dichotomy of confident cowboys and this authentic Chinese woman from Midland, Texas, no one could have predicted what was going to happen in her first class.[218]

English was a distant second language for the young Chinese teacher. She awkwardly tried to explain that she was going to teach the class a common Chinese

Myopic Me!

nursery rhyme with accompanying hand gestures. As she began to teach, she looked at Morgan in shock.

"You know this song?" she asked Morgan in Mandarin.

Morgan looked down at her hands that were moving in front of her as she continued to complete the song. In that moment, the classroom dissolved, and she was a little girl in the orphanage once again. Tears streamed down her face, while in the flashback she saw and heard the other kids in the orphanage singing and moving their hands; she was not able to stop the flow of images. The class just sat and watched silently as Morgan seemed to be in another world.[219]

Those cowboys could not imagine her hidden pain over the ones who had died from malnutrition. She remembered them like frail phantoms from lost memories. They could not conceive of the orphanage where workers simply quit feeding the ones they judged as being too weak.

Now, Morgan was learning Mandarin with cowboys who could not possibly be expected to understand the nursery rhyme's significance.[220] Those audacious classmates could not imagine that God might choose their classroom to reveal Morgan's lost past and her deep wounds.

While she was singing that little song again, she recalled bits of her own brutal childhood while her tears flowed. Nonstop flashbacks, sensory floods arrived without permission from that room where no cowboy could ever go.[221]

God never forces Himself on us, a Gentleman, always waiting for us to draw near to Him with whatever seed of faith we have. Yes, He is the Hound of heaven, pursuing us when we wander; but God is no bully, as Walt Whitman contended,[222] for Jesus came to gather many orphans to the Father's house. Anyone who believes in Jesus' finished work on the Cross is being adopted. He always comes to set us captives free.[223]

Some of us are more in need of that freedom than others; and Jesus said we should always come in the manner of little children—for we were all orphans, once adopted into God's glory.[224] Hallowed is His name. Wei Wan had appeared in this waking vision, still unaware of the

Chinese Orphanage.

fullness of that glory, brought bodily back into that past to see that her Father had not forsaken her.

Once again, she could feel that powerful feeling of being responsible for her starving crib-mates who would be carried off for burial when the two women finally arrived in the morning. Their reappearance in this morality play in West Texas brought her into the unlikely juxtaposition of China with her room filled with real cowboys.

The children who had no names had been left behind to die! She could now remember every face, remember every tear and every sound, and she heard again the faint breathing in that great room where death visited the sick ones on cue. She could remember those smells of green soup and the unbathed children pressing together in multiple cribs in a single room.

She remembered that she had finally crawled through the transom opening in the wall, stacking boxes and the bowl they used as a toilet. With that boost she could reach the portal, slipping down on the counter on the other side. Furtively, the tiny girl gathered a bit of food and some clothes before returning to her crib. She passed through that opening, lowering herself down onto the kitchen counter until the next time.

She returned each time from her nocturnal treks with cookies, crackers, and clothes for the little ones, keeping a few alive for one more day.[225] Her memories coalesced again in the front of her classroom, and Wei Wan could assess the meaning of those boots, with many by now planted firmly on the floor as they leaned forward to see what would happen next.

She knew that the irreverent cowboys could never grasp the synaptic flood from her past that had already changed her life forever. Hidden, buried, un-remembered, her stillborn history emerged with the movement of her hands in an involuntary lullaby. Bewildered, they were now standing up to see.

Singing her nursery rhyme again, her brain had reassembled thousands of misfiled synaptic bits connecting her to many poignant events constituting far too much of her life. It was not fair! She had become their protector; she had no choice.[226]

Pilfering extra rations, she learned to hoard food and clothing, hiding the leftovers under her crib mattress where she knew the women would never look.[227]

Myopic Me!

Her miraculous adoption by medical missionaries in Texas had intervened from the sky, when a giant metal bird landed nearby to bring her home to Texas. She had gained a new family. She had siblings, and a father and mother who suddenly loved her, as if she had won the lottery. She had left the orphanage behind, and her memories of that former nightmare quickly faded, as if it had never even happened. Given a list of names to choose from, Wei Wan chose the name "Morgan."[228]

> Several months later [after arriving in Texas], Morgan tried to copy our daughter, Julia, age 3, doing a cartwheel in the living room. Morgan's arms snapped due to vitamin deficiencies. I set her forearm bones and placed a cast on her arm. Though a year older than her new siblings, Morgan was considerably lighter due to the poor nutrition. We found that Morgan was sneaking food out of the pantry at night and hiding it under her bed and in her closet. She had learned hoarding in the orphanage.[229]

Before I knew these intimate details about Wei Wan's early life, I was standing again in the New England bookstore where I did most of my writing.[230] That orphanage, and our visit a year before to West Texas, seemed pretty far away as I compose my first draft of the young woman's story.

I did not know her name or many of these details on that morning; but the cart full of books in front of me revived my impulse to describe God's great mercy which I had witnessed in her post-Freedom testimonial that morning.

Standing over that cart, full of personal stories from unknown authors, I could imagine "Morgan" writing her story down one day. The chapters of her amazing and painful book would describe those childhood experiences in China for sure. My knowledge that morning would have her writing the stories of her journey to freedom with others who made the eight-week commitment in faith.

I didn't know then, that she could write an entire book beginning with the college classroom flashbacks, the flood of mental and emotional content, launched from that nursery rhyme. She was born again

Chinese Orphanage.

as Wei Wan, and she would describe how God's wisdom had taken her back to that store of pain and fear in order to move her forward as the new creature in Christ.

Those memories deeply connected her to God's presence and His ultimate freedom. He had been there all the time. Because of her deep need to understand her twenties-self, God had to revisit her tears in front of those cowboys who could not share her anguish—God spurred her on to understanding that He was never that distant and indifferent God she had imagined He was.

No abstraction now, He had become her Deliverer and her Friend. He arrived in her tears to comfort her, in her rotten ear drums to restore her hearing,[231] and in her heart and mind to set her free. Morgan could see His intimate hand at work in her life now—she was His beloved child, His courageous & compassionate Wei Wan, his miraculous Morgan.

When she finally writes it all down, a fitting title will surely acknowledge that her survival, her freedom, and her fruitful life have all come through unmerited favor. Wei Wan the castaway, left by unknown parents in that orphanage, forgotten inside the 1,400,000,000 people inside China, had survived. Had anyone looked for Wei Wan among all those people? But God never left her or forsook her there in that single room, and He was always with her. Hallelujah!

"Well done, Wei Wan. You have been very close to the kingdom of God for a long time." With a stuttering Mandarin teacher watching the miracle unfold in her first class,[232] Jesus had come to her as Wonderful Counselor and Mighty God. Morgan could vaguely feel God's wrath being lifted from her life. She could see the Son rising on a new chapter of her life.

I had already been working for an hour, drinking my coffee, and typing this chapter on my MacBook Pro. I got up to stretch and walk a bit. *An Unlikely Story Bookstore and Café* presented me with a beautiful cart full of new books in the center of the sixty-foot first floor.

As the strong morning sunlight leaped across South Street in Plainville striking the colorful covers of the books in front of me, I thought about the young Chinese woman's story. I could smell the strong scent of the bacon cooking in the downstairs kitchen, wafting up through the vents.

Myopic Me!

The children in that orphanage in China would not recognize that breakfast smell, for they were never served any meat. White rice and green soup had left them wandering in the valley of the shadow of death, with many of them dying of malnourishment,[233] and all of them being wounded from severe isolation from the comfort of a mother's arms and a father's protection.

I did not need to walk cross the floor to contemplate how difficult it had been to *Keep Her Safe* from *The Shadow Man*.[234] Those two titles jumped out immediately. That young woman we heard speak in Texas had implicit knowledge of this *Shadow Man*. Now her amazing parents enveloped her in a strong Christian support system. She inherited their strong church family for encouragement and teaching.

She had an important story to tell, and I pondered the significant commitment each of these authors had made to tell their stories. What could make them get up every day to write for hours, editing for days and weeks, and undoubtedly struggling with publishers during tense phone conversations? What subjects could bring these authors to complete this sacrificial work? My random collection of titles was useful:

> *The Lying Game; The Girl Who Takes an Eye for an Eye; The Power; Keep Her Safe; Glass Houses; Shadow Man; The Blinds; What We Lose; All the Dirty Parts.*[235]

The answer to my question could be summed up with two words in the cases of *Shadow Man; The Blinds; Glass Houses*.[236] Each author had committed at least a year to these two words which describe their books. Each random title seemed to have some relevance for Wei Wan's orphan story.

I thought that Morgan [I did not yet know her name] would someday be willing to share her experiences, living inside *Glass Houses*, sharing God's grace and mercy. Her medical missionary father and his wife had surely tried to *Keep Her Safe* as she discovered her new American legs in West Texas. Her fiancé encouraged her to open up her life to *The Power*[237]—to the power of God Who could deliver her from the clutches of an unseen spiritual enemy.

After we experienced first-hand her dramatic Saturday, bathed by many prayers, and receiving God's deliverance through the Word, we

Chinese Orphanage.

witnessed the disarming of *The Shadow Man* who had operated in relative secrecy in those ninety souls who participated in the nine week freedom journey. *The Lying Game*[238] Random Collection of Novels: See Bibliography for more information. had blinded many who had started the journey unaware of the power available in Jesus' name.

When we stop lying to each other, as Jesus commands, then *All the Dirty Parts* will be brought into the light of Christ. *What We Lose*[239] during the Freedom Weekend turns out to be worthless anyway! Morgan's story resonated with me as I heard her boldness, and I realized her new freedom in Christ is worth sharing. She had become the embodiment of Christ's freedom!

Her eyes had been opened to see the orphan spirit and the spirit of death that had sought to consume her. A spirit of prostitution had lied to her about love and affection, trying to convince her that she is worthless, a castaway in this life. Even though she had been adopted by medical missionaries who loved her,[240] the enemy had told her that she deserved her punishment in a single room in China for five years.

That death-crib, where multiple nameless crib-mates had died during the night, had stripped her life of hope. On that Sunday morning, that encroaching fear of death had been driven from her life. Sin had been defanged as she declared the propitiation through Jesus' blood on the Cross.

She repented of her sins, declaring Jesus as her LORD, for she was certain that Jesus had sent His Angels to watch over her crib. Her life came from Him, and belonged to Him. He anointed her for good works which He would show her during the remainder of her life. Like Samuel, sleeping beside the Ark of the Covenant,[241] she had gotten closer to God than she could have possibly known.

He had called her from the shroud of death, and lifted her from the idolatry of this crooked generation. This courageous little girl had become a bold young woman, who stood there in front of a room full of family members and participants to tell what her God had performed.

Like David, she had finally uttered, "Search me, oh Lord! Show me if there is any wicked way within me!"[242] She had come to see how sin had hunkered down in her doorway, looking to devour her.[243] The spirit of Cain, the wanderer was still chasing her, all the way from China to Texas.

Myopic Me!

> "My punishment is too great for me to bear! You have banished me from the land and from your presence; you have made me a homeless wanderer. Anyone who finds me will kill me!"[244]

But she was learning that the Lordship of Christ extended to every spiritual force in the universe—nothing could touch her as she confessed His great Power and Authority, name above every names. That cursed spirit of the wanderer, East of Eden, could no longer touch her. It had nothing to do with geography, for it applied in the kingdom of God, protecting her from the destroyer.

> Their king is the angel from the bottomless pit; his name in Hebrew is *Abaddon,* and in Greek, *Apollyon*— the **Destroyer**.[245]

After her college years, she won the *Timothy Project* hosted by *World Missions Alliance.*[246] She submitted a sixty-second video explaining why she felt called to missions, winning a free Mission's trip to China. She broke down and cried when she won.

She told me that her trip was eye-opening to see all the ways China had modernized; but she also saw the reticence to permit true Christian freedom in that giant experiment in Capitalism under an all-powerful, and utterly secular Communist regime.

On that Sunday morning in Texas, we had heard her story about dating in her college years, seeking to find her true love in a perfectly legitimate American manner. She had become an American girl now, a Texas girl, in point of fact.

Searching for Mr. Right on the other end of a phone call had become her accepted model for finding the right man to marry. She had been checking social media, and talking with friends about every boy who called her during that period of her adult life.

She continued to look for that deep relationship, offering closeness and sincere affection. She hoped that a boy could quench her deep need for love. After all, she had faced starvation daily, deprivation, isolation unending; and she had received no affection for the first five years of her life.[247]

During those years she had felt responsible for the little ones who were abandoned in that room. Two women came twice a day. They departed, leaving orphans to sob and cry. She had become the mother hen for a brood of nameless infants and children who were unwanted, unloved, and unknown.

Sleeping in a crib with one or more toddlers, she grimaced every time the women came to carry her lifeless crib-mate's body away, one after another, day after day, year after year.

Our return from New England to Midland had been prearranged for this Freedom Weekend.[248] That Sunday morning had introduced us to this bold young woman, full of courage, having supreme confidence, when she shared what God had done in her. This former captive broke open in our midst like that nard poured out on Jesus feet. The perfume of Christ filled the room.[249]

She knew what starvation looked like. None of us could really imagine what she had been through. Starvation had slept in her crib for five years. She knew how withering diseases slipped through the ribs of the crib during the night to silence the fitful breathing beside her.

During those years, she never left that room or felt a breeze on her face; now she wanted every pleasant sensory experience from the wide world around her.[250] She wanted to be loved and receive affection from another human being.

Offered freedom by her wonderful family, she could not imagine the danger lurking when freedom's door was slightly cracked for the predator's long tentacles into her crib to steal the best morsels. She could now see that her dating choices had left her very vulnerable, and her exposure impacted her family as well.

When her fiancé suggested that they sign up for "Free Indeed" at their local church, Wei Wan could not imagine why she needed to do this. It seemed entirely unnecessary. She was convinced, "I am already free!" After all, she had escaped from an orphanage. She could teach the class on freedom in West Texas. "Do you think I am not free?" she asked her fiancé.

After a bad experience in the dating world, being pursued by a frightening predator, she had briefly become discouraged about her quest to find companionship and love. Her adoptive father had gone straight to the police seeking protection for his family,[251] but not much later, Wei Wan finally found the right man to marry.

He explained that they would join with three or four others in small group settings in homes to focus on their growing relationship with Jesus Christ as Savior, Deliverer, and Lord. Each week they would seek Him, becoming more aware of His authority and power, while learning more about His promises and His freedom. He reminded her that Jesus came to set the captives free. She looked confused. "Do you think I am a captive?"

He felt a great burden for Morgan, and his love for her made him want the best for her; her questions were hard to answer, but he knew this would be very important for the two of them. "There is no condemnation in Christ," he told her. "It is His mission to lead us into all truth."

"That's what we'll do. Do you remember how you wept when you had those flashbacks at Texas Tech—when you were flooded with memories from those years at the orphanage?" She looked him in the eye to see if he was crying. She blotted the tears from her own eyes.

He continued speaking after wiping a new tear away from her eye, "You will be able to confront those nightmares and fears, those spiritual consequences of nearly starving to death, being so terribly isolated from a parent's love and affection, and being the one who had to protect dying toddlers in your crib."

He knew enough about those years as an orphan to see that this freedom journey could have lifelong benefits for their upcoming marriage. An undiscovered continent lay below the waterline of her life, and she did not fully understand those spiritual depths. His faith and love opened her eyes.

Wei Wan could see his loving concern for her, and she agreed that this commitment might be good for them to share. She felt close to him. She felt very good having someone care about her welfare—someone who would be with her in this journey that would culminate in the "Freedom Weekend."[252] She knew this was the next step in her life, in their lives together.

Not knowing many details about Wei Wan's life at this point, I did what writers do. I pondered writing a chapter that would present an accurate portrait of this grown woman. I could not fully imagine that tiny, rickets-infested, undernourished child who had been forgotten in a remote Chinese orphanage who I saw during the Sunday testimonies.[253]

When we heard her share her experiences that morning, she had just finished the eight-week course with ninety others from her church and community. She had met in the house of our long-time friends, and they had faithfully presented Jesus' Lordship over every predatorial incursion into their lives.

Together, they had discovered the spiritual doorways left open in their life journeys. Not all of them had been in orphanages, but each one had been an orphan, exposed to spiritual powers that had overwhelmed them at some point in their past.

> And Jesus went away from there and withdrew to the district of Tyre and Sidon. And behold, a Canaanite woman from that region came out and was crying, "Have mercy on me, O Lord, Son of David; my daughter is severely oppressed by a demon." But he did not answer her a word. And his disciples came and begged him, saying, "Send her away, for she is crying out after us." He answered, "I was sent only to the lost sheep of the house of Israel." But she came and knelt before him, saying, "Lord, help me." And he answered, "It is not right to take the children's bread and throw it to the dogs." She said, "Yes, Lord, yet even the dogs eat the crumbs that fall from their masters' table." Then Jesus answered her, "O woman, great is your faith! Be it done for you as you desire." And her daughter was healed instantly.[254]

After our ten days in West Texas, I still knew very little; but I could see that Jesus had stood guard with a Sword, guarding the doorway to the sheepfold.[255] Wei Wan, Morgan, was in His flock, one of His beloved sheep. He had protected her from destruction, and He was anointed to set her free.[256]

She now understood how the enemy had planted the inordinate need for love, that craving for security, and how God had somehow produced a fierce compassion and protectiveness in her. She also understood that

Myopic Me!

the burden was too great for her—that Christ alone can bear the weight of all those needs.

But He wanted little Wei Wan to know that she had been His hands and feet in that orphanage. She had delivered the drink of water to the nation of China, the least of those in that orphanage—the ones the women had left to die. She had been Christ to a few in that terrible poverty and hopelessness.[257] In her own discomfort, she had brought comfort and hope.

12

Born to Be Free!

> A slave is not a permanent member of the family, but a son is part of the family forever. So if the Son sets you free, you are truly free. Yes, I realize that you are descendants of Abraham. And yet some of you are trying to kill me because there's no room in your hearts for my message. [258]

> Well then, should we keep on sinning so that God can show us more and more of his wonderful grace? Of course not! Since we have died to sin, how can we continue to live in it? Or have you forgotten that when we were joined with Christ Jesus in baptism, we joined him in his death?[259]

Lost memories may have much in common with spiritual strongholds. They are often lost for good reasons. Many were too painful or powerful to process in younger years. Only in a safe environment can we touch those live wires, to adjust the voltage accordingly.

These spiritual wounds, influences, or strongholds, are addressed by Tom Vermillion and his team, bringing together people from the local churches, and sometimes including non-Christians who are seeking freedom in Christ after reading, *Born to be Free*.[260]

> A shattered self-image, toxic relationships, emotional brokenness, and a painful past seal us off from the abundant life Jesus promised if left unchallenged by

the power of God. *Born to Be Free* is for those who are no longer willing to settle for life as it is, but who desire to walk in the peace and fullness God has promised—a life transformed by the healing and freedom purchased by his blood for every follower of Christ.[261]

Ann and I participated in the Freedom Weekend, the final Saturday gathering of around ninety participants with their small group leaders. We had been involved in small groups and deliverance ministry for decades, and we looked forward to their nine-hour Saturday finale. We listened, prayed, and watched all day, very aware of a young Asian woman's dramatic deliverance, though we had not met her.

Our friends were ministering offline with her when she was freed from an orphan spirit, before they addressed a spirit of death. She had vomited earlier when and a spirit of fear had left her, and Kathy and George had spoken to each spirit directly. This young woman from a Chinese orphanage had pitched forward into the large trash can in front of her. Now, face down in that trash can, folded at the waist, she was silent and immobile. She had been discarded as trash in China, and now she was discarding the trash of that great lie in Midland-Odessa.

They told us afterward that they had watched for a moment in astonishment, expecting her to straighten up. When she did not, they spoke to the spirit of death that held her in this inanimate pose, rebuking death in Jesus' name. Her new freedom became her bold testimony the next day at the private Sunday celebration with all those who had been involved for eight weeks.

The Good News was a palpable thing when she got up to share her spiritual journey to freedom. She was unashamed of the Gospel, completely open, articulate, bold, fearless, and free. It was stunning to hear her, telling her simple story like that famous blind man whom Jesus healed.

Able to see for the first time in his life, he told the religious authorities, "I don't know whether he is a sinner, but I know this: I was blind, and now I can see!"[262] Her commitment allowing God to sift her as wheat had already borne good fruit.

She left behind the victimhood, so common in her generation, and she gave up that fear of abandonment, and the amorality so prevalent

Born to Be Free!

among her contemporaries in Texas. That death that had lied to her, with its foreboding threats was also silenced. Spiritual warfare had declared victory in Jesus name over her life.

> For we are not fighting against flesh-and-blood enemies, but against evil rulers and authorities of the unseen world, against mighty powers in this dark world, and against evil spirits in the heavenly places.[263]

A few days later in his office, Tom Vermillion talked with us about his book, *Born to Be Free*.[264] I observed that his book is mere Christianity, mere freedom, and mere spiritual fluency, though there might be more than a few Christian readers who would say that it is extreme Christianity. Yet, his story is beautifully biblical—and full of the Wonderful Grace of God.

> "The Spirit of the Sovereign Lord is upon me,
>   for the Lord has anointed me
>   to bring good news to the poor.
> He has sent me to comfort the brokenhearted
>   and to proclaim that captives will be released and
> prisoners will be freed."[265]

"Who are these prisoners?" Morgan, the Asian girl could have asked before her journey. The culture that speaks to every young person in her generation though psychology would emphasize the Dark Triad. In a *Psychology Today* article,[266] these three spiritual strongholds are of great interest.

Of course, these researchers apply their own terminology for the captives they study in their research. Their terminology is adopted as the standard within our secular dialectic, and their symptoms are referenced when describing abnormal personality traits [captivity].

> Psychopathy is characterized by high impulsivity and low empathy; narcissism is the personality trait of individuals with an inflated sense of their own self-worth [the upper end of the bipolar syndrome, with a warning

Myopic Me!

> from Paul in Romans 12:3-"don't think you are something when you are nothing"]; and Machiavellianism is characterized by manipulative and exploitative behavior[267] [demonstrated by Judas, Pontius Pilate, and Caiaphas, with Saul/Paul pursuing every follower of the Way; Peter pulling the sword, cutting off the ear of the Temple guard, with Jesus saying, "Get behind me Satan!"].

This Dark Triad is a useful portal into these aberrant, selfish, and cruel human characteristics. These same traits and qualities are standards for understanding aberrations in our leaders and public figures. Usually when we discover them in our friends or spouses, we have to come to grips with the destructive potential for each one.

They come like a hawk to hook the flesh, the heart, and the mind. These demons subdue children and adults alike, with talons ripping up many lives. Little Wei Wan, Morgan, had been exposed to the talons of demons in the orphanage, and even in her adult experiences in Texas, without realizing what was happening.

I looked up the word, "talons," to better craft an understanding of this word which could help us understand spiritual oppression, and even possession, by demons which seek to make us captives. "Talons" describe the familiar "claws" of a predatory bird, and the adult bird uses talons to immobilize the prey before carrying it to the nest to feed the babies. "Talons" is a good fit for this spiritual context, where we become immobilized, before we are devoured by a spiritual enemy seeking to destroy our souls and bodies. It reminds us that God warned Cain, telling him that sin was at his door looking for someone to devour.[268]

As I continued clarifying the definitions for "talons," I discovered a secondary application for this vivid word. Talons are internal elements for the common locks used in our doors. These talons are the slipping mechanisms which are displaced by the shape of the key in predetermined ways so that the door can be opened. These talons yield in a customized way when the well-crafted key dives into the lock.

The one who has the properly cut key can enter the room to steal, kill, and destroy—or to bless. Jesus said that He wants to give us a "rich and satisfying life." Thus, the key can open the door to permit great

Born to Be Free!

spiritual carnage or to permit great spiritual benefits. The door is not evil. The lock is not evil. The key is not evil. The spirit of the one, the One who knocks on the door, is all that matters.

> "Look! I stand at the door and knock. If you hear my voice and open the door, I will come in, and we will share a meal together as friends. Those who are victorious will sit with me on my throne, just as I was victorious and sat with my Father on his throne."[269]

Notice that Jesus does not use a key when He comes knocking on your door during the night. He is the key, and He is a gentleman, waiting for you to open the door for Him to come in to dine with you and to become your friend! Morgan let Jesus come into her story, and into the rooms of her life during those nine weeks. I saw it firsthand. Ann and I were there when she let Jesus into the fragile rooms of her heart.

The key is Jesus' voice, and it is always His voice. For those who mock the Christian's hearing of Jesus' voice, here is your proof that He speaks to us. Frequently, He speaks when we find ourselves in our own version of Wei Wan's death-crib as well.

Jesus knows that the enemy will also come to that crib to steal the soul of a child abandoned there in fear and emotional anguish. In a very feminine way, the talons of the lock on a child's heart may surrender to the masculine key of the enemy, allowing spiritual beings to enter through that open portal to do much harm.

Tom Vermillion's book addresses these invisible night raiders, these invisible gamma rays from the dark spiritual realm. Wei Wan experienced all of these in the Chinese orphanage, the one-room prison, with no parental love or protection. Tom references every scripture to remind us that God's mission is to set us free from every predator that has stolen a portion of our inheritance. This is fundamental to the assertion of Christ's Lordship in the believer's life.[270]

This is not necessarily the mission of any church, but every church should seek to set the captives free in Jesus name: Isaiah 61 has spoken to the body of Christ with full authority according to Christ's divine mission. Tom's team even makes an annual visit to a nearby high-security prison population [before the Covid-19 restrictions interfered with every schedule to bring the Gospel of Christ to a lost and dying world].

"I don't believe in demons!" we exclaim in our ignorance. Satan simply smiles. While we invent a thousand rationalistic explanations for our uncontrollable symptoms, our OCD patterns we can't stop repeating, we may never think to study for clues in God's Commandments.[271]

> Four Commandments were give concerning our relationship with God—forbidding the worship of other gods [to include demons], constructing idols, refusing the Sabbath Rest, or taking the Lord's name in vain.
>
> Six Commandments concern our relationship with our Neighbor—with a command against stealing, killing, lying, adultery, and coveting, with a command to honor our parents, gaining a long life.

God knew that our crimes of adultery, of idol worship, and our rebellion and sins would hurl us into the line of fire of the demons which never take a nap, and never cease their mission to steal, kill, and destroy our souls, bodies, and relationships. The other primary spirits mentioned in the Bible may come into the souls of man through similar open doors from titillation or trauma. Ignorance of this list is what the enemy counts on, for knowledge brings to bear the authority of Christ's powerful name.

> 1. spirit of antichrist, 2. spirit of error, 3. spirit of bondage, 4. spirit of prostitution/sexual immorality, 5. spirit of fear, 6. spirit of death, 7. spirit of haughtiness, 8. spirit of jealousy, 9. spirit of lying, 10. spirit of stupor, 11. spirit of deafness and dumbness. 12. spirit of divination, 13. spirit of infirmity, 14. spirit of heaviness.[272]

Jesus stepped between Morgan and her accusers, for He loves her and is her Advocate. Morgan is now a born again, spirit-filled woman in Christ, who is opened to Christ's authority in every part of her life. She knows the story of the woman caught in adultery, and she knows

Born to Be Free!

the woman at His feet, worshiping Him before anyone else could understand His sacrifice.[273]

The Scripture says that the woman caught in adultery had seven demons cast out before her spiritual cleansing from demons was complete.[274] The seven demons would come from our list of fourteen, and I consider these to be possibilities: 1. Prostitution/sexual immorality, 2. Love of money, 3. Fear, 4. Death, 5. Heaviness, 6. Divination, and 7. Lying.[275]

There was only One who was sinless when the woman was thrown at Jesus' feet. Jesus stood between her and her accusers when those men asserted the laws of God in her open and shut case.[276] They were serving Satan at the exact same moment that they were pretending to serve God. How is that possible? How is it possible for Jesus to tell Satan to get behind Him in the exact moment when He was looking into Peter's eyes?[277]

Those protectors of the Law quickly understood that they too were Lawbreakers. They looked down to see Jesus writing a list of sins in the dirt between their feet. They looked down to see their own personal sins writ large in that same dust where this immoral woman lay waiting. They realized that they might be stoned to death, if Jesus had His way with them. They deserved to die with her. Each one dropped his stone, beginning with the highest ranking man present, until every stone had been left there at Jesus's feet.

In that dust, the Prostitute became the adopted daughter of God. Though she would surely refer to this experience many times thereafter, she was spiritually disconnected from that word forever. "Prostitute" had been her name, but she no longer answered when the men called upon her for love.

If you try to research her identity in the Scriptures you will see what God has done to frustrate your efforts. It is intentional, for God is making new creatures. Wei Wan is become Morgan, and Morgan has become Wei Wan. She is not simply a woman from West Texas. She is a child of God. He made it nearly impossible for us to make that former connection between our version of Prostitute/Mary and Saul/Paul, and our former identities. We are free indeed!

The Catholics and Episcopalians might sternly inform you that the woman in adultery is not Mary Magdalene—that they could have no

Myopic Me!

DNA in common. And they are right. God broke this traceability so that no Bible-sleuth from the future will connect their dots together again. This Humpty-Dumpty will resist everyone who gives a hand.

There is this intentional scriptural disconnect for a reason. When our sins are forgiven, we are disconnected from our past life—we are, as God's promise insists, become New Creatures! The Bipolar Identity[278] in Christ subsumes, integrates, and transforms that wounded, sinful creature, making us into His Masterpiece. Jesus made the prostitute over in the very image of God—Jesus said, "Mary chose the better part."[279]

That better part is to be at His feet in praise of His name. We are now traced to the Throne Room of the Father in heaven through our adoption into Christ. It is said that Mary became a leader in the first Church, and that may be true. But there is a gulf between her old and new identities.

The woman, whoever she is, whom Jesus protected, had poured out the perfume from her former life on Jesus' feet. This perfume became the living sacrifice poured out as the ideal worship of the Lamb of God, no longer representing the seductive scent of the woman who pleasured men for money. This waste of a "year's wages" brought great discomfort for one famous lover of money, Judas Iscariot.[280]

While the tears were still rolling down her face, Jesus could see the silhouette of the Cross in His mind's eye. A week later His hands and feet were affixed with spikes, and a crown of thorns had been pressed down hard upon His head. Mary was standing beneath that cross, a few feet from Her Savior and Lord, when Judas took great care in hanging himself from a dead tree.

Judas, too, was outside Jerusalem's walls, when his intestines burst through his stomach wall, while his body hung from the rope of bitterness. He could not forgive, for he knew nothing of Grace. The demons had ruined his adoption into God's family, blinding him one last time with thirty silver coins.[281]

The indelible script had already been written into his withered soul when Judas took the bread and ate it. "Satan entered him. Then Jesus told him, 'Hurry and do what you're going to do.'" Judas is a special case, for he ate the bread of brokenness, never drinking the New Wine of forgiveness through Jesus' blood.

Judas loved the world, and he never recognized or worshiped Yeshua Messiah, Christ Jesus. He saw Jesus, the "good teacher," everyday; but he never SAW the Son of God. He never said, "You are the Messiah, the Promised One, the Christ of God." He could never say with the Centurion, "Truly, you are the Son of God!" Judas praised the idol of Mammon, Money, and wanted to be important in the world's terms. He could not defend himself against the demons Satan sent to destroy him.

Neither can we. We need Jesus to set us free. We need the revelation of Christ to lead us to our Ananias to lay his hands on us, removing the scales from our eyes, and empowering us with the Holy Spirit.

> But whenever someone turns to the Lord, the veil is taken away. For the Lord is the Spirit, and wherever the Spirit of the Lord is, there is freedom. So all of us who have had that veil removed can see and reflect the glory of the Lord. And the Lord—who is the Spirit—makes us more and more like him as we are changed into his glorious image.[282]

Orphans, no more, we become daughters and sons of God through Adoption Prime, God living inside of us. There is nothing like it in the Chinese version or the West Texas version! This adoption is eternal, powerful, glorious, and full of good works, in Jesus' name, Amen!

13

The Hernandez Murder.

> "Beware of false prophets who come disguised as harmless sheep but are really vicious wolves."[283]
>
> Don't lord it over the people assigned to your care, but lead them by your own good example.[284]
>
> One day Cain suggested to his brother, "Let's go out into the fields." And while they were in the field, Cain attacked his brother, Abel, and killed him.[285]

A very famous cover-up occurred—well-known in New England. It was the coverup perpetrated by Aaron Hernandez who killed his friend in order to keep him from talking. For me it has become the parable of Aaron Hernandez, the forty-million dollar New England Patriot's football star, who shot Odin Lloyd in the back with five 45-caliber rounds a mere half-mile from my open bedroom window at 3:25 a.m. in 2015.

I woke up at the exact time of the murder and went into the bathroom for my nightly pilgrimage. Though it is unlikely that I actually heard the gunshots, I did make a note of the time. The front window was open wide in the direction of that murder site, permitting cool air to enter the bedroom. I learned a few days later that the victim had died at that same early morning hour—the witching hour for the dark witches flying around over New England.

The helicopters circled overhead for a couple of days searching for any evidence of what had happened. Odin [name of the Norse/Germanic god associated with death, the gallows, and sorcery, among others[286]] knew too much about Aaron's secret life, so Hernandez shut him up permanently. Odin's family forgave Aaron, saying that faith would get them through the pain and the loss of a son and brother.[287]

What was Aaron thinking? What was in his mind? What loose cannon stripped its moorings to fly across his crazy deck chairs at that time of the morning? He had not taken those thoughts captive to Christ, of that, I am certain. Under the influence of synthetic marijuana[288] when he killed his friend, his thoughts belonged to the highest bidder—Satan.

It is possible that brain injuries from football played an important role in his condition of mind. Ann McKee, the head of BU's CTE Center which has studied the disease caused by repetitive brain trauma for more than a decade, describes Hernandez's brain as "one of the most significant contributions to our work" because of the brain's pristine condition and the rare opportunity to study the disease in a 27-year-old.[289]

> In a diagnosis that linked one of football's most notorious figures with the sport's most significant health risk, doctors found Hernandez had Stage 3 CTE, which McKee said researchers had never seen in a brain younger than 46 years old.[290]

Odin Lloyd apparently knew about the shooting of two men in a BMW outside a strip club in Boston. The men may have spilled their drinks on Hernandez. Eye for an eye, drink for a quart of blood. Makes perfect sense to me, or it did a half-century before. I knocked a classmate ten feet across the floor of the mess hall when he laughed at me while I was on the way to knock out the offender who had intentionally dumped a drink on my uniform at The Citadel.

For Hernandez, the shooting up of the BMW occupants might simply have been gang-related animosity. Hernandez did not attempt to hide his tattoos boasting his connection to the "Bloods" gang,[291] and their revenge-rules provide the best explanations for his insane actions. Cain would have been proud, though sullen, calling out to Aaron:

> "Hey, Hernandez! Great game with the Patriots last week! Hey, I saw Sin waiting at your door looking for

someone to devour. Looks like Sin found his boy! Too late to master it now, right?"

Of course, Hernandez would have shot him dead on the spot before he returned to Homeward Lane, a half-mile from my house. He likely suffered from muddled-motives, with synthetic marijuana twisted around his father-wound, driven by the vengeance code of his gang, and addled by the synaptic catastrophe flashing in his brain which scientists antiseptically refer to as "CTE."

His sexual life might have been the root of these many roots, remaining a partial secret, for Odin Lloyd knew all about Hernandez the "schmoocher" continuing a gay-bisexual relationship with a male high school friend.[292] This theory contends that Aaron attempted to cover up his secret sexual affliction by executing Odin Lloyd—shooting him in the back, standing in the North Attleboro industrial park at 3:25 a.m.

Who does that to an enemy, much less to a friend? Oh, that's right, it's not a new thing. Cain did the exact same thing to his brother with a rock. If Cain had access to a 357 magnum he would have used it. The spot where Odin died is a half mile away, half-way to our church facility in the Industrial Park in North Attleboro. This is a very nice area, with a pristine Park and excellent upper end neighborhoods all around. Aaron's neighborhood runs in the near-million dollar range for houses.

Less than a half a mile from my open bedroom window, a synthetic marijuana butt was found on the ground, and Hernandez's DNA was later identified in the lab. The Forty-millionaire, Hernandez, might have thought that Lloyd's death would eliminate several loose-cannons rolling around on his carefully arranged deck in North Attleboro. Aaron was dead wrong, as the subsequent trial would prove.

Several books have been written describing nearly every one of his secrets. Months before these events, our Senior Pastor had been serving in the Patriot's practice facility leading a Bible study for team members. Hernandez had walked by the small gathering, asked them, "What's going on?" Matthew Slater told him, "Bible study. Want to join us?" Aaron's voice turned sour, "Bible study! No thanks." He slouched away, possibly mumbling about the futility of such activities.

After the mindless murder of his friend, this second hand story seemed to validate the hardening of my heart toward Hernandez. "Now,

Myopic Me!

he's a scoffer and a murderer!" I thought out loud. I now officially despised him. I forgot about the Roman Centurion who had thrust his spear through Jesus' side and His heart when it was as dark as night.

He could have held his own with Aaron's gangbangers, and he would never have joined any sissy Bible Study either. But the Centurion was there with his gang when world changing events unfolded on the Hill of Skulls, while the blood of Jesus ran down his elbow from his own spear.

> And behold, the curtain of the temple was torn in two, from top to bottom. And the earth shook, and the rocks were split. The tombs also were opened. And many bodies of the saints who had fallen asleep were raised, and coming out of the tombs after his resurrection they went into the holy city and appeared to many [I got up to go to the bathroom when Aaron killed his friend a half-mile away]. When the centurion and those who were with him, keeping watch over Jesus, saw the earthquake and what took place, they were filled with awe and said, "Truly this was the Son of God!"[293]

These Roman gangbangers ruled the whole world, and not just this remote neighborhood outside Jerusalem's walls. He declared with a certainty, "Truly, this was the Son of God!" For him, that Lamb's blood had brought the revelation of the Way, the Truth, and the Life. His heart had softened, and awe overwhelmed his stoic perspective. I had felt nothing but vitriol for Aaron the gang leader once the North Attleboro police charged him with first-degree murder.

It was easy to classify Aaron as one of "those People," though I knew only a little at that time about his troubled life. I had seen his tats, of course. I had very recently observed him at a preseason practice session behind Gillette Stadium, where I concluded he was a real team player.

Though I arrived very early to watch the practice session from the hill alongside the end of the practice field, I could see his apparent commitment to the team. I had just left my appointment with the family doctor at the nearby medical center just beyond the stadium. Watching the team's preseason practice sessions is a big deal, or was a big deal, during this extended winning tradition in Foxborough at Gillette Stadium.

Every preseason practice would be attended by around fifteen-thousand curious fans daily, and I was one of a dozen who had shown up very early for this edition. I really admired his work ethic, watching Aaron there a half hour before any of his teammates showed up. He was returning punts from Ryan Allen, who was crushing the ball 60 to 70 yards down the field every time.

Catching these towering punts is a true skill which Julian Edelman describes in his 2017 book, *Relentless, A Memoir*.[294] The special teams punt receiver has to catch the ball "with his feet"—this seemingly impossible feat with feet was one of Julian Edelman's few coaching inputs received directly from Coach Belichick during the early part of his career in Foxborough, selected in the seventh round.[295]

Julian quickly discovered the simple wisdom in his counsel. Unless your feet are planted in perfect position when the ball returns to the earth, no amounts of good hands will help you field the punt arriving fast out of the blue sky or the snow-squall. Teachability is a foremost characteristic of those who make the Patriot's team, and is also a fundamental attribute of those whom God will bless.

Come as a little child to Gillette and to the Church as well. Come as a teachable child to the Bible-study, and to the game of life. But this team player, this teachable child, Aaron Hernandez, had hardened his heart to God during that season of his life. On that particular practice day, the gifted physical specimen had snatched the punts from the sky before exploding down the field. The spear would soon pierce his friend's **back**, five times, and Odin's blood would run out on the ground. The gangbanger would dispatch his friend with a super loud 45-caliber revolver in the Industrial Park!

Aaron's bow-legged running style did not affect his speed or balance on the football field, and Julian Edelman reported that his route-running skills were unprecedented, making Aaron a very challenging prospect for the best defensive players in the NFL. His speed and 245 pounds of muscle made Aaron a formidable receiver at the pro-level.[296]

At that time, I knew nothing about his father dying when he was in Middle School in Florida. Nevertheless, Aaron had blamed God. He had picked up the same rock that Cain left in the field, to kill his brother

Odin, who was the good guy. That gang-heritage he chose a few years later had destroyed whole neighborhoods and even entire cities across the nation, but he became a gang leader for the "Bloods gang,"[297]

Gangs produce revenge-driven soldiers, and the more power the gang gets, the more central that murder becomes. Revenge is the ultimate proof text of their power and control. Violence begets violence, and the cycle accelerates without end. I hate the gang tattoos, and all they stand for—knowing that God calls us into the ultimate gang, or family. He calls us into the ultimate team, or body, which is the Church—His Gang is bonded through His blood into this unity. Aaron's gang was the ultimate counterfeit, bonded through the blood of from revenge. His gang's name is the ultimate offense, referring to themselves as "Bloods."[298]

The night when Hernandez was arrested, my small group members were gathered a half-mile from the murder site, and they were far more gracious than I. More than one said she was already praying for Hernandez's soul to be saved. Aaron had not killed himself yet, nor had his trial concluded his guilt at this point. Their prayers seemed authentic and sincere, and they were also praying for his victim's family. They had already said that they forgave Aaron.

Sitting in the family room with these brothers and sisters in Christ, we were having our sissy, Bible-centric meeting where we looked at our notes from the weekend sermon, studying the scriptures from the perspective of our own lives and from current events. To show my wrath toward Aaron, I held my hand in the shape of a pistol, with the wrist rotated to the horizontal; I demonstrated how he had killed his friend a few nights before.

Following their example, I started praying for him as well. I don't know that I had prayed for him at all before my fellow Christians gave me a better example of Christ's love. When I started praying, the words flowed in the following manner, beginning with my honest confession.

> "Our Father, we all deserve death according to Your Own justice! You said, 'Not one is good, only the Father.' I have spent much of my life fantasizing that I am good. I have imagined at times that I was something when I was nothing. Your words make clear that

> I am depravity without your grace. Any goodness has come through Your Spirit working in my life. You paid a great price for my freedom. I do not deserve Your kindness. Have I not hated strangers, plotting murder in my heart? Have I not committed adultery with my neighbor far too many times? Like Aaron Hernandez, have I not been selfish, predatory, and proud in this life in the same way as Aaron? Have I not sought revenge, or tried to cover up my crimes?"

I prayed again at the end of the meeting for Hernandez's soul to be saved. I remembered that Paul wrote about a Love that keeps no record of wrongs. I said out loud, "How can Revenge gain a foothold if there is no record of wrongs?" God's love does not plot revenge. God asks us to believe in His Son, remembering His forgiveness from the Cross. The blood of Jesus washes our record clean: He keeps no record of our wrongs.[299]

> "Our Father, each of us deserves your wrath, for Your assessment is true. We have all gone our own way. My heart is perpetually wicked until Christ's Spirit controls me. If I am left alone for a moment without the Spirit's good counsel, I invent treachery and evil plans. Not one of us deserves to spend eternity in the joy of heaven! Father, I pray You change Aaron Hernandez's heart. Bring him to a place of deep repentance and acceptance of what You have done for him through Jesus' Cross."

According to the compassion and faith shown by my group, I prayed for his redemption. They brought me to repentance with their own testimony of faithfulness. I had to pray from that same Spirit of mercy now.

> "Our Father, let Aaron know how much You love him. Call him to Yourself out of his sinful and broken life! Father, change my own heart toward him, so that I do not wait so long to pray for my enemies! Forgive me for my failure to be as Jesus was on the Cross, beseeching

> You: 'Father, forgive them, for they know not what they do.' Father, forgive Aaron, for he acted in ignorance, consumed by his own blindness and idolatry."

Through this recent experience, I remembered with fresh understanding that God gave His life for us sinners. He died for those who are far off, not just for those who are near. He did not come for the righteous, but for sinners. The self-righteous are those who have already been justified by their own personal salvation efforts—in their own minds; in Hernandez's case, he saw salvation coming through his role as a gang leader, according to gang rules, gang law, brutal gang justice—salvation through the gang.

This is idolatry. He was an idolater and an evil-doer just as I was when I prayed on my knees in Atlanta fifty-two years before, "Jesus, forgive my idolatry!" Jesus died for everyone who draws near through faith. His salvation is for those who are convinced that He is the only way to God's heaven.[300]

After King David inseminated Bathsheba during an adulterous night in the Palace, he became concerned that their secret rendezvous would be exposed by her pregnancy. Though Bathsheba's husband, Uriah, was fighting David's war against the Philistines, David could not allow this loyal soldier to return home to find his wife pregnant. The king would certainly be implicated, and that could not be allowed to happen.[301]

The prerogative of kings came to the forefront in his coverup. While I declare today that David is a biblical hero, and that God loved David to his final breath, the king's character was surely wrecked. The miracle is this: God's Son, Jesus Christ, would be born in the City of David according to God's promise to honor David's house. Why? Though David committed adultery before murdering Bathsheba's Hittite husband, God would keep His promise to David and to David's son, Solomon.[302]

God forgave David's heinous sins when he repented before the prophet Nathan, who showed him that he deserved the death sentence for his sins against God and man. God honored him greatly through his repentance. Therefore, what is the riddle of God's love for us sinners?[303]

Because we are created in His own image, under the ancient covenant with Abraham, we have this opportunity to become the very children of God. The reason for His love for us comes down to one final criterion, one necessary and sufficient reason, and that through the blood of His only Son. Jesus said that we would be measured, "By the same standard [which we apply to others], you will be measured."[304] When Jesus comes, the standard set is impossible—only Grace can defend us then.

Aaron's case seems unforgivable when I list his crimes and his depravity. But God is the only just God, and there is only one way to come into His presence. Though Aaron Hernandez was not known for his faith and love—probably killing several men during his brief lifetime—yet he wrote, "John 3:16," on his forehead before hanging himself.[305] Was this an answered prayer for my small group members and for me? Did God forgive all of his sins, even the final one, taking his own life?

When they cut him down from the window of his solitary confinement cell in Shirley, MA, this scandalous message becomes the final bookend of his tragic life. Is it possible that the scandal of God's grace overwhelmed the scandal of Aaron Hernandez's sinful and hidden life?[306] This grace of God through faith had certainly impinged on David's life—like Abraham, David believed God was His Savior and King.

It is also clear that Aaron, could not, would not, live for Christ, becoming the Living Sacrifice. He chose Death. Grace certainly impinges on the scandal of my own life, but does Aaron's final message speak of his surrender to Christ before he died? Was this another one of Aaron's deeply held secrets?

> "Therefore David blessed the Lord before all the assembly; and David said: 'Blessed are You, Lord God of Israel, our Father, forever and ever.'"[307]

This reference to "our Father" is common in Isaiah and other books of the Old Testament. God's glory as the "Good, Good, Father" is spoken again and again; and "The whole earth is filled with his glory!"[308] Hernandez had asked God, "Why did you take my father?"[309] The Father had answered, "I have always been your Father."

The grand misconception in the fallen world is 99% of us are blaming God for the busted Apple we still reach for too often. Sin and corruption had deceived Aaron Hernandez, and Satan had come to steal,

Myopic Me!

kill, and destroy him. But God's desire is to save us from ourselves. He came to save sinners.

The Garden of Aaron's youth was ruptured when his father died. Aaron turned bitter, opening himself up to the prerogative of demons—and evil gangs. Demons love unforgiveness and bitterness, and revenge, in the same way that dogs love piles of animal poop on their daily walk.

Aaron bit into the forbidden fruit, and the corruption of that lie of revenge. He chose gangs early, and often, to mete out vengeance. Violence became the god of his chaos. Life was cheap in his philosophy of the gang, for his father died young, when he needed him most. His physical and mental attributes set him up as a natural leader and a cruel murderer.

In Julian's book, *Relentless*, he has nothing but good things to say about his former teammate,[310] but death had left an ugly furrow in Aaron's soul, and Hernandez had sown to his bitterness, taking two or three lives—finally killing himself in his solitary confinement cell. While Aaron suffered brain damage from concussions, his biggest injury may have been the loss of his father at that critical moment in his life.

No excuse for murder, it is unclear whether Aaron ever forgave his father, his friend, or himself. Unforgiveness is a noose slipped over his own neck. Truly, he dug two graves. Only God can lift the death he pulled around his soul, and that through the **Blood of His only Son**.

14

History & the Mall in Washington.

> Here is another story Jesus told: "The Kingdom of Heaven is like a farmer who planted good seed in his field. But that night as the workers slept, his enemy came and planted weeds among the wheat, then slipped away."[311] . . . Then, leaving the crowds outside, Jesus went into the house. His disciples said, "Please explain to us the story of the weeds in the field."[312]

History has become so much more important to me since Google made a door into all those libraries of humankind. Those dreary World History classes which nearly stopped my little educational wagon at Clemson University are in the past now. My perspective has changed dramatically. My education continues to the present day, and has never ceased in the fifty-three years since.

"Professor, please explain the meaning of the weeds in the field." But the professor continued with his sacrosanct notes, not turning to the left or to the right for any interruptions of his perfectly practiced presentation. He assumed that we would receive the World from the spoon he held up to our partially open mouths. His Pablum of dates and placenames repelled me in this survey of the history of the world where no context or reason ever coaxed me to dive into his dull waters.

The broad-brush course in history was required for graduation, and I had to take that final course in summer school to complete the educational requirements. I hated the detailed memorization of dates and

Myopic Me!

actors seemingly without much aim or purpose. I hated what this professor labeled as history!

But today, it is different. History is the narrative of men's inhumanity to man. It is the story of the weeds in the field growing beside the grain. It is the story of how men come together to form a great nation, forged in a thousand intractable arguments.

It is the story of terrible bloodshed, temporarily bringing peace between warring parties. It is the story of complacency, regurgitated from generation to generation; and it is the story of power, shifting across the landscape of the world with its dark shadow. It is the story of men falling down before their God just in time to avoid being swept over the hard lip of Niagara Falls into the history of fallen men.

It is the story of God's love for His creation, the battle to extricate our souls from the grips of evil forces. It is the Good News of ultimate victory over darkness and evil. History chronicles the stories of courage which the students in the hard Formica desks could not fully appreciate during their academic careers.

In that hot October sun in 1997 on the Washington Mall, we could feel the distant fire burning our skin, reminding us of that fire which Elijah called down from heaven on Mt. Carmel. On that amazing day of male liberality in D.C., we did not perceive each other with the filtering of the world system, seeing the other's economic or educational stratum.

There was no in-crowd, nor any inferior categories to divide us. Politics and factions played no role in our encounters with each other. Our moral self-worth did not come from any self-righteousness, knowing that God Himself is the only true Promise Keeper!

The Mall filled up with tears during the day, as men wept over the dark heritage of the suffocating slave ships from Africa and the West Indies. My wonderful black brother in Christ from Winston Salem, by way of his Pittsburg church, was there on the platform with the others leading a million men into the heart of worship.

Sharing his songs and experiences as a famous Pittsburgh pastor, every heart was broken as he led us into the Spirit's unity. I remembered our affectionate meeting in our shepherd's home fifteen years before, when he was the speaker at a local Christian conference.

Love and gratitude marked our time together, and we knew him as a man of the Spirit and a truly humble brother. We could all see that grace had come to him through much sacrifice for Christ and for the Church. But there together on the Mall, we were like a million Israelites filling the plain below Mount Sinai with the fire of God flowing down.

The blinding April sun left us stunned in the surreal proximity with the congressional business that unfolded nearby in the Capitol. We could feel the rumble of history, a nation in the balance of God's invisible hand. We knew that our purpose at the Nation's Capitol was invisible to many people across the nation.

The very present fire of Jesus Christ arrived during our prayers and worship time during the day. The "hobbling" which Elijah addressed that day on Mt. Carmel was also relevant in 1997, and is even more urgent in 2021. Elijah's question directed to the people of Israel and to the prophets of Baal rung with clarity and authority as we realized we were not exempted or innocent ourselves:

> "How much longer will you waver, hobbling between two opinions? If the Lord is God, follow him! But if Baal is God, then follow him!" But the people were completely silent.[313]

Elijah framed the issue succinctly for every generation, and he brought into focus our hobbling between various religions that leave us limping. Materialism is a religion that cripples our souls. Factionalism is a religion that makes us hot under the collar, building hostilities as fast as peacemakers can tear them down. Each of these was at work in 1997.

But Elijah was not really talking about religion. He was addressing Lordship. If we missed God's instruction to build the Ark for the coming flood, then even Noah's family would not have survived? Details are important to God. Loose specs sink ships. If we edit His instructions, building our boat two-hundred feet long, instead of four-hundred fifty-feet long, then we will not survive the storm.

If there are two internal decks for the animals, instead of three, then how could the future ecosystem thrive? Details matter to God! We were confronting those subtle curses from the fathers meted out upon the sons and daughters. We were there to tear down the strongholds of Segregation and Abortion, two abominations that are anathema to God.

Myopic Me!

We prayed as one man against the powers and principalities and spiritual influences from many dark kingdoms arrayed against God's purposes in America. The Lord of Lords was specifically asking us if we would put aside every false teaching concerning His glory.

> "Will you gather as One, with black believers and white believers standing in the gap together in the unity of the Holy Spirit giving My Son all the glory? I remind you all, as a remnant delivered from the slavery of sin, 'to whom much is given, much is required.' Stand in the Gap for justice, mercy, and righteousness, and no longer participate in the shadow kingdoms promoted by this crooked generation."

A special relationship was expanded with a black brother who traveled with us from our Attleboro church on the overnight train—we spent the early part of the day together talking about the Lord's purposes while we drank our Starbuck's coffee. The crowd was diverse as well, yet there was no particular self-consciousness about race in this Christian gathering.

A reporter for the Los Angeles Times decided to interview the black participants he spotted during the day, and he filed this report:

> There was a fairly significant number of blacks in the crowd, many of whom came from evangelical Christian churches. Several said they felt comfortable in the predominantly white setting of Promise Keepers rallies because they believe that the group is earnest in its call for racial healing.[314]

There was a concerted effort during the day, praying for God's forgiveness and for His will to be accomplished in His Church. Two verses stood out for me. The first is the prayer of Jesus in the Upper Room for unity.

> " . . . now protect them by the power of your name so that they will be united just as we are . . . I am praying

> not only for these disciples but also for all who will ever
> believe in me through their message. I pray that they
> will all be one, just as you and I are one."[315]

Our pride had blinded many, keeping us from discerning one another as sons and daughters of the Most High God. We rejected or feared or hated one another because of the different shading of our skin or the neighborhood from which we came.

Segregation is a legal commitment that we will henceforth regard one another without consideration as members of God's family, deserving honor as His sons and daughters. When the secular state passes such a law that builds walls, the body of Christ tears down every wall of hostility.

Therefore, God will judge the Church before the nation. The Church is called to the mission of honor, love, faithfulness, justice, and mercy. While the nation removes unalienable rights, God's Church extends the boundaries of family to embrace every member.

Segregation is no mandate to the Church, for the laws of man cannot abridge the Laws of God. The Church will ever answer to Christ who is the Head. "For it is my Father's will that all who see his Son and believe in him should have eternal life. I will raise them up at the last day."[316]

It is very hard today to step back from that intrinsic dividing wall that is not unique to the American story, for it is part of the sin-wall between man and the Holy God. Sin ends the intimacy of Cain, unless you master it.

> "Why are you so angry?" the Lord asked Cain. "Why do
> you look so dejected? You will be accepted if you do
> what is right. But if you refuse to do what is right, then
> watch out! Sin is crouching at the door, eager to con-
> trol you. But you must subdue it and be its master."[317]

A powerful spirit of deception entered the hearts of many church leaders in the nineteenth century. It was very much like that spirit which entered Judas Iscariot during the Last Supper—the love of the world rather than the love of God and neighbor.

Myopic Me!

That spirit of deception flew from the promulgation of a false gospel called "Separate but Equal," broadcast to America upon the ugly carrier wave of Racism. This Racism erected a wall of hostility that has persisted for one-hundred forty-three years since 1896—fomenting fear, emasculation, and murder.[318]

Jesus speaks, then and now, to one city at a time, one nation at a time. You can read all about it in Revelation 2 and 3. He is interested in healing the American church, while discipling the nations. The crowd filling the Mall from the Capital steps to the Washington Monument was hobbling as we stood and kneeled for hours, confessing our sins, and our father's sins.

The nation was limping into Washington D.C. from every Christian background and geographic perspective. We were no longer silent, like the Israelites on Mt. Carmel, or hanging back, like the Israelites at the base of Mt. Sinai, or misconstruing Jesus' identity like the disciples on Mt. Tabor. We were stepping out of the national silence in behalf of Unity, Life, and Reconciliation.

We were gathering to draw near to God while we could still hear His voice, confessing our sins to one another that we would be healed. We remembered that God is not always in the wind or the earthquake or the fire, but He sometimes speaks with a whisper. His whisper terminates evil rulers, silencing the Jezebels in every era.[319]

Elisha followed Elijah, and the old prophet threw his cloak over the younger man's shoulders without a word. That is enough for God, for Elisha would be the forerunner of Jesus Christ, and the Kings would come from Persia to cast their crowns at Jesus' feet, their incense, gold, and myrrh laid down as the first of many tithes for the work of the King of Kings.

In God's whisper, His still small voice, He accomplishes the purging of idolatry in every age.[320] On the Mall, 1,400,000 arrived who had not bowed the knee to Baal Hadad, the God of Convenience—the Abortion goddess of the age. Seeking God's vision, they prayed for their families, their churches, and their nation.

There, in the final days of the twentieth century, that contemporaneous crowd, as numerous as the Israelites in the Wilderness, stood waiting for their Elijah to speak. But Elijah came one more time to throw his cloak over a few shoulders in Washington. When we said we wanted to tell mom and pop goodbye, he said, "Do what 'chu gotta' do."

Standing in the gap between the four-hundred-fifty Baal prophets in the Capitol that day, we stood our ground in the valley of Checks and Balances that were ricocheting through the three Branches of the Government, twisting in the Red Tape and Deep State and the Broken Fourth Estate.

We could hear the tuning forks adjusting the Public Ear with lies, and the Re-election cycles were already whirring as the Capitol filled up with rancor, divisions, and self-cancelling ideologies. We remembered Elijah's fear of Jezebel, and we all knew her name in Washington.

We could hear her complaining in the nation's Capitol, while the streets and villages filled up with the vestiges of Virtue, Freedom, and Faith. We prayed against the factions plotting revenge and self-destruction inside every Senator's office.

With one foot set down in the shadow of Baal and another foot standing in the fire from the One True Living God, the servants of the people were busy voting pay increases and more protections for their perpetual positions of power. They stood in front of the cameras hurling rocks across the aisle at their brothers and sisters.

God's powerful display convinced a few of them, and His fire coming down from heaven swayed the others to flee. Ahab, the evil king, was sent packing when he saw a cloud the size of a man's hand, before the black sky and lightning erupted, and the heavens unleashed a fierce storm with violent wind. Elisha, with seven-thousand others, will execute God's judgment on Ahab and Jezebel and on the idolatry of the Baal gods.[321]

Jesus is speaking to Elijah with a whisper, cueing the dogs to do their part, like street cleaners at Jezebel's house. They will lick up her brains and all her evil schemes and murders which have spilled out on the ground. "Beware, Jezebel. The dogs can smell your evil thoughts!"

Whether God comes to raze a nation, or to raise a vision among the remnant who make Him Lord, we could not know on that day. There is nowhere to hide from God's searching eyes, and no president or majority leader can hide from the reach of His still small voice.

His name is above every name, knowing the Past, Present, and Future, seeing everything from Alpha to Omega, as He rules over His

Myopic Me!

own creation. When He whispers, kings fall from thrones; when He whispers, the Jezebels fall from their second story windows into the toothy grins of the dogs waiting below.

During the 401-year period since the Rock of Christ collided with Plymouth Rock, the cost for standing between the Baal Hadad prophets and the still small voice of God has gotten too steep. But God reminds us that seven-thousand have not bowed the knee.[322] There are seven-thousand who remember the night when Elijah stood with Moses and Jesus, and God made clear to all, "This is my beloved Son. Listen to Him!"[323]

> Six days later Jesus took Peter and the two brothers, James and John, and led them up a high mountain to be alone. As the men watched, Jesus' appearance was transformed so that his face shone like the sun, and his clothes became as white as light. Suddenly, Moses and Elijah appeared and began talking with Jesus. Peter exclaimed, "Lord, it's wonderful for us to be here! If you want, I'll make three shelters as memorials—one for you, one for Moses, and one for Elijah." But even as he spoke, a bright cloud overshadowed them, and a voice from the cloud said, "This is my dearly loved Son, who brings me great joy. Listen to him." The disciples were terrified and fell face down on the ground.[324]

America is no longer listening to Jesus' Words. His Words are thrown down like garbage into an alley. He is speaking, but we are not listening. On the Mall in Washington, God was speaking to everyone who wanted to build a booth rather than listen to His Son.

Our identity from our local churches or from our individual commitments was being subsumed into this larger identity as functioning members of an American church which had failed to truly listen to God's Son—now we were Standing in the Gap for all of those who had erred in the past, bringing great harm to families and to whole segments of the culture during the Epoch of Segregation. The fractures existing in that larger church had persisted for many decades, but we prayed with faith for God's deep healing.

History & the Mall in Washington.

Not seeking a magic trick, we had come to hear from God's Son. We gathered according to His final prayer in the Upper Room, on the night when Judas Iscariot betrayed Him for thirty pieces of silver. Jesus prayed for the unity of the Spirit to come to the generations who would follow the powerful testimonies of those disciples present, all but one of whom would die for their faith in Christ.

We were very aware of the proclamations of the Founding Fathers as we kneeled to pray during that day. What did these words mean in the Light of Day?

> We hold these truths [what truths?] to be self-evident, that all men are created equal, that they are endowed by their Creator with certain unalienable Rights, that among these are Life, Liberty and the pursuit of Happiness.[325]

Tradition holds that Peter blurted out his plans for three memorials while standing on Mt. Tabor, but I have wondered out loud if Jesus did not go to tear down the "high places" which Solomon permitted on the hills and mountains around Jerusalem. Trying to please his seven-hundred wives, he built shrines for the worship of their gods, and he may even have sacrificed his own children—to the god Chemosh. Yet, the peaks of mountains and the valleys belong to God.

In this book, I searched to learn that I have referenced Moses twenty times; Elijah, twenty-three times; and Jesus, two-hundred and fifty-two times. Is this enough emphasis on Jesus? No. It would be impossible to make Him enough the Center of this book, of who we are, and of all that is visible and invisible!

Even though Elijah was present, and Moses was there beside Him, God told Peter, James, and John: "This is my Son. Listen to Him!" Moses was silent. Elijah was silent. Jesus was silent. But God was adamant: "Tune your ears when My Son speaks. It is important. It is not just temporal life that is at stake, but eternal life. He is the Way, the Truth, and the Life, and no one will come to Me except through Him. Worship Him in Spirit and Truth, and Follow Him all the days of your life."

I heard someone recently baptized use the all too familiar phrase, "I made Jesus a part of my life;" and I grimaced, saying, "No He's not

Myopic Me!

part of your life! He is all and in all. He is the Center of all that is, the Word with God and the Light of the World, the Maker of heaven and earth. In Him you have your very being."

Jesus' voice is the Voice that will not be silenced in the Valley of Death or on the mountain of where the Anathema gods are on display for every age of man. When Peter, terrified, blurted out about the booths, the tents, the statuary of the three men, he failed to note the identity of God's Son—he called Him, "Rabbi." No rabbi, Jesus is the Son who pleases God. And it is impossible to please God without faith.[326]

Standing with the one who delivered the Ten Commandments [Moses], the one who restored the Law [Elijah], and the One who was the Fulfillment of all the Law and the Prophets [Jesus], only One voice was propitious and worthy of the attention of men and nations.

The Word from Jesus' mouth is the Word made flesh, moving into our neighborhoods and our Capitol Mall, holding our lives together, and reconciling all things in Himself. Statues are anathema, abhorrent, to God; but worse still is our propensity in Church and out to misconstrue Jesus' true identity.

Paul wrote in Romans 1 that no one has an excuse in America for misconstruing God's Truth, for His eternal power and divine nature have been made known to us!

> Yes, they knew God, but they wouldn't worship him as God or even give him thanks. And they began to think up foolish ideas of what God was like [even though He sent His Son]. As a result, their minds became dark and confused. Claiming to be wise, they instead became utter fools. And instead of worshiping the glorious, ever-living God, they worshiped idols made to look like mere people and birds and animals and reptiles [the anathema idols and abominations].[327]

Every idol is an abomination which God despises. If we want to understand what happened on Mt. Hermon or Mt. Tabor, we have to focus our microphone on every word from Jesus' mouth. We have to give up our craving for all these vain projects which boast about our near-misses with men of earthly renown.

History & the Mall in Washington.

Are we not obsessed with ***Myopic Me!*** But it is the sad human condition, and only God can refocus our self-lust and our compulsive need to be the center of every story! Only God can cause us to fall face down on the Mall to worship the King of Kings.

> Peter exclaimed, "Lord, it's wonderful for us to be here! If you want, I'll make three shelters as memorials—one for you, one for Moses, and one for Elijah." But even as he spoke, a bright cloud overshadowed them, and a voice from the cloud said, "This is my dearly loved Son, who brings me great joy. Listen to him." The disciples were terrified and fell face down on the ground.[328]

This Good News rises above every petty dispute of men, as God cries out from the Cross, "Forgive them for they know not what they do." On the Mt. of Transfiguration, Peter was taking the ultimate vacation Selfie-shot, name-dropping on a cosmic scale, while God was illuminating the One True Living God whose face shone as brightly as the sun! Today it's Social Media vs. the Words of God: No contest!

This was the problem we were facing while we were on the Mall in Washington—before the Twitter-feed dominated. Every Peter among us was distracted, looking forward to building three booths when we got home. While God was seeking to elevate His Son in our hearts, the Transfiguration was revealing that Christ's spiritual identity, His glory and beauty, His radiance and true dimensions as God's Son, were too much for us to bear.

To see the fullness of His beauty and form and glory would have overwhelmed one point four million men. We could only handle this partial view, in the same way that Moses could not look directly at God, hiding in the cleft of the rock. Peter, sputtering, was looking for a project with his hands to keep from dying in the bright light transfiguring the Son.

Fear will always precede wisdom, and fear comes before God's glory. Building booths is merely the proof that we will do almost anything to avoid truly **Listening to Him**. During that day in Washington, we were on our knees looking down a lot because the sun was so bright on our faces. I must assess, flawed of course, that we saw very little of God's face

Myopic Me!

that day, though we were very tired when we arrived home at 4:30 a.m. in Attleboro Station. Mark and I had slept sitting up straight in our seats.

One million four-hundred thousand men had a few hours there on the Mall to capture the selfie shots with God for those few hours there after we had tumbled out of our trains at Pennsylvania Station, or from our automobiles from Interstate ramps. We had come, inevitably, to build our own monuments on the Mall in Jesus' mighty name. Those Congressmen and Senators who joined us during lunch to pray and worship could go back into the Capitol to speak or vote with new resolve.

George Washington, who spent his own money to fund the National Army, would have come out at lunch to pray with us if he had been there on that day. He would have bowed his knee to the God who stood with Elijah and Moses on the summit of the mountain. This first President of the United States would have given his "Amen" to the God who said, "Listen to Him.'

God revealed to us that He is the Lord of the Rain. He is the Father who loves His Only Son. On one occasion, a small group bowed to pray, and I joined with these strangers as the father turned to address his son. "Son, please forgive me for all my sins against you over the years. I have harmed you, too often driving you away from Jesus and from myself as well. Please forgive me son! 'Lord Jesus, forgive my sins against my one and only son.'"

Though I did not know a single person whom I prayed with during that day, many tears were shed over past injuries and over myriad unnamed offenses. This surreal day, with that massive "family" sharing their most intimate secrets with each other, witnessed the entire mall being mended with grace.

On that Mall, in the Land of the Free and the home of the brave, we were bowing down before our Maker, the offspring of Abraham by faith, and God was telling us that we had exchanged our unalienable rights for a bowl of soup.[329] Sixty-million babies had already died for a bowl of Jacob's stew, and our inheritance was in great jeopardy.

> "From among all the families on the earth,
>   I have been intimate with you alone.
> That is why I must punish you
>   for all your sins."[330]

History & the Mall in Washington.

Nations fall, but God disciplines the believers who should know better—and should act accordingly. But what I find amazing in this verse from the prophet Amos is God's desire for intimacy with us—we are *Made in the Bipolar Image of God*[31] and yet we choose lesser things to worship!

God breathed life into Adam's lungs, and each of us got our oxygen from our mother's hemoglobin. We don't get the divine genealogy of that first breath of life from God Himself. Because of Cain's great sin, our greatest idolatry is to avoid any accountability of sonship, even for those crimes we committed. Though we kill our own brother, our own child in the womb, we still demand to be left alone.

We shout in God's face: "Am I my son's guardian?" The idolatry of Eugenics[332] is our Golden Calf of Convenience, and our Urgent bowl of stew. With God standing right there beside us, we insulate ourselves from His full identity, calling Him, "Rabbi;" and we go about our own vain lives building booths without a clue. For your Body's Freedom, you will even murder your own son.

> Then the LORD God formed the man from the dust of the ground. He breathed the breath of life into the man's nostrils, and the man became a living person . . . male and female He created them.[333]

We were confronting those subtle curses from our grandfathers visited upon the sons and daughters. We were tearing down those ancient and modern strongholds of Segregation and Abortion, two abominations that are anathema to God.

We prayed as one against the powers and principalities, and the dark kingdoms arrayed against God's purpose in America—City full of Light, positioned high on a Hill. Now, God was warning the Church to stop demoting His Son of glory—"Listen to Him!"

> "Will you gather as One, with black believers and white believers standing in the gap together in the unity of the Holy Spirit giving My Son all the glory? I remind you, as a remnant from slavery, 'to whom much is given, much is required.' Stand in the Gap for justice, mercy, and

Myopic Me!

> righteousness, and no longer participate in the shadow-land kingdoms promoted by the god who promises that you will never be inconvenienced again—the god who demotes the One who fulfilled the Law and the Prophets."

There was a concerted effort during the day to pray for God's forgiveness and the accomplishment of His will. One message stood out for me—the prayer of Jesus in the Upper Room:

> " . . . now protect them by the power of your name so that they will be united just as we are . . . I am praying not only for these disciples but also for all who will ever believe in me through their message. I pray that they will all be one, just as you and I are one."[334]

Segregation had been a legal pronouncement that we [they] would henceforth regard one another without honor. The secular state might pass a law establishing Segregation, and God judges that nation. For the Church it is a whole 'nother ball game. The Church answers to Christ, who is the Head. He prayed for honor, unity, and love. He said,

> "Anyone who believes in God's Son has eternal life, for that dividing wall in the Most Holy Place is torn down."[335]

The scar of Segregation still shines bright red as the nation slowly heals in 2021. It has been one hundred and forty-four years since "Separate but Equal" became the law of the land in 1877, and that confident slogan made many people feel good about themselves. Segregation laws were later passed in 1896, forming a legal separation between blacks and whites in American schools.[336]

The hopeful ideas following the Civil War were subsumed in these real and perceived racial differences.

That Hostility presented the Wall of jealousy and victimhood dividing men for multiple generations. That hostility reinforced the infinite wall of sin already established between man and God.

This hostility is not unique to American racial politics, for it is a subset of the fundamental gulf between the Holy God and sinful man. This gulf is nothing new, but it is nonnegotiable! There is no suspension bridge or rope ladder which could safely ford this chasm. The distance affects everything, from blindness to hearing, deafness to vision. Without a vision, the people perish. Without the Cross, to cross, there is no way to reach God's throne of Grace. Sorry for this foray into "dogma," but it doesn't seem to sink in on the first hearing, or the second. Is it your third?

"Are you for us or against us?" Joshua asked. **"No,"** God's warrior Angel [or Jesus] answered. He left us asking this question over and over again, but He always answers us in the same way that He responded to Joshua. "No," or "Neither." We look perplexed, baffled, that He will not take our side of the argument, supporting our Faction. But God does not show favoritism, and Factions are Anathema to God. There's that word again, that Abomination again. Anathema again.

His favor came to Abraham, Noah, Moses, and David. Why? They listened to His voice and did what He said. Or is it simpler than that? They received His favor. Today, He does not say, "Biden!" Neither does he say, "Trump!" He says, "Neither!" It is our responsibility to say, "Yes!" If He wishes to use Trump or Biden to accomplish His purposes, that is His sovereign business; and our job is simply to say, "Yes, Lord, show us Your glory!"

Many "Christians" today say, "No, we will produce an 'Ismael.' We can't wait any long for God to act. We don't trust Him, and we never hear Him speak in the storm or the earthquake or the fire." They fashion another Abomination out of their gold jewelry and golf clubs.

Some of us Israelites noticed that God makes no favorites of white men or black men, preferring to look at our hearts and our character. He refused to promote our political party or our legislative agenda as His own. He will use whomever He pleases to get His good and perfect will accomplished, even promoting Nero with his big matches and antisocial personality disorder. He was the spiritual offspring of King Ahab in Israel.

> "[King Ahab] erected an altar for Baal in the house of Baal, which he built in Samaria. And Ahab made an Asherah [mother goddess, Queen of heaven]. Ahab did

> more to provoke the Lord, the God of Israel, to anger than all the kings of Israel who were before him."[337]

God's archetype for the evil King is found in King Ahab, and the apogee of Ahab's idolatry is the Queen mother, the Asherah, his Jezebel. Abhorrent is every distraction from One thing: "This is my Son: Listen to Him!" As for the rule of Queens, I must admit, we did discuss among ourselves in Washington the exclusivity of our masculine gathering. "Where are all the women of God on the Mall today?" we wondered aloud.

God answered us, alluding to Eden and Gethsemane, reminding us of those two missions for strong men, where the serpent was present to beguile with his culturally sanctioned arguments to the contrary.

You will not surely die & You will surely die for nothing!" One man silenced him, and the other man ignored him. One man ignored God's words, and the other embraced them.

Adam failed to listen to God's Command, and Jesus drank the cup of suffering, listening to the Father's hard reminder of the essential Cross. On the Mall, men who might have been wary of God's ostensibly effeminate kingdom were reminded of the cup which Jesus drank to the dregs. "Listen to Jesus' voice!"

Men were called to accountability, confessing sins and failures in their roles as men. They were exhorted to stand before the Lord for a reckoning that might change the course of their relationships with the Church, with their nation, and with their families.

Men who already appreciated the efficacy of cold beers and ball games, hard work and an occasional frustrating round of golf or a pick-up basketball game—these men who could still hear the concussion of the shells exploding inside their hunting blind or under their Humvee— men such as these were called into the hard work of prayer, and the joy of worshiping the King of Kings.

These men, whose fathers had taught them nothing beyond the dove in the field and the fish in the breathable bucket, were called out of their man-caves for a weekend. For a few hours they could see themselves as men of God, hearing the Savior's voice just as well as their wives could hear Him.

While we met for a few hours on the Mall, hundreds of young women were using tax payer funding to have their babies torn apart from their

History & the Mall in Washington.

wombs. Nearly one million four-hundred thousand babies were torn apart from their safe harbor during that annual cycle by the abortion harvesters—Planned Parenthood.

> You can get an in-clinic abortion at many Planned Parenthood health centers. Our caring doctors and nurses are experts at providing safe abortion and providing support throughout the process. You can also get an abortion from some private doctors or gynecologists, family planning clinics, and abortion clinics.[338]

An inordinate percentage of the abortions occur right there in the District of Columbia where we were bending our knees in prayer. Slavery, Segregation, and Abortion had left a devastating swath through a nation's freedom—not to mention the furrow cut through the heart of the Church.

Mother Teresa declared, "No act is more devastating for the mother than the killing of her own baby."[339] The mother will later suffer the deepest grief that is known in the universe of men when she fully grasps what she has done. Because of our complicity in these murders, the nation and the Church is being called into repentance. "But I have done nothing!" many are complaining, but God's record of our sins is far more accurate than our own assessment.

> "The people of Israel are struck down.
>   Their roots are dried up,
>   and they will bear no more fruit.
> And if they give birth,
>   I will slaughter their beloved children."
> My God will reject the people of Israel
>   because they will not listen or obey.
> They will be wanderers,
>   homeless among the nations.[340]

We think America will always be here, but it won't. God is judging America. It won't be political, so that we blame the other Party. It will happen because we <u>all</u> turned away from Him. Do you think every Dem is for God? Is every Republican a believer in Christ? Of course not.

Myopic Me!

One evidence is the fifty year love affair with killing our babies for our own convenience. God is the Judge. He pulls the plug on nations, and He always has. The Jebusites are no more. The Hittites do not exist today. There is no Roman Empire, no more Ming Dynasty in China; the Greek Empire is gone and the Weimar Republic is no more.

There is no Soviet Union and no Burma on the world map. They are all gone! They all forgot their God who is Lord. When we kill our babies we forget to love, refusing His foremost commandment. Whereas Slavery and Abortion inspire the crowds to come to Washington, each person gives up a little freedom to be there.

> "Any country that accepts abortion, is not teaching its people to love, but to use any violence to get what it wants."[341]

15

Factional Hostility.

When Joshua was near the town of Jericho, he looked up and saw a man standing in front of him with sword in hand. Joshua went up to him and demanded, "Are you friend or foe?"

[14] "Neither one," he replied. "I am the commander of the Lord's army."

At this, Joshua fell with his face to the ground in reverence. "I am at your command," Joshua said. "What do you want your servant to do?" The commander of the Lord's army replied, "Take off your sandals, for the place where you are standing is holy." And Joshua did as he was told.[342]

But if you are led by the Spirit, you are not under the law. The acts of the flesh are obvious: sexual immorality, and debauchery; idolatry and witchcraft; hatred, discord, jealousy, fits of rage, selfish ambition, dissensions, **factions**.[343]

When Joshua encountered God's pre-incarnate Son, or an Angelic Being, before the battle in Jericho, he fell on his face in reverence. Something new would be born from the singular reality which Joshua discovered upon their meeting. He had imagined there was an

Myopic Me!

Us and a Them, a battle between Good and Evil, which could be won through great courage alone.

Now, he understood that the battle belongs to the Lord of Heaven's Armies. God showed him that his perception of "two sides" is a convention born in the Garden of Eden when Adam and Eve blamed God, the Serpent, and one another.

Jesus came into this hostile world telling us the same thing: "Neither one. I am neither for you or against you. I am the Savior of the world. My Father did not send me to condemn the world, but to save the world. I am the Light of the world, and those who recognize Me will gain eternal life. Those who do not recognize me, never coming to know Me, will be lost forever in eternal darkness and death."

Aborting the Unborn is the single issue which makes it very easy for me to play the fool at the ballot box, voting for whomever will vote against this plague of death. "Which **Faction** are you representing?" I will answer, "Neither one." I just vote according to the candidate's stance on this one issue of Life.

There are always a thousand flaws in <u>every</u> candidate, each having a litany of high crimes and misdemeanors; but the stain that runs with the blood of the unborn is the stain that ruins my conscience if I vote any other way. So, Abortion has its factions and its statistics of Death, but this national stain will destroy us all.

Life has its factions, but the fetus has no cry, no vote, and no defenders—even the mother turns on her tiny passenger. The fetus can only kick the mother, reminding her of her shame or her joy. There is no Fetal Party Platform, and there are no rallies held for the approximately five million fetuses in the wombs of the pregnant women in America at any given time.

When I explained this political exigency to my friend, her blue state rhetoric subsided immediately. She agreed that it is terrible that the baby is lost in the arguments; but I am sure that she continues to vote her conscience against her own better judgment.

Does she have a higher priority than life? Is it women's rights, or something else? Is it gay rights? Is it simply liberality that she loves, or transvestite rights, or something else? I don't actually know what makes her vote with such ferocity, resisting every alternative for good government. But she always votes for death.

Factional Hostility.

Machiavelli is our unspoken puppet-master, for this *Prince*[344] is the Prince of Darkness who jerks the puppet strings in our Republic. He pulls, and we hop. He votes to accomplish the "good" outcome, using the most pernicious means. Even his good is suspect. "It's okay! It's for the good of the Faction! Our candidate will be elected, and our candidate's known evil is better the the unknown potentialities of the other candidate—and that other Faction!!!"

Can there be such a thing as self-government where the Prince pulls the strings? When the primary element of this government is Me, can anything good arise? Well, the Founding Fathers addressed that concern by limiting my influence to this one vote. I can't do much damage. The disciplinary actions of the election process only comes every four years for the President—every two for the Congressional positions. We vote to represent ourselves within that self-strangling outcome.

We Americans bring our freedom, our virtue, and our faith to bear on each election, applying these intentional filters to our candidates. Together these produce this Golden Triangle.[345] How does this influence my single vote? Will I look after my own needs, or will my faith drive specific choices? Will freedom disappoint my family, causing me to vote in ways that will cancel their futures? If they vote for new freedoms, will my virtues constrict their legal boundaries.

The Founding Fathers adopted "The Golden Triangle" as a linch-pin for the self-governing process.[346] The Golden Triangle delineates three engines operating within the government which undergird the Republic, like Father, Son, and Holy Spirit undergirding the operation of God's character, intentions, and relationships.

These Founding Fathers were describing something urgent in 1775, and in 2021, that is interactive and relational—something which points to the necessary and sufficient functions of the electorate and the branches of the Republic. The Golden Triangle is not merely defined by common geometry, but by three necessary and sufficient legs for every Stool: These legs are Virtue, Faith, and Freedom. Take one away, and the Republic fails.[347]

The problem which arises is very predictable. Each one of these legs becomes enlarged into a grotesque factional display, where Freedom becomes the only thing that matters. Virtue then, reacts as the vanguard, establishing or enforcing laws to set appropriate limits. Faith is not

Myopic Me!

silenced, and rises, unsheathing the two-edged sword of truth, revealing the existence of absolute boundaries promulgating the love of neighbor and neighborhood.

Factional Hostility rises again like that Confederate Flag, or like that Nazi Swastika, or the Japanese flag with the fiery image of the sun, so hated by every American sailor in the South Pacific who watched torpedoes fall into the ocean a hundred yards from their vulnerable steel hulls.

Can a nation truly be self-governing for the good of all the people? The Founding Fathers of our Republic pondered these same questions, and they envisioned this Golden Triangle—with those necessary and sufficient engines or elements, or legs— or filters—which keep the Republic functioning through every insistent wind of cultural change.

Virtue, Faith, Freedom:[348] Freedom is good, and everyone loves freedom, but it has limits, does it not? What happens when a nation limits unalienable freedoms which have been promised by the Declaration of Independence or the Constitution?

When is it okay for your neighbor to kill your son, or rape your daughter, or seduce your child with sexual pornography? Do you have no issue with petty theft, but oppose the broader larceny that produces chaos? When can free speech be silenced, or free religion quashed?

You can see that law is not explicitly mentioned in this Golden Triangle. The sharp edge of Virtue is this expansion of Torts, Prohibitions, and Ordinances. Virtue demands that, "You shall not drive drunk or high on cocaine more than one hundred miles per hour in a school zone—no matter who you are or how hot your car is!"

With every law offered for the neighborhood, a faction is quickly assembled to defend the threatened personal freedoms. "We have seen how Europe handles terrorists, and we want to open our borders like they do." The demand is assimilated into the Faction's larger goals. It is subsumed into the Machiavellian script.

"We want no discrimination," even though discriminate is a scientific word meaning detect, separate from the background, isolate for further study or analysis. It is, in fact, a fundamental part of the critical thinking process! But the dictionary has become obsessed with victimhood, and has become a new virtue, ironically restricting freedom of speech across the land.

Factional Hostility.

Jesus provided a much simpler list, not rejecting the torts from Leviticus, but pointing the finger of Grace—totally absent in this list of taboos and intolerances below. He said to Love God with all your heart, soul, mind, and strength, and your neighbor as yourself [This, for many, is the brick wall of Hostility—always juxtaposed with God's Holiness].

Jesus could already see these categories below while He hung on the Cross, for they had restricted His Justice, His mercy, and His free speech concerning the Commands of God—Love the Lord your God with all your heart, soul, mind, and strength, and love your neighbor as yourself. Yet, Jesus would speak forgiveness over the sins of that crowd, healing the thief beside Him.

> Social Acephobia Adultism Amatonormativity Anti-albinism Anti-autism Anti-homelessness Anti-intellectualism Anti-intersex Anti-left handedness Anti-Masonry Antisemitism (Judeophobia) Aporophobia Audism Biphobia Clannism Cronyism Drug use Elitism Ephebiphobia Fatism Gerontophobia Heteronormativity Heterosexism HIV/AIDS stigma Homophobia Leprosy stigma Lesbophobia Misandry Misogyny Nepotism Pedophobia Perpetual foreigner Pregnancy Reverse Sectarianism Supremacism Black White Transphobia Non-binary Transmisogyny Vegaphobia Xenophobia.[349]

This list is discrimination by any other name. But discrimination is a basic critical thinking skill. LOL. We are made to discriminate. Discrimination is a foremost characteristic of the intelligent and attentive human being. We are also created to love one another, and to love our neighbor as ourselves. Part of discrimination is to discern the neighbor's deepest need and most pragmatic need, addressing both.

Is it good to encourage hundreds of children to travel a thousand miles by themselves to pass through our southern border? Is that encouragement actually bringing great harm? This type of discrimination is essential, and this pragmatic love is active and alive, exposing the very motives of the heart.

Thus, Virtue will resist every perceived incursion of evil by any of the pejoratives in the perverse list above, and any appearance of

Myopic Me!

wickedness, licentiousness, and perversion will be measured as threats to the human condition, potentially bringing harm to self, family, neighborhood, or city. Thus, if someone is addicted to heroin, love will seek a solution, while discrimination will protect the populace from larceny, violence, and HIV/AIDS, hepatitis B, and hepatitis C.[350]

Incredibly pertinacious in asserting their rights, perversity gets its arguments directly from the python, twisting the lie around the truth. The exercise of free speech is effectively applied with the locking of factional arms, soon added to an expanding Platform for perceived freedoms. Once applied, these are promoted in every speech and every march in the streets, and their removal is unlikely.

These powerful Factions oppose every Virtuous voice. They challenge definitions of good and evil, right and wrong, edifying and corrupting. They force the society to decide the question: When is behavior bad? When is the Ugly American a thing? When is the European Ugly! What about China; or does China get to operate by a different cultural mandate than the rest of the world?

"Thou shalt be okay with every citizen placing their revolver on the bar, while downing a dozen tequila shots." Ugly Texan? Ugly Californian! "No churches shall be allowed within the City." Where will the lines to be drawn?

Should tax money be used for the sex change operation of a rapist or murderer who is locked up for life in prison? Should murderers be allowed to roam the neighborhoods, taking pot shots at the pedophiles? Should a serial killer be executed without a trial? When is free speech not free?

Is it okay to break all ten of the Commandments prescribed by God for the Israelites, dishonoring your parents and refusing to keep the Sabbath day of rest? Should Coveting be prosecuted before the adultery or the murder even occurs? The beauty of the Israelite Laws stunned the kings of the world.

The God of Israel was accorded greatness because of the wisdom delineated through the Ten Commandments and the tributary torts enumerated in Leviticus. Today, there are factions which despise the Ten Commandments, calling into question every taboo listed in Leviticus.

What happens when Freedom abrogates every boundary marker established by Virtue? When the Law is cast aside, which new Freedom

Factional Hostility.

will replace its restraints? What happens to Virtue when Faith in God is shifted to a reliance upon Technology and Materialism? Is it okay to educate children with sexually explicit videos? Should young people be shown how to install condoms before having sex with men, or with classmates on the school bus?

Virtue arises in the midst of such discussions as these. Is virtue part of the profile of the current American populous? Has Virtue been cast down like something intolerable, while Freedom shouts down every objection? Virtue has to provide more than "virtue signaling," where some token of virtue is asserted to gain a political advantage. But what should be done when true Virtue is mocked as absolute evil within the culture?

What happens to the world where Virtue is despised—where the virtuous one is spit upon by the mob? Virtue raises many questions of morality, ethics, and righteousness, gaining a new status in a tilting Republic. The Virtues are labeled evil, while every freedom without limit is construed as good. Virtue recommends goodness, but Freedom silences every upright claim. Goodness is cast out, so that every desirable depravity can be practiced through entitlement.

These questions apply to the populace of the Republic. Is the populous virtuous, moral, good, or has that ship sailed? Faith is a big deal for all people, but the Atheist puts his faith in the non-existence of a Supreme being. He pushes all the chips into the pot for Materialism. The Atheist's faith is strong, but he rejects God's authority or involvement in the affairs of men. Still, he lives by faith. Faith is the assurance of what is unseen, and he can't see God or the lack of God.

The faith of the Christian comes with the promises of God, the laws of God, and the Word of God. The ultimate message from all of those laws and ordinances is directed to Love of God and Love of Neighbor. Jesus said, "Bless your enemies, don't curse them." He also said, "You will have no other gods before me—make no idols for worship."

> A group of protesters was filmed chanting the words "pigs in a blanket, fry 'em like bacon" during an August 29, 2015, march to the grounds of the Minnesota State Fair. The march had been organized by the independent Black Lives Matter group in St. Paul, Minnesota.[351]

Myopic Me!

When does the slogan become the crime? When does our righteous demand remove every evidence of good sense? The democracy of hell, with its terminal freedoms, is a counterpoint to Christ's offer for redemption and release of the captive. Even murder is washed away by His blood.

Peace is possible through His name for the one who has formerly shed peace like it was the Coronavirus. Do you see any peace in these events or their aftermath? How does hate become so selective in these human hearts? What and where is this Love which God ordains for neighbor?

> "Love isn't something natural. Rather it requires discipline, concentration, patience, faith, and the overcoming of narcissism. It isn't a feeling, it is a practice."
> [Fromm, Eric, *The Art of Loving*][352]

Death is always promoted in the excremental liturgy promoted by our present culture. Where the wages of sin is death, the ignorance of this universal spiritual law changes nothing. Sin, left to its own devices, is equal to death. Sin is only removed by believing in Jesus as Savior and Lord, name above every name. Sin comes in many forms, each one separating us from fellowship with God. Factionalism is a sin we commit openly in America.

We call it political party, ideology, minority group, action group, power grab, and a bunch of other names. God calls it factions. Is there a good faction? Ask the same Angel Joshua asked: "Are you for us or against us?" The Angel answered, "Neither." God does not show favorites, and neither should we. What should we be for? God's will and purpose, glory and pleasure.

Paul the Apostle inserts "Factions" in the same catalog of potential sins, works of the flesh, that includes "sexual immorality." These works of the flesh can keep you out of heaven! Don't doubt for a moment Factions is a religion of death, approved in every rebellious version of our universal brokenness.[353]

It becomes an idol in our schedules, our bank accounts, and our dividing walls of hostility, even separating us from God's love. Our idols will increasingly demand our full attention. Idols pull rank on Virtue and

Factional Hostility.

Faith, demanding absolute Freedom for ***Myopic Me!*** The psychiatrist calls this an obsessive-compulsive disorder.

Life and Death divides us. We disagree on Life and on Lordship. We built this wall by choosing Death instead of Life in the Garden. Adam and Eve swept us into a new world East of Eden.[354] Now, even the Christians are confused over the protection of Life under Jesus' Lordship. Abortion rights reflect, almost entirely, the sexual or materialistic priorities of our present age. My body, my sexual freedom, and my career are higher priorities than human life made in the image of God.

How can that be? How can that not be? It has always been so. It is not merely our religious differences which result in our enmity, though religion imposes its own version of Shariah Law. Those Do's and Don'ts will castigate the absolute freedom which Christ has won for us. Faith and Virtue will continue to be essential for our Republic to survive. Freedom will always run amok into license, and license into depravity.

> But the Scriptures declare that we are all prisoners of sin, so we receive God's promise of freedom only by believing in Jesus Christ.[355]

I told you this, but it carries more weight when Paul is reproving the Galatians who have become foolish, bewitched, returning to another gospel than the one they received. The gospel of the world is found in factions telling each other they are right; they are good; they are heroes and saviors; they are gods, knowing both good and evil.

Examine all the various religions on the earth, and imagine which ones will actually function to bring virtue and freedom within our Republic? The ancient religions which practiced child sacrifice and sexual rituals with temple prostitutes are often preferred today.

The Aztecs cut out the beating heart of a young girl to appease their gods, and many factions have lost touch with the true religion: Justice and mercy, plus faithfulness toward the weakest among us who have done nothing wrong. Muslims and Jews today practice legalistic rituals without really knowing God, rejecting or ignoring the One True and Living God, Jesus Christ.

Which forms of religious freedom will actually produce virtues—good things for all the people? Paul spoke of this true religion as being

Myopic Me!

unencumbered by any Do's and Don'ts. He clarifies the essential outcomes of freedom.

> You say, "I am allowed to do anything"—**but not everything is good for you.** You say, "I am allowed to do anything"—**but not everything is beneficial [edifying]**.[356]

In Russia, or the Soviet Union, the experiment in Liberty failed, or is still twisting in the wind, with little patience for virtue or faith or freedom being demonstrated by Vladimir Putin. Russians had the desire for freedom, and many had faith, but they could not live without the familiar corruption and coercion learned through multiple generations of Communistic and tribal periods of their history.

Liberty, in the Republic, does not arise from a formula mixed like cookie-dough to be spooned onto a greased baking sheet. It is a miracle of God's divine intervention. Every American should know the story which Eric Metaxas recounts in his book, *If You Can Keep It.*[357]

The miracle in America came when Jesus was preached across the deep woods of Kentucky and Georgia and Pennsylvania on horseback during the 1750s and beyond. Grace, not religion, brought the promise of unity to all men. A system of Law which accounts for Grace and mercy, justice and faithfulness made sense to these born-again Christians.

As John Wesley took the message of God's grace to brave men and women, lives were transformed by this Good News which many of these settlers had never heard. This was no stodgy message which George Whitefield, the cross-eyed 23-year-old Englishman took to the new territories in America when he was ostracized by the English church.[358]

There, he had spoken to thirty-thousands of people on one occasion, bringing them to tears when they realized that they were God's Masterpiece by believing in His Son who died on the Cross for them! They realized that through Grace they were valued in the eyes of the God Who created all things! This message came to America through divine choreography of the same kind that might have reached you when you got down on your knees by your bed and cried out to the God of heaven to save you.[359]

Factional Hostility.

God gently led him into amazing grace after George had led a couple to Christ as he shared the verses from John 3:16 with them: "For God so loved the world that He gave His only begotten Son so that all who believed in Him might live and not die." They experienced true and total revelation when they heard the words from John's Gospel—they heard the one word: "believed."

They understood the Good News—if a man **believes** in God's Son he will not die, but will have everlasting life. Not understanding this verse himself, George read on from John 3:16 until he found the thief on the cross. He discovered a man (the first man) entering heaven with Jesus.[360]

He entered heaven on the basis of one thing: he *believed* in Jesus as being God's Son sent to save him. The thief never went to a church service. He never shared communion in a church. He never tithed a dime. He never did one good thing for the poor or preached a sermon. But he believed in the One Whom God sent Who was bleeding on the cross beside him.[361]

George Whitefield explained to these early Americans that no one could buy salvation with any portion of their salaries, or through any number of communion services. He could list no religious accomplishment or acts of generosity—yet he would arrive in heaven through the bloody cross of Jesus. He became a Masterpiece of God's grace when he believed.[362]

Eric Metaxas, a great prophetic Gospel voice into the American landscape, made the following claim concerning George Whitefield's twenty years of sacrificial service in the new colonies and territories of America.

> We might also say that Providence brought [American Colonies] (knowledge of self-government and faith) into existence. We might also say that providence brought them into existence through the life and work of a single man, very little known to us today. We are talking about the life and work of the man named George Whitefield, without whom the United States simply could not have come into being.[363]

Myopic Me!

The mutually exclusive perspectives of the diverse settlers were unified by a miracle our historians have ignored or denied! It should be obvious in 2021 how difficult it is to agree on anything when an undercurrent of Abortion politics seems to float all boats within a single party, while the ostensible greed of a hundred billionaires is the fault-line running through the other.

While you and I try to shift the blame to one person or another group, the social and cultural differences cannot explain the full meaning of the trouble infesting our current world. "That woman you gave me!" one yells, pointing to his wife or girlfriend, or sexual partner. Meanwhile, the other screams, "The devil made me do it," holding up the apple, or the heroin, or the marked bills from the ATM.

We are inflamed at the boundaries between the Law and every untrustworthy citizen. Our inequities arise from our iniquities.[364] It is God Who raises up rulers, but He also tears them down again when they get too big for their sudden thrones.

My political exigency is very simple, and I look for some support for this idea in the candidate's plans and performance, past, present, and future. Has he or she done anything good regarding the issue of Life? Mother Teresa speaks with such clarity addressing this boundary marker.

> "But I feel that the greatest destroyer of peace today is abortion, because it is a war against the child–a direct killing of the innocent child–murder by the mother herself. And if we accept that a mother can kill even her own child, how can we tell other people not to kill one another? How do we persuade a woman not to have an abortion? As always, we must persuade her with love, and we remind ourselves that love means to be willing to give until it hurts. Jesus gave even his life to love us."[365]

I have long concluded that the status of our nation pivoted since 1973, with one disaster after another following the *Roe vs. Wade Supreme Court Case*. That precipitous moment in jurisprudence propelled a nation into decades of extreme hostility.

Factional Hostility.

This hostility has unabashedly rejected God's counsel, dividing men and women and political parties, while expelling the baby from the safety of the womb—the least of those among us expelled into a shocking death [formerly alive through the breath of life from the mother's hemoglobin].

> Because of your great sin and hostility,
> you say, "The prophets are crazy
> and the inspired men are fools!"
> The prophet is a watchman over Israel for my God, yet
> traps are laid for him wherever he goes.
> He faces hostility even in the house of God.[366]

The harm is incredibly complex in America, as it was in Israel, with reverberations into the social and spiritual caldron of the age. The cause of this self-immolation takes us back to the days of Cain, and to his progeny in Sodom. The aftermath of *Roe vs. Wade* is witnessed in the shadow of America's first military defeat in Vietnam, the Oil Rationing, giving OPEC great power over American life with the creation of that Oil Cartel in the Middle East. We lost our energy independence, bringing us into many dark alliances with paralyzing dependencies.

Today, the Factions are demanding absolute obeisance. We imagine every four years that the President will become the savior, but the Presidency always reveals the defects and spots of self-righteousness, boasting, and deep-pocket corruption, which God despises.

Anticipating this, the Founding Fathers established a political process which is bounded by the Legislative, the Judicial, and the Executive branches. This is for good reason. Like the Golden Triangle, these three are essential defusers of ultimate power, which ultimately corrupts.

The Founding Fathers were not ignorant of our fallen status, yet they depended upon Grace alone in a wild and untamed land—untamed to the present day. They knew that we would battle at the boundaries—at the Dividing Wall of Hostility. They understood the deadly cargo of sin spilling out along this interface.

Though we have added a lot of asphalt and many high-rise buildings, our lines for heroin addicts in our cities are getting very long. Each faction is sure the evil one is ruling the other faction, and they are right.

Myopic Me!

"You may think you can condemn such people, but you are just as bad, and you have no excuse! When you say they are wicked and should be punished, you are condemning yourself, for you who judge others do these very same things."[367] But righteousness comes from God.

> America needs no words from me to see how your decision in Roe v. Wade has deformed a great nation. The so-called right to abortion has pitted mothers against their children and women against men. It has sown violence and discord at the heart of the most intimate human relationships. It has aggravated the derogation of the father's role in an increasingly fatherless society. It has portrayed the greatest of gifts — a child — as a competitor, an intrusion, and an inconvenience.[368]

Mother Teresa's words are Light and Salt in a world that is dying—and her words should reverberate in every part of Jesus Christ's Church. Our factional darkness will not extinguish the Light of Christ shining in the heart of the Church. God is watching American turn her back on her own progeny in the name of racism, eugenics, convenience, and factionalism.

> The time of Israel's [America's] punishment has come; the day of payment is here. Soon [America] will know this all too well. Because of your great sin and **hostility**, you say, "The prophets are crazy and the inspired men are fools!". . ."The glory of [America] will fly away like a bird, for your children will not be born or grow in the womb or even be conceived."[369]

Mother Teresa spoke into this taproot issue of American hostility to God at the Prayer Breakfast in Washington DC in 1997—the same year 1.4-million of us men gathered on the Mall in Washington to pray for God's forgiveness for the sins of the churches and the nation.

We were facing the monolithic idolatry of Segregation that has contributed to this war against the sanctity of life. It has contributed to the spirit of eugenics that is secretly being applied across the globe. It looks

Factional Hostility.

new, but it is ancient in origin. The Fall of the Roman Empire is often referenced by leaders who seek to head off the fall of America. They generally conclude the following reasons for the Fall.[370]

1. Invasions by Barbarian tribes
2. Economic troubles and over reliance on slaves
3. The rise of the Eastern Empire [China]
4. Over expansion and military overspending
5. Government corruption and political instability
6. The arrival of the Huns and the migration of the Barbarian tribes [Central American Cartels]
7. Christianity and the loss of traditional values
8. Weakening of the Roman legions [paid army][371]

These all miss the point. God tears down nations when they fail to honor Him who is their Creator. Idolatry comes, and factions form sides in response to the various idols of the nation. Divisions erupt, and unity fails. Outside influences are introduced when spiritual doors are opened wide to enemies that come flooding into the culture and the government and the system of laws. The Fall is the inevitable outcome.

> "What is taking place in America," [Mother Teresa] said, "is a war against the child. And if we accept that the mother can kill her own child, how can we tell other people not to kill one another." February 1997– National Prayer Breakfast in Washington attended by the President and the First Lady.[372]

16

Persecution of Christians.

> Even those closest to you—your parents, brothers, relatives, and friends—will betray you. They will even kill some of you. And everyone will hate you because you are my followers. But not a hair of your head will perish![373]

Hatred of Christians is on the rise, and One mark of the End Times is the pervasiveness of Hate-laws and Cancel Culture[374] which blame Abel for every every evil thing in this life.

> Cancel culture (or call-out culture) is a modern form of ostracism in which someone is thrust out of social or professional circles – whether it be online, on social media, or in person. Those who are subject to this ostracism are said to have been "cancelled". The expression "cancel culture" has mostly negative connotations and is commonly used in debates on free speech and censorship.[375]

Like Cain before them, they fail to see the sin at their own door.

> "Why do you look so dejected? You will be accepted if you do what is right. But if you refuse to do what is right, then watch out! Sin is crouching at the door, eager to control you. But you must subdue it and be its master."[376]

Myopic Me!

The crosshairs of those laws is positioned over the scripture-believing Christians! It seems crazy to the Cancel Culture, forgetting that after the resurrection Jesus gave the following command: "Teach these new disciples to obey all the commands I have given you."[377]

While the culture encourages the rise of Shariah Laws in certain parts of the country, especially in the Detroit area, such Laws tend to demean women and even recommend honor killings. Meanwhile, the Laws of God, aimed at protection of every relationship, are being torn down little by little. This is one evidence of the End Times. Expect to see:

- Great Deception
- Great Distress
- Great Divisions
- Hatred and Defamation of Christians
- Depravity rapidly permeating the Culture[378]

Christians will become the single target of a society which rejects hate in every other form! In Egypt, laws against Christians are very aggressive. ISIS, an extreme relative of the Muslim Brotherhood, has acted many times on this hatred. The video stream was seen by millions who watched the beheadings in horror. What provoked it? The tattoo of the cross on the wrists of these victims led to these infamous executions.

> TV cameras and lights were in front of the captives and they were each forced to kneel as their masked captor stood behind them holding the knife to their throat. The whole ordeal was videotaped by ISIS in a slick, Hollywood-style production. Each of the captives were asked to renounce Christ. When they refused to renounce Christ, they were beheaded one by one, their blood spilling out on the beach. One dark-skinned captive from another African nation was taken by mistake. He did not have a tattoo but was rooming with others who did. He was the last to be asked to renounce Christ or die. He saw 20 other young men beheaded, one by one. He told the ISIS captors, "Their God is my God!"[379]

Persecution of Christians.

The issue in the earth is believing. One believes, and another does not. Actually, the issue in the earth is sin, but a subset of sin is unbelief. "Don't imagine that I came to bring peace to the earth! I came not to bring peace, but a sword."[380] This produces the most profound hostility of all. It is a matter of life and death. It is a deciding between the Savior and the Destroyer.

> "'I have come to set a man against his father, a daughter against her mother, and a daughter-in-law against her mother-in-law.'"[381]

In a country where Scripture-believing Christians are referred to as "deplorables" and "chumps," can the scene with ISIS be far behind? In former times, christians turned their backs on an entire race of people, making them separate but equal, segregating them from every school system in the land where there were white kids!

When researchers visit the lifers in prison in Louisiana, they find with disturbing consistency that these men and women reference their difficulties with their fathers as deep, unhealed wounds. The absence of the father, the abusiveness of the father, or the drunkenness of the father, appears again and again in their overlapping histories—these antisocial disorders [like Jeffrey Dahmer the cannibal], are common to forty-percent of the prisoners.[382]

These inmates on death row or serving life sentences have experienced the breakdown of this fundamental relationship with their father. Governmental support too often encourages the dissolution of father-led families! Life itself is degraded in the nation where brothers and sisters can be executed in the mother's womb.

In the book, *A Defense of Abortion*, author and philosopher David Boonin wrote: "A human fetus, after all, is simply a human being at a very early stage in his or her development."[383]

> If we acknowledge the humanity of the preborn child, one must further ask – does every human being have a right to life? Or is this right held only by those humans with particular characteristics that come and go at various points throughout their lives?

Myopic Me!

Pro-life apologist and frequent Focus on the Family Broadcast guest, Scott Klusendorf, shared the following:

> Pro-life advocates contend there is no morally significant difference between the embryo you once were and the adult you are today that would justify killing you at that earlier stage of development. Differences of size, level of development, environment and degree of dependency are not good reasons for saying you had no right to life then but you do now.[384]

The proliferation of Abortion has long been the battleground for a nation's soul, demeaning life by certain peculiar scientific positions. Only God can then, or now, heal the breach. The deep harm of Segregation—the false gospel of many white people in decades past—spawned by economic and scientific exigencies of the same kind produced a long shadow on the landscape of America.

The Americans represent the very first true melting pot of racial and ethnic diversity in human history. Whereas Sweden still holds on to a caucasian homogeneous society, the American experiment is stumbled by the ancient heritage of African slavery in the South mostly.

> "The human body has many parts, but the many parts make up one whole body. So it is with the body of Christ. Some of us are Jews, some are Gentiles, some are slaves, and some are free. But we have all been baptized into one body by one Spirit, and we all share the same Spirit."[385]

To the Galatians, Paul reiterates this explanation of the body of Christ.

> And all who have been united with Christ in baptism have put on Christ, like putting on new clothes. There is no longer Jew or Gentile, slave or free, male and female. For you are all one in Christ Jesus. And now that you belong to Christ, you are the true children

of Abraham. You are his heirs, and God's promise to Abraham belongs to you.[386]

When Paul spoke abrasively to the Corinthian church about their behavior sharing the Last Supper, he emphasized "honoring or discerning the body of Christ [the Church]." His meaning is often misinterpreted, for Christians have understood that this is referring to Jesus' body on the Cross or in the Upper Room or in Transubstantiation, as the Catholic church doctrine insists.[387] I believe that Paul was upbraiding them for their failure to discern their diversity.

> For if you eat the bread or drink the cup without honoring [discerning] the body of Christ, you are eating and drinking God's judgment upon yourself. That is why many of you are weak and sick and some have even died.[388]

The Church for years, for decades, for centuries, dishonored the body of Christ, excluding some on the basis of their race, their social status, or their standing in the larger homogeneous community. It is impossible to view this verse without consideration of the Church composition and resulting unity since Paul is addressing the disgraceful behavior of some in the Corinthian church. Hostility is blatantly present in their behavior toward one another.

Though terrible wounds have been partially mended by dramatic changes in America, the damage is still evident daily. Therefore, today we still see the angry offspring of slaves whose hopes have been dashed again and again as the political parties exploit them for any political advantage.

Born into this aura of enmity, the most prolific of all the slave ships in human history is exposed. The curse arrives in the hold of the slave ship of Sin. One of the foremost versions of this broken state is victimhood. It is not new. It infected the very first family on earth.

The foremost symbol of hatred in the world comes stillborn from Cain's sullen anger and jealousy—his victimhood. He would wander the earth forever, him and his offspring, looking for someone to blame, always complaining about the unfairness of life.

Myopic Me!

When "slavery" somehow overwhelmed the "love of our neighbor as ourself," God's words were knocked out of step with this pervasive reality. God disapproved of our love of this world, our racial divisions, and our social discrimination according to geography and differences in political ideology—a world where social justice collides with equal justice, inequality with equity, and all hell broke loose with hiding, blaming, and hating.

> "Our Father, Your name brings glory beyond our pale comprehension. You take our breath away. You reside in perfection, love, justice and eternity beyond our world of hurting and being hurt. You accepted every offensive word, and every cruel blow, so that we may embrace Your reconciliation. You have given us the Ministry of Reconciliation, and have called us to forgive as we have been forgiven. Therefore, Father, we pray for those we have been injured physically and spiritually. There are too many names to list. We pray Father, that the things we have done will not bring them down, but that You will put praise of Your Son into their mouths. Heal their memories and wash us all with Your blood. Amen."

17

The Black Angel.

At dawn the next morning the angels became insistent. "Hurry," they said to Lot. "Take your wife and your two daughters who are here. Get out right now, or you will be swept away in the destruction of the city!" When Lot still hesitated, the angels seized his hand and the hands of his wife and two daughters and rushed them to safety outside the city, for the Lord was merciful.[389]

"Don't forget to show hospitality to strangers, for some who have done this have entertained angels without realizing it!"[390]

"Write this letter to the angel of the church in Pergamum. This is the message from the one with the sharp two-edged sword . . . you have some Nicolaitans among you who follow the same teaching [of Balaam]. Repent of your sins, or I will come to you suddenly and fight against [you] with the sword of my mouth."[391]

The night before Peter was to be placed on trial, he was asleep, fastened with two chains between two soldiers. Others stood guard at the prison gate. Suddenly, there was a bright light in the cell, and an angel of the Lord stood before Peter. The angel struck him on the side to awaken him and said, "Quick! Get up!" And the chains fell off his wrists. Then the angel told him, "Get dressed

Myopic Me!

and put on your sandals." And he did. "Now put on your coat and follow me," the angel ordered.[392]

When the young black man appeared in front of me, I was storing the laptop and bluetooth speaker in my Bean bag. I had just presented the Gospel to a hundred homeless folks at the Rescue Mission in Providence, Rhode Island. A few volunteers were clearing the folding chairs and rolling out the pads for the women who would stay through the night.

Resting my elbows on the wooden podium, I could see that he would have a private audience with me. The young man introduced himself, saying, "I am a Servant of God." I was surprised, of course, and I listened intently to learn his mission. "Servant of God?"

Was he visiting from another church or did he come from some kind of cult, I wondered? When he spoke, looking directly into my eyes, his words changed my demeanor. There was surely a third possibility that had not crossed my mind. He was an Angel from God.

> "You had them all hanging on every word of your testimony. You should have had them all repent as you did, confessing their idolatry on their knees."

His words struck me. He woke me up, like the Angel who struck Peter from a sound sleep in his jail cell between the sleeping guards. "Who am I speaking to?" I still wondered. He had struck me with this singular instruction. "Make them **all** repent as you did!" Was he right? Didn't I do that?

I had shared my own testimony from 1968 when God sent a man I barely knew, traveling five-hundred miles on an overnight train to Peachtree Station, telling me about God's love. During that twenty-four hour period, fifty-plus years earlier, my brother-in-law had talked to me about Jesus' love, sending me that same night to see the only man he knew in Atlanta, Georgia—a city of three-quarters of a million people.

At the Rescue Mission, the Holy Spirit **had** been very present in the room that night, and the response had been overwhelming. That night in Atlanta, I related that I had got down on my knees in a little chapel. I

The Black Angel.

was in a church I had never heard of, on a street I had never visited, in a city I barely knew.

In the Rescue Mission, I had gotten down on my knees in the aisle next to the toughest looking man in that crowd. With boldness, I lifted up my hands to the heavens: "God forgive my sin of idolatry. Take over my life and show me how to live." I asked them to pray with me, praying their own words.

This was my reenactment from Atlanta, and I wondered now if I failed to call them to repentance, getting down on their knees beside me? The Angel's words were rolling around in my head, and I truly wanted to hear what he was telling me. I knew it was important for me to fully apprehend what God was saying.

During 2019, I had spoken at the Rescue Mission many times, but the urgency for the Good News that night was invisible to everyone but God. In a couple of months the Covid-19 Pandemic would sweep the dead from the face of the world, and God sent his black Angel ahead of this catastrophe to try to rescue everyone in the room that night.

Over half a million Americans would die from the Covid virus [current number at this publishing date], and some of those in the room would also die. More Americans than in WWII, Korea, and Viet Nam combined have died by March 2021.

Many of those who died had ignored every warning concerning the Death Angel that would come for them. This is nothing new, for Jesus spoke one of His most dramatic parables addressing this common arrogance of every ill-prepared man. He related the words of a rich land owner whose early retirement seemed to be all set.

> "I'll sit back and say to myself, 'My friend, you have enough stored away for years to come. Now take it easy! Eat, drink, and be merry!'" [Stage left, the Coronavirus arrives from China] "But God said to him, 'You fool! You will die this very night. Then who will get everything you worked for?' Yes, a person is a fool to store up earthly wealth but not have a rich relationship with God."[393]

Myopic Me!

Still not sure that the black servant of God was an Angel, the intensity in his eyes captured my attention completely. In the manner of a confident drill Sergeant in Basic Training, his command gave me no option but an affirmative response: "Yes, Drill Sergeant!" I still had no idea that this instruction would rock my world. He had captured my full attention with the authority in his chastisement. Behind his restraint, I sensed a monumental authority speaking to me.

"You went as far as your faith allowed you to go." Then he hesitated. "I've said too much already." He watched me, and I could feel him scanning my soul for any doubting. "I have more to say, but I am being restrained from saying any more."

What else would he have said? If there were no restraint, would he reprove me further, pointing out some other shortcoming or failure? I was shaken to the core. I knew that God was actually speaking directly to me with feedback I needed to hear. The Angel had deftly enunciated a sacred calling which seemed very personal, yet I later realized that it applied to every believer.

The Angel understood that God called me to teach and preach. He understood that a crucial biblical admonition had been spoken by Jesus commanding every disciple to take the Gospel to every nation, preaching repentance from sin, and calling each new believer to be baptized.

Jesus even demonstrated how that baptism should look: with the Father, the Son, and the Holy Spirit all present there in the Jordan River—buried in death, and raised to newness of life, being filled with the Holy Spirit with the mission of God remaining.[394]

He was reminding me that the Spirit of God is the one who restores every word to our memory for this very purpose. Every word spoken is His, and He always speaks Jesus' Words, glory, and Cross, bringing conviction of sin. He also convicts us of the righteousness we inherit from Christ.

The Holy Spirit convicts us in our repentance of the judgment to come. Yes, and sorry if you don't believe there is a hell which is one option for that judgment. On that day, the only name that matters will be Jesus' name. Jesus is the One who took the keys to sin and death, to hell and heaven. He is the keeper of the Book of Life.

This is the Holy Spirit's fundamental duty, for He is our Comforter, Counselor, and Advocate. When we confess our sins before men, accepting

The Black Angel.

the finished work of Christ, our sins are forgiven, and we become new creatures. Actually, the Holy Spirit is restraining the Antichrist in our day as well.

This Angel had deposited God's message in my heart and mind. He was now observing how I would respond. Would I have enough faith to finish each message with the high calling to lead others to repent? I had offered no resistance to the Angel's counsel, and I said that I agreed with every word he had spoken.

His crucial message was demonstrated when the tax collector cried out in the synagogue. "God have mercy on me a sinner!"[395] His seven words brought him justification before God. Jesus emphasized this to his core disciples. The "bad man" confessed his sins, seeking the mercy of God, and publicly expressing his faith in God's Salvation. He was visibly, humbly, repenting of his sins before God and before the self-righteous people standing near him.

This is God's high calling for every believer who shares what Christ has done. It is the mission of every preacher of the Good News. My necessary and sufficient response to Jesus' forgiveness is to communicate to others this life-changing forgiveness I have received.

Though I felt jubilant before he approached me, I knew he had given me something much deeper than this flicker of vanity. "Lead them ALL into REPENTANCE as you demonstrated." I stared in amazement knowing that this was not really new information, yet it felt authoritative. Still, my mind questioned God's wisdom, "Didn't I just do what you wanted me to do, with forty people coming to faith?"

The cover image for this book is my blended painting completed several months after the Angel had spoken to me. I found a photograph of a young black man from my search on the internet to give me a starting point. I knew when I started painting that I could transform that stranger's face into the Angel's face. This absolute confidence belied the fact that I had never succeeded in accurately painting any human face. I had no gift for the task.

As I put the final touches on the painting, I could see the Angel's face appearing under each brush stroke. This supernatural moment of recognition had the Angel's eyes actually looking at me again. I spoke out loud, "This is the Angel who spoke to me!" I felt the flush of God's love coming over me as if he were actually there in the room.

Myopic Me!

Gradually, I understood better what he had shown me. He had revealed by the Spirit that God always fits the battle for the souls and bodies of those created in His image along an ephemeral Dividing Wall. It is the formidable geometry of Sin. This dividing wall is immovable, an infinite plane between life and death. Repentance is the oil of the Holy Spirit that calls down Grace from Jesus' Cross upon the sinner.

When the convicting symbolism of the Cross brings repentance, the Good News causes every man to get down on his knees. It is a miracle when any man repents, for Pride is so formidable. The Oil of the Holy Spirit softens **Myopic Me!** This infinite help from God saves us there on our knees. It is a spiritual thing, and it is a physical thing.

God tells us that, "Every knee will bow, and every tongue will confess that Jesus Christ is Lord." It happened when Saul encountered the risen Christ on the Damascus Road. It happened to the Jews at Pentecost in Jerusalem when the Holy Spirit came with tongues of fire. It happened to me in the chapel at the Church of Our Savior in Atlanta fifty-three years ago.

When Jesus forgives us, His naked and bloody body has been nailed to the Cross, showing us the physical and spiritual reality of what God's love looks like! It makes no sense, for we see ourselves as physical beings only, with no spiritual potential at all. But God gives us this inexplicable Good News, not wanting our tiny faith to hinder the miraculous moment when His Spirit brings rebirth.

Physically getting on our knees reminds us that He is Lord. He rose from the crucifixion, ascending into heaven. The government is upon His shoulders—that includes every government, everywhere, for all time. He is the reconciler of all things, and He will return to receive His bride from out of the world.

On that night at the Rescue Mission, God reproved me, saying that my little faith should never become a barrier in that critical instant when Grace comes into a man's heart. The Angel commanded me to take seriously that moment of divine conviction, when that dividing wall is torn down, and Death is exchanged for Life.

On that night at the Rescue Mission, God was the One who saves, but I was His worker in the Harvest Field. Those vulnerable people would quickly scatter again for a night's sleep under their favorite highway overpass. Some of the women would sleep on the floor in that very room. God

The Black Angel.

sent His Angel to see if I might properly divide the Word, obeying everything which Christ commanded.

Would I step into their confusion, boldly instructing them to receive this Good News through repentance on their knees? Many of the one-hundred departed that night with their prescription meds in a pull-tie bag on their belt loops. Most would trudge miles on foot across the city in the growing cold. They would bed down in their big plastic bags, sealing out the freezing temperatures.

The Providence Rescue Mission was established by my friend Sean who got rescued in this same northwestern Providence neighborhood. He had lost his right-mind on Wall Street, drinking his way into the gutters of a very familiar daily hell.

He was accustomed to gaining his daily provision through personal efforts, innate intelligence, and dwindling savings after leaving his Wall Street job. He remembers those days when he wanted to position himself as far away from Christians as he could possibly get.[396]

Providence means "God's provision," and some who visited the Rescue Mission that night did not know that God had actually come to rescue them from the death that never ceases to pursue their souls. It is the death that goes on after the grave.

Today, the rescuing is made more challenging with the Covid-19 virus spreading across the world, but God's Good News cannot be silenced by a Pandemic, and even the Gates of Hell cannot prevent the spreading of this Gospel of His mercy and great glory.

> God promised this Good News long ago through his prophets in the holy Scriptures. The Good News is about his Son. In his earthly life he was born into King David's family line, and he was shown to be the Son of God when he was raised from the dead by the power of the Holy Spirit. He is Jesus Christ our Lord. Through Christ, God has given us the privilege and authority as apostles to tell Gentiles everywhere what God has done for them, so that they will believe and obey him, bringing glory to his name.[397]

Myopic Me!

Do you have family members who have faced the novel virus at home or during their hospital stay? Of course you know someone who has been through this bitter eye of the needle. What did you say to them? "Get well! Love you! See you soon." What might you have said? What could possibly be more important than, "I love you!"

Maybe we say, "God loves you so much He sent His Son to die for you. He sent His Son to suffocate on the Cross so that your sins could be forgiven. Repent, and believe, for the hour has come; and this Jesus is alive, and He has taken possession of the keys to Death and Hell. He is calling you into His great Light, and He will never leave you or forsake you! Take His hand, and be born again!"

It is no accident that God sent a black Angel to speak to me, for I grew up in the South where black men were not allowed on the streets during my entire youth. Therefore, the black man carries in his skin all the symbolism of an ancient hostility from the slave ships.

He carries the bondage of the Israelites toiling as slaves in the Egyptian sun. They slaved in the mud of sin at the bidding of the Pharaoh, who was Satan-personified, demanding that Egypt worship him as their God.

The black Angel's human counterpart had come to America, not as a man seeking religious freedom, but as a man in chains brought out of the hold of a slave ship. But the Good News shouts down the slaver's whip, breaking the hold of this universal slavery which still holds peoples from every race, nation, and tribe.

In the Garden of Eden the fig leaves belied a more serious consequence of disobedience. Adam and Eve had spawned a race of men who would know the good and the evil. They would need a Savior to rescue them. God understands that every race, including African, Caucasian, Asian, Native American, will trace their roots into an ancient slavery to sin.

> "All of you were slaves. All of you came from the Mud Pits. All of you arrived in America as slaves to sin. All of you came from Mt. Ararat addicted to wine. All of you can trace your genealogy to Adam and Noah and the men who wished to have sex with the handsome Angels in Lot's house. Therefore, repent of your sins so that you might be saved from this crooked generation! Believe in God's Son, receiving Jesus as your Savior and Lord.

The Black Angel.

Surrender your life to Him, for He is Messiah and the Lord of All. Bow your knee to Him, and be filled with the Holy Spirit who is your Comforter and Advocate."

Every eye had been focused on me as I walked through those chairs at the Rescue Mission speaking about my own rescue from that same slave ship. Even the gay man in the room that night had quit his nervous chittering with his neighbor, finally turning toward me to hear what God was saying **to him**. His face opened up like a flower, and his eyes stopped their darting to and fro.

He heard something he had never heard before, and the Holy Spirit convicted him of sin and Righteousness for the first time in his life. After leading them in prayer on my knees, I asked how many had prayed for God to save them, and at least forty hands went up with shouts of celebration!

Then, together they all rose like a flood, flushed into the dining room—the scent of that roast pork loin met them from that other large room with the adjoining kitchen. For some of them, the mandatory Gospel message was finally behind them, and their opportunity to repent had been lost for another day.

I had been thrilled by their powerful response, certain that the Holy Spirit had filled that room with His powerful testimony of Jesus. My heart was full of joy knowing that I unburdened myself of what God had given me. The Angel's arrival out of nowhere flipped my jubilation to hearing this urgent message from God.

When God speaks from heaven, I want to listen. When Jesus speaks, I want to be on my knees. He was there calling me into a much deeper faith and understanding. Nuance is a word that reminds us of the still small voice of God which says, "Build a boat . . . for the Great Flood is coming!" Only one will hear this word in the noise of the Cancel Culture, the culture of victims and snowflakes like I had been a half-century before.

God's Servant was there to give me biblical counsel that my testimony is never a careless thing, for it is a miracle of God's love birthing an eternal relationship with me and with others who hear it. Heaven comes down to earth to pierce the Dividing Wall of Sin through the blood of Jesus.

My testimony is powerful to the tearing down of strongholds in another person's life. My repentance from idolatry is a reminder to others that God is calling their souls and bodies out of slavery. It is a miracle that

Myopic Me!

moves the Angels in heaven to celebrate. But this Angel in Providence wanted to tell me that God does not want **anyone,** not even that gay man, to perish. Not even me!

"Where is your faith?" Jesus asked. The disciples were shaken by Jesus' rebuke of their unbelief, for they had failed to set the boy free from the demon of deafness and dumbness. The symbolism of that boy being thrown into the fire is a reminder of the fire of hell that Satan wishes for everyone who has not come to repentance believing in the Son whom God sent.

Jesus saw that devilish victory, and He quickly overturned it, sending the demon out of the boy immediately. Now, my faith was being challenged by the Angel in Providence. "Where is your faith? Why did you stop short of what God requires?" I knew by the time I got into my eighteen year old G35 Sport Coupe to drive home, that the Angel had come directly from God.

When I got home, I opened the scriptures to search for every occurrence of the word "repent." I found two amazing delineations of what the Angel had spoken to me. When Peter preached the Good News in that first sermon in Jerusalem, he was speaking into the confusion that rose after the Wind of the Holy Spirit had moved through the gathering. The crowd of three-thousand thought it humorous that a number of the gathered people were speaking in unknown languages.

Peter's Pentecost sermon started by explaining what had just taken place. Then, he informed them that they had crucified Jesus, God's Son, in Jerusalem. They were convicted by the Holy Spirit immediately:

> Peter's words pierced their hearts, and they said to him and to the other apostles, "Brothers, what should we do?" Peter replied, "**Each of you must repent of your sins and turn to God, and be baptized in the name of Jesus Christ for the forgiveness of your sins**. Then you will receive the gift of the Holy Spirit. This promise is to you, to your children, and to those far away—all who have been called by the Lord our God." Then Peter continued preaching for a long time, strongly urging all his listeners, "Save yourselves from this crooked generation!"

The Black Angel.

Those who believed what Peter said were baptized and added to the church that day—about 3,000 in all.[398]

When I read this, I understood that the physical act for them was being baptized. They were baptized to mark their repentance from sin, turning to God. Not only was it important to get them on their knees, but the baptism is a crucial act of submission to the Lordship of Christ.

The second place I discovered, concerning the call to repentance, was equally dramatic, bringing into focus the actual words of the great Apostle. Though Peter was the owner of a lucrative fishing trade, he was not an educated man according to human standards. He spoke to the large crowd with the same authentic authority as Christ.

Standing in the Temple in Jerusalem with the crippled man whom God had just healed as Peter and John prayed in Jesus' name, Peter shared a personal story. Every Jew recognized the man crippled since birth walking and leaping and praising God in the Temple. The crowd was deeply moved to see what God had done for this man.

> "Through faith in the name of Jesus, this man was healed—and you know how crippled he was before. Faith in Jesus' name has healed him before your very eyes. Friends, I realize that what you and your leaders did to Jesus was done in ignorance. But God was fulfilling what all the prophets had foretold about the Messiah—that he must suffer these things. **Now repent of your sins and turn to God, so that your sins may be wiped away.** Then times of refreshment will come from the presence of the Lord, and he will again send you Jesus, your appointed Messiah. For he must remain in heaven until the time for the final restoration of all things, as God promised long ago through his holy prophets."[399]

I had instructed everyone to pray, putting their confession into their own words, confessing their sins, and asking God to forgive them. I was on my knees with my hands raised to heaven there in the aisles between them when I called for prayer. I believe now that I should have told them to get on their knees beside me! That seemingly insignificant physical

Myopic Me!

act was the missing and utterly significant action required. Surrender. Physically surrender!

God works in the physical. He gives instructions with a divine consequence. "Lazarus, come out!" Jesus instructed the dead man, His dead friend. But I had not instructed them as God desired.

How astonishing that the God of heaven sent His Angel to instruct me! He had shown me the importance of being on our knees to mark our physical surrender. The Holy Spirit had then led me to reread the Scriptures where Peter told them to be baptized immediately after their repentance, asking God to save them.

These were emblems of our surrender to the Lordship of Jesus. These were physical actions that would remind us, mark us, with the reality of an invisible and supernatural rebirth that had come to us. I understand better today that we are sheep, and our Shepherd uses His rod and His staff to lead us into green pastures. Peter would later learn this same lesson:

> The angel struck him on the side to awaken him and said, "Quick! Get up!" And the chains fell off his wrists. Then the angel told him, "Get dressed and put on your sandals." And he did. "Now put on your coat and follow me," the angel ordered.[400]

Peter's experience in the jail is a picture of our own salvation that comes with blunt instructions from God. Peter's chains fell off immediately. But he had to be led by the Angel every step of the way. He got dressed, and obediently followed the Angel's instructions for the rest of his life. He was set free, but he barely understood what was happening. He would never forget the miracle that set him free, or the Angel who directed his steps into freedom!

18

Confess your sins to one another.

Confess your sins to each other and pray for each other so that you may be healed. The earnest prayer of a righteous person has great power and produces wonderful results. Elijah was as human as we are, and yet when he prayed earnestly that no rain would fall, none fell for three and a half years! Then, when he prayed again, the sky sent down rain and the earth began to yield its crops.[401]

Why did Elijah pray against rain when the nation needed rain so badly? The answer is simple: To reveal the power, nature, and sovereignty of God. What is my purpose when I pray against the rain? It is to reveal the character and sovereignty of God. The nation of Israel was divided between the sovereignty of Baal and the sovereignty of the One True and Living God.

A few weeks after I experienced the Angelic conversation at the Rescue Mission, I drove into the dark at 6:00 p.m. in the upper parking lot of our hundred-thousand square-foot church facility. I would moments later be leading the Communion service at Waters Church during our monthly night of prayer, worship, and teaching.

Speaking to around four-hundred present, I would be sharing about the character and sovereignty of God in sending His Son to deliver the nations from the slavery of sin and death. I felt God's power coming into

Myopic Me!

my own weakness. I remembered Peter's words written to the young church in Jerusalem.

> The Lord isn't really being slow about his promise, as some people think. No, he is being patient for your sake. **He does not want anyone to be destroyed, but wants everyone to repent** [He does not want to seal up the Ark before you enter in through Grace].[402]

As I entered the driveway in the darkness enveloping the church facility, I asked God to forgive me for making preaching bigger than the Christ who is being preached. Though preaching the Gospel is a command from Christ, that project should never be larger than Christ who is the Way, Truth, and Life. Christ is the reconciler of ALL things, including my internal priorities. He is Supreme, the Light of the World, the Savior, and the Lord. He is the Head of the Church. There is none above Him. He is the Center of all that we do.

Therefore, if <u>anything</u> becomes more important in our lives than Him, that thing is instantly exposed as an idol, as an adversary of the relationship and purpose of Christ in us. Tim Keller, in two of his wonderful books, *Preaching* and *Center Church*, explains that the Gospel is not everything, but it is the crucial thing for every local church, literally impacting everything.[403] The Gospel reveals that Christ is calling us to repentance.

> "The time promised by God has come at last!" he announced. "The Kingdom of God is near! **Repent** of your sins **and believe** the Good News!"[404]

My own confession of Jesus' Lordship set me free from striving and cowardice; therefore, on this night I wanted God to forgive me for making preaching into an idol that brought me to covetousness and fear.

My prayer in the darkness was real. It was absolutely sincere, emboldened by the Holy Spirit. It was simple, like faith is simple. It was powerful, for even a mustard seed's worth of faith can move a mountain. God's faithfulness and power—awaits our sincere prayers. No one heard me pray this prayer but God Himself. Jesus' warning had come to me from Revelation.

Confess your sins to one another.

> Wake up! Strengthen what little remains, for even what is left is almost dead. I find that your actions do not meet the requirements of my God. Go back to what you heard and believed at first; hold to it firmly. **Repent and turn to me again.** If you don't wake up, I will come to you suddenly, as unexpected as a thief.[405]

I felt His strength, not my weakness. I entered the facility deeply aware of His love and forgiveness. That confession had brought me closer to Him. I climbed out, went in, and we started in the nearly empty worship area praying out loud.

After the Communion service was over, two people came directly to me to tell me that it was the most powerful and moving communion they had ever experienced. The Senior Pastor was the first one to express his joy, recapping from memory what I had said, which I only partially remember now.

> "You touched on everything, from Christ's Power over sin and death to slavery in Pharaoh's mud pits where we see our own slavery to sin. You shared how the Lamb's blood protected the Hebrews from the Angel of Death, and how the blood of the little lamb kept in each Hebrew house, had been spread over the doorpost with a hyssop branch. You explained how this foreshadowed the hyssop branch dipped in vinegar to quench the thirst of Jesus, the Lamb of God, on the Cross whose blood flowed down to cleanse the sins of everyone who believed in Him. You spoke of His power over slavery, sin, and death. You spoke of His substitutionary sacrifice, the only way to the Father. You exalted God's Son as Supreme. Everything! You covered it all!"

For my part, I can merely write these paragraphs to make clear the fleshly struggles that only Christ can resolve—He is calling us all to repentance from our alliances with the evil one and from our idolatry linking us to a crooked world. God's still small voice spoken to Elijah is despised and ignored in our world as it was despised and ignored in Noah's days.

Myopic Me!

There is no formula for personal gain or spiritual success, nor should you even look for a formula to enhance your status as the foremost ***Myopic Me!*** in your own church body—you should not encourage that demigod from the Garden of Eden.

> "God knows that your eyes will be opened as soon as you eat it, and you will be like God, knowing both good and evil [Satan reassured Eve]." ... So they sewed fig leaves together to cover themselves [futile attempt to resolve sin and broken relationships—buy a new pair of shoes, a new pair of jeans with holes in the knees, or purchase that new technology we have had our eye on—our new religion to prove we are worthy, to justify our way of living, defining our own acceptability by the good works we perform in our own strength].[406]

Instead of following Eve's example, receiving encouragement from Satan, you should look to please Jesus, listening to His Words, trusting His promises: Listen to Him! The world surrounds us with such compelling and strident voices that are forever speaking: "Follow us. Listen to us. Do what we do. Agree with us, or else!" I say to you, "Follow Him. Listen to Him. Keep your eyes on Him. Repent and return to Him."

Like those lust-filled visitors to Lot's door that night, the voices of this world are demanding that we obey them, sending God's Angels to slake their lust.[407] They still demand to know who we think we are, becoming the judge of them. And we must remember that God warns us we are just like those we condemn.[408]

The men of Sodom were so angry, they didn't see the fire which God was preparing in the sky, moments from releasing His wrath upon them from heaven.[409] When Lot's family left the city, the wrath of God was released to burn up every one of them.

This is a foretaste of the wrath of God which can only be avoided though Jesus' blood on the Cross. He took God's wrath for those who believe. In Sodom, Lot could only escape the fire by God's favor and mercy shown to Abraham.

Why does God send His Angel and His prophet? He sends them to rescue. The Angels rescued Peter in the jail. They rescued Paul and Silas

Confess your sins to one another.

in the jail. They rescued Daniel in the Lion's Den. They rescued me and those homeless people in the Rescue Mission in Providence. They come because the hour is late, and the time is short.

God is still calling us out of the unrighteous city and out of the prisons and jails before the fires fall from heaven on the final day. He is calling us to a City whose builder is God. He does not want a single person to be lost, but He knows we are among those who will rebel. God is looking to save everyone who says, "Lord, forgive me, for I have sinned and fallen short of the standard established by Your Son Jesus. Take over my life!"

> "Praise, glory, and honor to You, Lord Jesus! You have made a way for us through Your Body and Your Blood, so that we might be reconciled with God our Father, through Grace and Mercy—These bring us to the confessing of our sins to one another and to You. You have made it possible for the worst of us to enter into the Father's rest intended for us from the beginning! You have opened a door into a new and better Kingdom, and a new and beautiful family, spotless and without blemish through the blood You shed on that Middle Cross on the Hill of Skulls. The efficacy of those other two crosses is merely to show us how very far we are from you, and how very near to you we are."

> "You died in our place outside the City Walls, where the refuse, the ritual trash, the filthy rags, and our unseemly materials are spread out in the sun. You made it possible for us to become the adopted children of God, giving us an inheritance of love and spiritual riches. You put an end to the hostility between us and our neighbors when You opened the Curtain in the Temple, allowing us to enter into God's presence. In His presence, we are healed of all unrighteousness."

> "Father, in the mighty name of Your Son Jesus, we pray that you fill each of us with Your Holy Spirit daily, empowering the weakest ones of us to become

Myopic Me!

Peacemakers, no longer committing our hours here on earth to every mission of hatred and revenge. We tear up our records of wrongs done against us, imagined and real lists of crimes against us.[410] God forgive us."

"We repent of digging two graves, of serving the cold dish of vengeance, of taking an eye for every eye. You have shown us how by Your own example how to turn the other cheek! We repent of gouging out our own eyes so that we would no longer see the log in our eye, keeping us from being able to remove the speck from the eye of our enemies. Through Christ's example on the Cross, let us also forgive those who abuse us, persecute us, or bear false witness against us."

"Oh God, let Grace abound in us. Help us now to become perfect with Christ who is perfect! Fill us daily with the Holy Spirit, that we might give away all the gifts of God to a world desperate for hope and love. Make us Holy and set apart for good works that You prepared for us to walk in. Hallowed be Your name, and glorious is Your good and perfect will here on earth as it is in heaven.

Let every Wall of Hostility be torn down in our lives and relationships, and let every blessing flow from us instead of this cursing that has hounded us since we picked up that first rock in the field of Cain blaming everyone for our sinful hearts, including You, Lord, for our sins and for our own failures. Let Your kingdom be advanced in our lives, churches, and families, in Jesus' name, Amen."

Permissions for Stories included in this book:

Where possible, written permission was received for quoting named or unnamed individuals, telling their stories, or using their famous quotations.

Cover art is by the author, and no known persons are depicted in the painting on the front cover. The back cover includes photos and paintings by the author, showing himself at various stages of life and ministry, and including images of his wife and child as a baby.

Bibliography/References:

"Aaron Hernandez's CTE Worst Seen by BU Experts in a Young Person: MED's Ann McKee says convicted killer's brain will advance research, November 9, 2017, Rich Barlow." The Brink: Pioneering Research from Boston University. bu.edu/articles/2017/aaron-hernandez-cte-worst-seen-in-young-person. Web. October 19, 2020, 1:45 p.m.

"Albert Einstein Quotes." Brainy Quote. brainyquote.com/authors/albert_einstein. Web. January 3, 2019, 2:33 p.m.

Alcorn, Randy. *Pro-Life Answers to Pro-Choice Questions*. June 1992. Publisher: Multnomah Books. ISBN: 0880704721.

"A Lesson from Blessed Teresa of Calcutta on Abortion, Linda O'Brien, September 3, 2007." Catholic Exchange. catholicexchange.com/a-lesson-from-blessed-teresa-of-calcutta-on-abortion. Web. October12, 2020, 8:45 a.m.

"Alice's Adventures in Wonderland." Wikipedia, the Free Encyclopedia. en.wikipedia.org/wiki/Alice%27s_Adventures_in_Wonderland. Web. March 1, 2018, 10:47 a.m.

"Alice in Wonderland (1951)." IMDb. imdb.com/title/tt0043274/?ref_=nv_sr_2. Web. March 1, 2018, 12:18 p.m.

"A Patient Safety Threat—Syringe Reuse." cdc.gov/injectionsafety/patients/syringereuse_faqs.html. Web. March 19, 2021, 11:25 a.m.

"A Reason to Believe: 'Can I Trust the Bible?' Tim Hatch." Sermon from the Fast Lane. sermonfromthefastlane.blogspot.com/2016/03/a-reason-to-believe-can-i-trust-bible.htmlWeb. February 9, 2021, 2:04 p.m.

Bartlett, Richard Paul MD. *The Doctor's Travel Journal: Miracles around the World, 2020*. RB Productions. ISBN: 978-1-61206-210-5.

Baum, L. Frank. *The Wonderful Wizard of Oz*. 1900. New York: Harper Collins Publishers and Book of Wonder. Republished 1987 by Peter Glassman. ISBN 0-06-029323-3.

"Because of Bethlehem: An Interview with Max Lucado, Jonathan Petersen." biblegateway.com/blog/2016/11/because-of-bethlehem-an-interview-with-max-lucado. Web. December 25, 2020, 3:21 p.m.

Bennett, Dennis. *Nine O'clock in the Morning*. Bridge-Logos Publishers (June 20, 2011). ISBN-10: 0882706292.

Bible, Amplified Bible (AMP). Copyright © 2015 by The Lockman Foundation, La Habra, CA 90631. All rights reserved.

Bible, New Living Translation, Copyright © 1996, 2004, 2015 by Tyndale House Foundation. Used by permission of Tyndale House Publishers, Inc., Carol Stream, Illinois 60188. All rights reserved.

Myopic Me!

"Black man shot dead by police in Philadelphia, sparking heated protests, October 27, 2020, Rachel Elbaum, Kurt Chirbas, Colin Sheeley and Julie Goldstein." NBC News. nbcnews.com/news/us-news/black-man-shot-dead-police-philadelphia-sparking-heated-protests-n1244888. Web. October 28, 2020, 10:35 a.m.

"Borg." Wikipedia. en.wikipedia.org/wiki/Borg. Web. November 12, 2020, 4:12 p.m.

"Cancel Culture." Wikipedia. en.wikipedia.org/wiki/Cancel_culture#:~:text=Cancel%20 culture%20(or%20call%2Dout,to%20have%20been%20%22cancelled%22. Web March 24, 2021, 2:30 p.m.

"Catholic Archdiocese of Boston sex abuse scandal." Wikipedia.en.wikipedia.org/wiki/Catholic_Archdiocese_of_Boston_sex_abuse_scandal#:~:text=In%20early%20 2002%2C%20The%20Boston,Spotlight%20scandal%20also%20pleaded%20 guilty. Web. November 13, 2020, 10:16 a.m.

"Christian Men Hold Huge Rally on D.C. Mall, James Risen, October 5, 1997." Los Angeles Times. latimes.com/archives/la-xpm-1997-oct-05-mn-39657-story.html. Web. October 5, 2020, 2:34 p.m.

"Chuck Colson." Wikipedia. en.wikipedia.org/wiki/Charles_Colson. Web. November 11, 2020, 12:42 p.m.

Colson, Charles W. *Loving God: The Cost of Being a Christian,* with Eric Metaxas. 1987. Zondervan. ISBN: 978-0-310-352631.

"Corona and the Spiritual, Tom Vermillion." Vermillion.com. Web. October 31, 2020, 1:45 p.m.

"C.S. Lewis, Greed, and Self-Interest, Dr. Art Lindsley, August 8, 2012." tifwe.org/resource/c-s-lewis-greed-and-self-interest. Web. January 5, 2021, 2:53 p.m.

Cummings, E. E. *The Enormous Room.* Dover Thrift Edition. 2002 [originally published in 1923]. ISBN-13: 978-0-486-42120-9.

Dickinson, Emily. *The Complete Poems of Emily Dickinson.* "254." Thomas H. Johnson, Editor. Back Bay Books. 1960. Little, Brown and Company, Boston. ISBN 0-316-18413-6.

"Did Caligula really make his horse a consul? Elizabeth Nix." History. history.com/news/did-caligula-really-make-his-horse-a-consul. Web. January 18, 2019, 11:57 a.m.

"Did Madonna Say She Would Vote for President Trump in 2020?" Snopes. snopes.com/fact-check/madonna-trump-2020. Web. February 5, 2019, 9:30 a.m.

Edelman, Julian, with Curran, Tom E. *Relentless: A Memoir.* New York, Boston: Hachette Book Group, Inc., 2017. ISBN 978-0-316-47985-1 (hardcover).

"8 Reasons Why Rome Fell: Find out why one of history's most legendary empires finally came crashing down. January 14, 2014. Evan Andrews." history.com/news/8-reasons-why-rome-fell. Web. March 15, 2021, 11:30 a.m.

"Elegy (film)." Wikipedia. en.wikipedia.org/wiki/Elegy_(film). Web. November 11, 2020, 1:41 p.m.

"Erich Fromm Quotes." Goodreads. goodreads.com/author/quotes/8788.Erich_Fromm. Web. January 23, 2021, 9:38 a.m.

"Fact-checking Trump's references to the anti-police chant 'pigs in a blanket, fry 'em like bacon,' Daniel Dale, July 2, 2020." CNN. cnn.com/2020/07/02/politics/

Bibliography/References:

fact-check-trump-pigs-blanket-black-lives-matter/index.html. Web. October 26, 2020, 5:10 p.m.

"Fences (2016) Rotten Tomatoes." rottentomatoes.com/m/fences_2016Denzel Washington. Web. November 11, 2020, 11:23 a.m.

"First Tuesday, November 10, 2020, Tim Hatch."". Waters Church You Tube. North Attleboro.. Web. March 24, 2021, 11:24 a.m.

"God is a mean-spirited, pugnacious bully." Goodreads. goodreads.com/quotes. Web. November 25, 2020, 10:28 a.m.

"Grandparents defend young woman who sued parents for college tuition." November 17, 2014." 6 ABC. 6abc.com/entitled-generation-college-tuition-action-news-special-report-wendy-saltzman/392148/#:~:text=21%2Dyear%20old%20Caitlyn%20 Ricci,years%20for%20her%20college%20tuition. Web. November 16, 2020, 3:46 p.m.

"Gravity." Wikipedia. en.wikipedia.org/wiki/Gravity. Web. August 19, 2018, 2:41 p.m.

"Gravity." IMDb. imdb.com/title/tt1454468. Web. March 4, 2019, 9:24 a.m.

Hancock, Brecker, Hargrove. *Perfect Machine.* "*Rockit.*" amazon.com/Herbie-Hancock-Michael-Brecker-Roy-Hargrove/e/B002E0IC18/ref=dp_byline_cont_music_2. Web. March 9, 2021, 10:14 a.m.

Hemingway, Ernest. *The Old Man and the Sea.* New York:1953. Simon & Schuster.com. ISBN 978-0-684-80122-3.

"He Preyed on Men Who Wanted to Be Priests. Then He Became a Cardinal, July 16, 2018, Laurie Goodstein and Sharon Otterman." New York Times. nytimes.com/2018/07/16/us/cardinal-mccarrick-abuse-priest.html. Web. November 13, 2020, 10:10 a.m.

Hitler, Adolf. *Mein Kampf*, July 18, 1925. Munich: Franz Eher Nachfolger. English translation, vol 1, Thomas Dalton PhD, 2017. CreateSpace Publishing. ISBN-13:9781974502967.

"Hitler hated Judaism. But he loathed Christianity, too, April 20, 2019, Michael S. Rosenwald." The Washington Post. washingtonpost.com/history/2019/04/20/hitler-hated-judaism-he-loathed-christianity-too. Web. November 26, 2020, 11:02 a.m.

"How do I get an in-clinic abortion?" Planned Parenthood. plannedparenthood.org/learn/abortion/in-clinic-abortion-procedures/how-do-i-get-an-in-clinic-abortion. March 17, 2021, 2:20 p.m.

"Induced abortions in the United States, September 2019." Guttmacher Institute. guttmacher.org/fact-sheet/induced-abortion-united-states?gclid=Cj0K-CQiA8dH-BRD_ARIsAC24umb-l0hFC4rcdOzckOKq7b2wy53u7uj-KQ0aO0yRx__8e-L2P-sFGdYaAvzcEALw_wcB. Web. December 12, 2020, 1:34 p.m.

"Is there a criminal gene? Up to 70% of jail inmates have disorder also seen in serial killer Jeffrey Dahmer–and it could be in their DNA, September 13, 2016, Stacy Liberatore," Daily Mail. dailymail.co.uk/sciencetech/article-3787469/Does-DNA-predict-end-jail-Scientists-closer-finding-genetic-roots-crime-reveal-40-inmates-disorder-seen-serial-killer-Jeffrey-Dahmer.html. Web. October 21, 2020, 8:28 a.m.

Myopic Me!

"Joe Biden Ben Carson Gay Marriage Response." Politico. politico.com/story/2015/03/joe-biden-ben-carson-gay-marriage-response-115833. Web. November 11, 2020, 4:32 p.m.

Jones, Rick. *Understanding Roman Catholicism: 37 Roman Catholic Doctrines Explained.* 1995. Ontario, Calif. Chick Publications. ISBN: 978-093795848-3.

"Joyfully Embracing God's Children, October 28, 2020, Jim Daley's Blog." Focus on the Family. email@contact.fotf.com. Web. October 28, 2020, 10:01 a.m.

Keller, Timothy. *Center Church: Doing Balanced Gospel-Centered Ministry in Your City.* Zondervan, 2012. ISBN: 978-0-310-49418-8 [Hardback].

Keller, Timothy. *Preaching: Communicating Faith in a Skeptical Age.* Viking. An imprint of Penguin Random House, New York, 2015. ISBN: 978-0-525-95303-6.

Kinney, Jeff. *Wimpy Kid.* wimpykid.com. Web. February 4, 2021, 9:01 a.m.

Lane, John D Jr. *Myopic Me! Captured by the Faith-Time Continuum.* Xulon Press, 2018. ISBN: 978-1-5456-3881-1.

Lane, John D Jr. *Myopic Me! Jerusalem with Solomon & Einstein.* Xulon Press, 2019. ISBN: 978-1-5456-6818-4.

Lane, John D Jr. *Myopic Me! Made in the Bipolar Image of God.* February 17, 2021. Xulon Press. ISBN-13: 978-1-6628-0362-8.

"Lay's TV Commercial For Lay's Classic Chip Love." iSpot. ispot.tv/ad/7VHa/lays-lays-classic-chip-love. Web. November 11, 2020, 2:54 p.m.

Leach, William. *Land of Desire: Merchants, Power, and the Rise of a New American Culture.* First Vintage Books Edition, September 1994. ISBN 0-679-75411-3.

"Lennon Leftovers: Repackaged but Not Reheated, November 7, 2004, Richard Harrington." The Washington Post. washingtonpost.com/archive/lifestyle/style/2004/11/07/lennon-leftovers-repackaged-but-not-reheated/74e06886-fdb0-47a7-95fd-05f1278375f8. Web. November 25, 2020, 10:15 a.m.

"Lewis Carroll." Wikipedia, The Free Encyclopedia. en.wikipedia.org/wiki/Lewis_Carroll. Web. January 28, 2019, 8:12 a.m.

"Life begins at birth — it says so in Genesis, August 7, 2018."

baltimoresun.com/opinion/readers-respond/bs-ed-rr-abortion-law-letter-20180807-story.html. Web. February 13, 2021, 3:13 p.m.

Machiavelli, Niccolo, translated by Luigi Ricci. *The Prince.* 1532. Oxford World Classics. Public Domain. Web. January 7, 2021, 9:45 a.m.

"Meet The Real Narcissists (They're Not What You Think), September 2016, Rebecca Webber." Psychology Today Magazine. psychologytoday.com/articles/201609/meet-the-real-narcissists-theyre-not-what-you-think?collection=1093092. Web. February 28, 2018, 4:23 p.m.

Metaxas, Eric. *Bonhoeffer: Pastor, Martyr, Prophet, Spy,* 2010. Nashville: Thomas Nelson. ISBN 13: 9781595551382.

Metaxas, Eric. *If You Can Keep It: The Forgotten Promise of American Liberty, 2016.* New York: Viking: Penguin Random House. ISBN 9781101979983.

"Michael Clancy, photographer of 'Baby Samuel,' is National Right to Life Convention 2011 Banquet Speaker,

Bibliography/References:

May 10, 2011, Karen Scoggins." NRL. nationalrighttolifenews.org/2011/05/michael-clancy-photographer-of-%E2%80%9Cbaby-samuel%E2%80%9D-is-national-right-to-life-convention-2011-banquet-speaker. Web. November 3, 2020, 12:33 p.m.

"Minkowski's space-time: From visual thinking to the absolute world, 1979, Peter Louis Galison." Historical Studies in the Physical Sciences. 10: 85–121. Web. March 1, 2018, 12:49 p.m.

"Narcissism." Wikipedia, the Free Encyclopedia. en.wikipedia.org/wiki/Narcissism. Web. May 18, 2018, 12:42 p.m.

"Narcissus (mythology)." Wikipedia, the Free Encyclopedia. en.wikipedia.org/wiki/Narcissus_(mythology). Web. May 18, 2018, 10:10 a.m.

"Nonverbal Communication: How Body Language & Nonverbal Cues Are Key, Feb 18, 2020 by Dustin Smith." Lifesize. lifesize.com/en/video-conferencing-blog/speaking-withoutwords#:~:text=These%20studies%20led%20Dr.,is%20%E2%80%9Cnonverbal%E2%80%9D%20in%20nature. Web. November 11, 2020, 1:51 p.m.

"No One Really Knew Jane Roe. Her shocking deathbed confession makes that clear, May 21, 2020, Callie Beusman." The Cut. thecut.com/2020/05/jane-roe-norma-mc-corvey-deathbed-confession-abortion.html. Web. December 5, 2020, 10:48 a.m.

"Odin." Wikipedia. en.wikipedia.org/wiki/Odin. Web. February 11, 2021, 12:35 p.m.

«Planned Parenthood leaders admit under oath to harvesting body parts from babies born alive, Micaiah Bilger, November 3, 2020." pregnancyhelpnews.com/planned-parenthood-leaders-admit-under-oath-to-harvesting-body-parts-from-babies-born-alive. Web. November 3, 2020, 12:36 p.m.

"Plato, The Cave." en.wikipedia.org/wiki/Plato#The_Cave. Web. October 27, 2020, 10:34 a.m.

"Plessey vs. Ferguson." Wikipedia. en.wikipedia.org/wiki/Plessy_v._Ferguson. Web. October 26, 2020, 3:03 p.m.

"Quiet Courage: The Yellow Flower of Syria, John Lane, August 30, 2014." Horror Scope with Good News. blogger.com/blog/post/edit/2899364129592320646/8494878921420458732. Web. December 11, 2020, 10:25 a.m.

"Quotes from Mother Teresa on Abortion." St. Joan of Ark Church. stjoanofarcchurch.org/Downloads/e8304718-37cb-4c45-81c8-4cb54ae8eb99.pdf. Web. October 21, 2020, 3:35 p.m.

"Quotes: Revenge." Goodreads. goodreads.com/quotes. Web. November 25, 2020, 10:28 a.m.

"Random Collection of Novels." Amazon. com. [*The Blinds by Adam Sternbergh* | Aug 1, 2017; *Glass Houses: A Novel* by Louise Penny (Author) Format: Kindle Edition; *Keep Her Safe: A Novel* Paperback – January 23, 2018 by K.A. Tucker (Author); *The Power* Kindle Edition by Naomi Alderman (Author) Format: Kindle Edition; *The Shadow Man*:by Helen Fields; *The Lying Game: A Novel* Kindle Edition by Ruth Ware | Jul 25, 2017; *All the Dirty Parts* by Daniel Handler | Aug 29, 2017; *What We Lose: A Novel* Kindle Edition by Zinzi Clemmons | Jul 11, 2017]. Web. March 13, 2021, 9:27 a.m.

"Real Change-Can a Man be Gay and a Christ-Follower?Sunday, February 26, 2012, John Lane." Sermon from the Fast Lane. https://sermonfromthefastlane.blogspot.com/2012/02/1010-pm-wedding-night.html. Web. November 11, 2020, 1:27 p.m.

"Reasons given for having abortions in the United States, January 18, 2016. Robert Johnston." wm.johnstonsarchive.net/policy/abortion/abreasons.html#3. Web. September 1, 2018, 9:56 a.m.

"Report: Fear of Being Outed Prompted Killing by Aaron Hernandez, April 22, 2017, Neal Broverman." Advocate. advocate.com/sports/2017/4/22/report-fear-being-outed-prompted-killing-aaron-hernandez. Web. October 27, 2020, 1:50 p.m.

Riead, William, Director. *The Letters, The Untold Story of Mother Teresa, 2014*. Big Screen Partners, V. Ltd. foxconnect.com.

"Roe vs. Wade." Wikipedia. en.wikipedia.org/wiki/Roe_v._Wade. Web. November 11, 2020, 12:56 p.m.

"Samuel." Holman Study Bible. studylight.org/dictionaries/eng/hbd/s/samuel.html. Web. March 16, 2021, 3:34 p.m.

"Separate is Not Equal: Brown vs. Board of Education." Smithsonian National Museum of American History. americanhistory.si.edu/brown/history/1-segregated/separate-but-equal.html. Web. November 11, 2020, 11:30 a.m.

Sheeran, Ed. *Shape Of You*. amazon.com/CD-Single-Ed-Sheeran/dp/B07FM42WGR/ref=sr_1_2?dchild=1&keywords=ed+sheeran+in+love+with+your+-body&qid=1615303337&s=music&sr=1-2. Web. March 9, 2021, 10:24 a.m.

"Start Healing, Living Whole-heartedly & Having Fulfilling Relationships." Dr. Mori Kovanen. drmarikovanen.co.uk/8-consequences-of-the-father-wound-on-well-being-and-relationships. Web. March 13, 2021, 9:52 a.m.

"Star Trek: Next Generation." en.wikipedia.org/wiki/Star_Trek:_The_Next_Generation. Web. November 19, 2020, 3:15 p.m.

"Steel 'cross' will stay at WTC memorial: court, July 28, 2014, Rich Calder." New York Post. nypost.com/2014/07/28/steel-cross-will-stay-at-wtc-memorial-court. Web. November 26, 2020, 3:53 p.m.

Swift, Jonathan. *Gulliver's Travels: Travels into Several Remote Nations of the World in Four Parts*. October 28, 1726. London, Public Domain.

"Template: Discrimination." Wikipedia. en.wikipedia.org/wiki/Template:Discrimination. Web. March 8, 2021, 4:00 p.m.

"The Big Bang Theory." Wikipedia, the Free Encyclopedia. en.wikipedia.org/wiki/The_Big_Bang_Theory. Web. March 1, 2018, 11:32 a.m.

"The Big Bang Theory." YouTube. youtube.com/watch?v=majaPLfQMzk. Web. January 4, 2019, 8:04 a.m.

"The connectomics of brain disorders, February 20, 2015, by Alex Fornito, Andrew Zalesky & Michael Breakspear." Nature Reviews Neuroscience. nature.com/articles/nrn3901. Web. November 11, 2020, 12:28 p.m.

"The Fallacy of Materialistic Determinism, February 1, 2012, Bojidar Marinov." The American Vision. americanvision.org/5540/the-fallacy-of-materialistic-determinism. Web. March 8, 2016, 3:32 p.m.

Bibliography/References:

"The High Cost of Facebook Exhibitionism, April 9, 2013, Susan Krauss Whitbourne, Ph.D." Psychology Today. psychologytoday.com/us/blog/fulfillment-any-age/201304/the-high-cost-facebook-exhibitionism. Web. September 30, 2018, 10:35 a.m.

"The Master's Expectations: Compassion! May 5, 2014, John Lane." Sermon from the Fast Lane. sermonfromthefastlane.blogspot.com/2014/05/the-masters-compassion-providence.htmlWeb. December 5, 2020, 2:07 p.m.

"The Most Post-Christian Cities in America: 2019, June 5, 2019." Barna. barna.com/research/post-christian-cities-2019/. Web. November 16, 2020, 12:37 p.m.

"The 25 Best Inventions for 2014." Time. time.com/3594971/the-25-best-inventions-of-2014. Web. February 3, 2021, 4:26 p.m.

"These Are The Most Godless Cities In America, January 22, 2014, Denver Nicks." Time. time.com/1541/godless-cities-in-america. Web. February 1, 2019, 12:34 p.m.

"The Size of the Human Brain: The size of the brain may not always indicate a measure of intelligence, Kendra Cherry, May 11, 2020." VeryWell Mind. verywellmind.com/how-big-is-the-brain-2794888. Web. November 3, 2020, 12:42 p.m.

"The Theory of Everything: The Quest to Explain All Reality, Course No. 1318, Professor Don Lincoln." The Great Courses. thegreatcourses.com/digital-library/course/view/id/13091/format/1. Web January 23, 2019, 10:48 a.m.

"The Tragic Cost of Her Cavernous Thirst, John Piper." Preaching. U-Tube.com. youtube.com/watch?v=B9nDLRWdNt4 Web. July 17, 2018, 3:58 p.m.

"The Wackiest Roman Emperors." Walks. walksofitaly.com/blog/art-culture/the-list-of-craziest-ancient-roman-emperors. Web. October 27, 2020, 11:48 a.m.

"The Water in You: Water and the Human Body." USGS. usgs.gov/special-topic/water-science-school/science/water-you-water-and-human-body?qt-science_center_objects=0#qt-science_center_objects. Web. November 13, 2020, 9:27 a.m.

"William Barclay, The Letters To The Corinthians," p. 2-3. Corinth, Greece in the New Testament–David Padfield, Padfield.com. Web. March 22, 2021, 1:14 p.m.

"The Wizard of Oz (1939), December 22, 1996." Roger Ebert. rogerebert.com. Retrieved August 30, 2012.Web. February 28, 2018, 5:20 p.m.

"The Wonderful Wizard of Oz." Wikipedia. en.wikipedia.org/wiki/The_Wonderful_Wizard_of_Oz. Web. February 28, 2018, 5:43 p.m.

"23 ways that DNA changed the world." Independent. independent.co.uk/news/science/23-ways-that-dna-changed-the-world-5352712.html. Web. January 2, 2019, 1:35 p.m.

"United States Declaration of Independence." Wikipedia. en.wikipedia.org/wiki/United_States_Declaration_of_Independence. Web. November 24, 2020, 3:43 p.m.

"University of Pittsburg Rainbow Alliance." Student Affairs. studentaffairs.pitt.edu/lgbtqia/studentorg/rainbow. Web. October 27, 2020, 2:47 p.m.

"Unwrapping Christmas: God's Good News Plan, Isaiah 53, John Lane, December 13, 2020," Sermon from the Fast Lane. sermonfromthefastlane.blogspot.com. Web. December 13, 2020, 2:06 p.m.

"U. S. Apparel Market, December 1, 2020." statista.com/topics/965/apparel-market-in-the-us. Web. February 15, 2021, 10:17 a.m.

Vermillion, Tom. *Born to Be Free: Discovering Christ's Power to Set you Free from a Painful Past.* July 30, 2013. Morgan James Publishing. ISBN-13: 9781614486046.

Vermillion, Tom. *FreeIndeed.* Mid-Cities Community Church, 2008. midcities.org.

Webster, Richard. *Freud, Satan, and the Serpent. From Why Freud Was Wrong: Sin, Science and Psychoanalysis* (1995), richardwebster.net. Web. December 12, 2017, 11:41 a.m.

"Who was the commander of the army of the LORD in Joshua 5:14?" Got Questions-Your Questions. Biblical Answers. gotquestions.org/commander-army-Lord.html. Web. December 22, 2020, 4:02 p.m.

Endnotes

1. "Quotes: Revenge."
2. Ibid.
3. Ibid.
4. Ibid.
5. "Lennon Leftovers."
6. "Did Madonna Say She Would Vote for President Trump?"
7. Matthew 5:38.
8. Mark 1:15.
9. Philippians 2:1-4.
10. Matthew 19:14.
11. Matthew 26:40-41.
12. John 14:12-14.
13. Mark 1:15.
14. James 5:16.
15. John 3:16-17.
16. John 14:15-17a.
17. Kinney, Jeff. *Wimpy Kid*.
18. "The 25 Best Inventions for 2014."
19. Ephesians 2:14.
20. Genesis 3:6-7.
21. Exodus 32:19-20.
22. Romans 5:17.
23. "William Barclay, The Letters To The Corinthians," p. 2-3.
24. Dickinson, Emily. *The Complete Poems of Emily Dickinson*. "254."
25. "William Barclay, The Letters To The Corinthians," p. 2-3.
26. Ephesians 6:10-12.
27. Genesis 3:6-7.
28. Biblehub.com. biblehub.com/interlinear/genesis/4.htm.
29. Genesis 4:10.
30. "U. S. Apparel Market."
31. Genesis 3; Genesis 9.
32. Exodus 32:25-28.
33. Genesis 4:9.
34. Matthew 5:3.
35. James 4:2b-3.
36. "C.S. Lewis, Greed, and Self-Interest, Dr. Art Lindsley."
37. "A Reason to Believe: 'Can I Trust the Bible?' Tim Hatch."
38. "C.S. Lewis, Greed, and Self-Interest, Dr. Art Lindsley."
39. Exodus 20.
40. "C.S. Lewis, Greed, and Self-Interest, Dr. Art Lindsley."
41. Hemingway. *The Old Man and the Sea*.
42. Hebrews 11:10; 11:16; 12:22.
43. Ephesians 2.
44. James 4:16.
45. John 5:19-21.
46. Ephesians 2:1-10.
47. Genesis 9.
48. Matthew 26:39.
49. Genesis 4.
50. Acts 9.
51. Ephesians 2:9-10.
52. Romans 12:13.
53. Romans 12:18-20.
54. Ephesians 6:2.
55. Ephesians 6:4.
56. Galatians 5:19-22.
57. John 3:17.
58. "Start Healing, Living Wholeheartedly & Having Fulfilling Relationships. Dr. Mori Kovanen."
59. Matthew 19:14.
60. Romans 8:31.
61. Luke 23:34.
62. Romans 12:14-18.
63. Hebrews 12:15.
64. Genesis 3:1.
65. John 8:44.
66. Matthew 27:27-31.
67. 2 Samuel a 16:6.
68. Psalm 139.

Myopic Me!

69 Isaiah 53:2b-5a.
70 Ephesians 4:26-27.
71 Isaiah 14:9-14.
72 Galatians 1:8-9.
73 Matthew 6.
74 Genesis 44:16e,33.
75 Genesis 45:5.
76 Hebrews 11:6.
77 1 Corinthians 1:21-23.
78 Matthew 10:16.
79 "These Are The Most Godless Cities In America."
80 "He Preyed on Men Who Wanted to Be Priests."
81 "Catholic Archdiocese of Boston sex abuse scandal."
82 Romans 1:16.
83 "These Are The Most Godless Cities In America."
84 "The Most Post-Christian Cities in America/2019."
85 "Quiet Courage: The Yellow Flower of Syria, John Lane."
86 Ibid.
87 Ibid.
88 Ibid
89 "The Most Post-Christian Cities in America/2019.".
90 Isaiah 54.
91 Ibid.
92 Exodus 20:17.
93 2 Samuel 11:4, 14-15.
94 "Because of Bethlehem: An Interview with Max Lucado."
95 Lane, Myopic Me! Captured by the Faith-Time Continuum. pp. 24, 120.
96 Psalm 46.
97 Psalm 139:7-10.
98 Galatians 5:13.
99 1 Corinthians 10:29.
100 "Lay's TV Commercial For Lay's Classic Chip Love."
101 Ibid.
102 Romans 12:1-3.
103 Isaiah 53:4-5.
104 Romans 6:13.
105 Romans 8:3.
106 Romans 7:24 [AMP].
107 "Nonverbal Communication."
108 "Elegy (film)." Wikipedia.
109 1 Corinthians 10:23.
110 Philippians 4:8.
111 "Erich Fromm Quotes." Goodreads.
112 "Elegy (film)." Wikipedia.
113 Ibid.
114 Ibid.
115 Ibid.
116 Ibid.
117 Hancock, Brecker, Hargrove. *Perfect Machine*. "Rockit."
118 Sheeran. *Shape Of You*.
119 "Elegy (film)." Wikipedia.
120 Jeremiah 49:4.
121 "Quantum Physics and Faith."
122 2 Kings 9:35-37.
123 "Elegy (film)." Wikipedia.
124 Ibid.
125 "Real Change-Can a Man be Gay and a Christ-Follower?"
126 Ibid.
127 Ibid.
128 1 Corinthians 6:9-11.
129 2 Timothy 2:3.
130 "Real Change-Can a Man be Gay and a Christ-Follower?"
131 Matthew 5:10-12.
132 "Real Change-Can a Man be Gay and a Christ-Follower?"
133 1 Corinthians 6:11.
134 "Real Change-Can a Man be Gay and a Christ-Follower?"
135 Ibid.
136 Ibid.
137 Romans 12:1.
138 1 Peter 1:4.
139 Romans 7.
140 2 Corinthians 5:1.
141 Matthew 6:20.
142 Ibid.
143 Romans 1:24.
144 Hosea 13:16.
145 "Michael Clancy, photographer of 'Baby Samuel.'"
146 Ibid.
147 Hosea 13.
148 Alcorn. *Pro-Life Answers*.

Endnotes

149 "Life begins at birth — it says so in Genesis."
150 Hosea 13.
151 Psalm 139:13-17a.
152 "Alice's Adventures in Wonderland." Wikipedia.
153 Genesis 2:21-22.
154 Luke 1:41.
155 "Michael Clancy, photographer of 'Baby Samuel.'"
156 "Samuel." Holman Study Bible.
157 1 Samuel 1.
158 1 Samuel 3:11-14.
159 "Michael Clancy, photographer of 'Baby Samuel.'"
160 Ibid.
161 Alcorn. *Pro-Life Answers*.
162 "Roe vs. Wade." Wikipedia.
163 Alcorn. *Pro-Life Answers*.
164 "Planned Parenthood leaders admit."
165 "Erich Fromm Quotes." Goodreads.
166 Ibid.
167 Psalm 139:1-6.
168 Psalm 139:7-12.
169 "Grandparents defend young woman who sued parents."
170 "Steel 'cross' will stay at WTC memorial."
171 Genesis 2:22-24.
172 Romans 1:18-20.
173 Alcorn. *Pro-Life Answers*. pg. 63.
174 Alcorn. *Pro-Life Answers*. pg. 79.
175 "No One Really Knew Jane Roe."
176 Alcorn. *Pro-Life Answers*. pp. 206, 207.
177 Ibid.
178 Alcorn. *Pro-Life Answers*. p. 30.
179 Alcorn. *Pro-Life Answers*. p. 68.
180 James 4:11-13.
181 Alcorn. *Pro-Life Answers*. p. 280.
182 Ibid.
183 Alcorn. *Pro-Life Answers*. p. 404.
184 Alcorn. *Pro-Life Answers*. p. 146.
185 Alcorn. *Pro-Life Answers*. p. 128.
186 Alcorn. *Pro-Life Answers*. p. 129.
187 Alcorn. *Pro-Life Answers*. p. 195.
188 John 14:6.
189 "23 Ways the DNA."
190 Metaxas. *Bonhoeffer: Pastor, Prophet, Martyr, Spy*. p. 472.
191 Alcorn. *Pro-Life Answers*. p. 221.
192 Alcorn. *Pro-Life Answers*. p. 231.
193 "Plaintiff in Roe vs. Wade Arrested at Notre Dame."
194 Alcorn. *Pro-Life Answers*. p. 181.
195 Ibid.
196 Alcorn. *Pro-Life Answers*. p. 19.
197 Alcorn. *Pro-Life Answers*. p. 14.
198 «Quotes from Mother Teresa on Abortion."
199 Alcorn. *Pro-Life Answers*. p. 134.
200 1 Corinthians 6:9-10.
201 Numbers 16:22-33.
202 Matthew 25:36.
203 2 Corinthians 12:10.
204 Metaxas. *Bonhoeffer: Pastor, Prophet, Martyr, Spy*.
205 "Chuck Colson." Wikipedia.
206 Colson. *Loving God*.
207 Ibid.
208 Ibid.
209 Colson. *Loving God*. Forward, Eric Metaxas.
210 Ibid.
211 Ephesians 6.
212 Metaxas, *Bonhoeffer: Pastor, Martyr, Prophet, Spy,*
213
214 John 8:36.
215 Ephesians 1:5.
216 Romans 8:23.
217 Bartlett. *The Doctor's Travel Journal*. p. 76.
218 Bartlett. *The Doctor's Travel Journal*. p. 77.
219 Ibid.
220 Ibid.
221 Ibid.
222 "God is a mean-spirited, pugnacious bully."
223 Isaiah 61.
224 Ephesians 1:5.
225 Bartlett. *The Doctor's Travel Journal*. p. 77.
226 Ibid.
227 Ibid.

228 Bartlett. *The Doctor's Travel Journal.* p. 81.
229 Ibid.
230 "An Unlikely Story Bookstore and Café." Facebook.
231 Bartlett. *The Doctor's Travel Journal.* p. 82.
232 Bartlett. *The Doctor's Travel Journal.* p. 77.
233 Bartlett. *The Doctor's Travel Journal.* pp. 77, 81.
234 Random Collection of Novels: See Bibliography for more information.
235 Ibid.
236 Ibid.
237 Ibid.
238 Ibid.
239 Ibid.
240 Bartlett. *The Doctor's Travel Journal.* p. to 79-81.
241 1 Samuel 3:1-4.
242 Psalm 139.
243 Genesis 4.
244 Ibid.
245 Revelation 9:11.
246 Bartlett. *The Doctor's Travel Journal.* p. 82.
247 Ibid.
248 Vermillion. *FreeIndeed.*
249 John 12:3.
250 Bartlett. *The Doctor's Travel Journal.* pp. 79-81.
251 Bartlett. *The Doctor's Travel Journal.* p. 83.
252 Vermillion. *FreeIndeed.*
253 Ibid.
254 Matthew 15:21-28
255 John 10.
256 Isaiah 61.
257 Matthew 25.
258 John 8:35-37.
259 Romans 6:7-8.
260 Vermillion. *Born to Be Free.*
261 Ibid.
262 John 9:25.
263 Ephesians 6:1-20.
264 Vermillion. *Born to Be Free.*
265 Isaiah 61:1-4.
266 "Meet The Real Narcissists." Psychology Today.
267 Ibid.
268 Genesis 4:7.
269 Revelation 3:7.
270 Vermillion. *Born to Be Free.*
271 Exodus 20.
272 Vermillion. *FreeIndeed.*
273 John 12:3.
274 Mark 16:9.
275 Vermillion. *FreeIndeed.*
276 John 8:1-11.
277 John 10:1-11.
278 Lane. ***Myopic Me!*** *Made in the Bipolar Image of God.*
279 Luke 10:41-42.
280 Mark 14:5.
281 Matthew 27:3-9.
282 2 Corinthians 3:16-18.
283 Matthew 7:15.
284 1 Peter 5:3.
285 Genesis 4:8.
286 "Odin." Wikipedia.
287 Report: Fear of Being Outed."
288 Ibid.
289 "Aaron Hernandez's CTE Worst Seen."
290 Ibid.
291 "Report: Fear of Being Outed."
292 Ibid.
293 Matthew 27:51-54.
294 Edelman. *Relentless, A Memoir.*
295 Ibid.
296 Edelman. *Relentless, A Memoi*r. *p.* 134.
297 "Report: Fear of Being Outed."
298 Ibid.
299 1 Corinthians 13:4-5.
300 John 14:1.
301 2 Samuel 11:6-24.
302 2 Samuel 12:24-25.
303 2 Samuel 12:9-14.
304 Matthew 7:2.
305 "Report: Fear of Being Outed.".
306 Ibid.
307 Deuteronomy 33:29.
308 Isaiah 6:3b.
309 "Report: Fear of Being Outed."

Endnotes

310 Edelman. *Relentless.*
311 Matthew 13:24-25.
312 Matthew 13:36.
313 1 Kings 18:21.
314 "Christian Men Hold Huge Rally." Los Angeles Times.
315 John 17:11b; 20, 21a.
316 John 6:40.
317 Genesis 4:6-7.
318 Ibid.
319 1 Kings 18:20-40.
320 1 Kings 19:11-14.
321 1 Kings 19:15-18.
322 1 Kings 19:18.
323 Matthew 17:1-6.
324 Ibid.
325 "United States Declaration of Independence." Wikipedia.
326 Hebrews 11:6.
327 Romans 1:21-23.
328 Matthew 17:1-6.
329 Genesis 25:30.
330 Amos 3:2.
331 Lane. **Myopic Me!** *Made in the Bipolar Image of God.*
332 Alcorn. *Pro-Life Answers.* pp. 15, 18, 124, 149, 223.
333 Genesis 1, 2.
334 John 17:11b; 20, 21a.
335 John 6:40.
336 "Separate is Not Equal: Brown vs. Board of Education."
337 1 Kings 16:32-33.
338 "How do I get an in-clinic abortion?" Planned Parenthood.
339 "A Lesson from Blessed Teresa of Calcutta."
340 Hosea 9:16-17.
341 "A Lesson from Blessed Teresa of Calcutta."
342 "Who was the commander of the army of the LORD in Joshua 5:14?"
343 Galatians 5:18-19 (NIV).
344 Machiavelli. *The Prince.*
345 Metaxas. *If You Can Keep It. pp. 60-63.*
346 Ibid.
347 Ibid.
348 Ibid.
349 "Template: Discrimination." Wikipedia.
350 "A Patient Safety Threat—Syringe Reuse." CDC.
351 "Fact-checking Trump's references to the anti-police chant 'pigs
352 "Erich Fromm Quotes." Goodreads.
353 Galatians 5:18-19 (NIV).
354 Genesis 3.
355 Galatians 3:22.
356 1 Corinthians 10:23.
357 Metaxas. *If You Can Keep It.*
358 Metaxas. *If You Can Keep It. pp. 82, 96-99.*
359 Ibid.
360 Metaxas. *If You Can Keep It. pp. 83-90.*
361 Luke 23:40-43.
362 Ephesians 2:8.
363 Metaxas. *If You Can Keep It. p. 77.*
364 "Unwrapping Christmas: God's Good News Plan, Isaiah 53."
365 "A Lesson from Blessed Teresa of Calcutta."
366 Hosea 9:7b-8.
367 Romans 2:1.
368 "A Lesson from Blessed Teresa of Calcutta."
369 Hosea 9:7,11.
370 "8 Reasons Why Rome Fell." History.
371 Ibid.
372 "A Lesson from Blessed Teresa of Calcutta."
373 Like 21:16-18.
374 "Cancel Culture." Wikipedia.
375 Ibid.
376 Genesis 4:6-7.
377 Matthew 28:20.
378 "First Tuesday, November 10, 2020, Tim Hatch."
379 Bartlett, *The Doctor's Travel Journal.*
380 Matthew 10:34.
381 Matthew 10:35.
382 "Is there a criminal gene?" Daily Mail.

Myopic Me!

383 "Joyfully Embracing God's Children." Focus on the Family.
384 Ibid.
385 1 Corinthians 12:13.
386 Galatians 3:27-29.
387 Jones, Rick. *Understanding Roman Catholicism. pp. 83-88.*
388 1 Corinthians 11:29.
389 Genesis 19:15-16.
390 Hebrews 13:2.
391 Revelation 2:12,15,16.
392 Acts 12:6-8.
393 Luke 12:16-21.
394 Matthew 28; Acts 1.
395 Luke 18:13 NIV.
396 "The Master's Expectations: Compassion!"
397 Romans 1:2-5.
398 Acts 2:37-41.
399 Acts 3:16-21.
400 Ibid.
401 James 5:16-18.
402 2 Peter 3:9.
403 Keller. *Center Church.* pp. *29-46.*
404 Mark 1:15.
405 Revelation 3:2-3.
406 Genesis 3:5,7.
407 Genesis 19:9.
408 Romans 2:1-2.
409 Genesis 9.
410 1 Corinthians 13:5.

CPSIA information can be obtained
at www.ICGtesting.com
Printed in the USA
BVHW031812110621
609374BV00005B/86